B + T 1-65 (Henley)

Portraits of the Eighteenth Century

LOUIS XV
From a portrait by Rigaud

PORTRAITS
OF THE
EIGHTEENTH CENTURY

Historic and Literary

VOLUME I

by
C. A. SAINTE-BEUVE

With an Introduction by Ruth Mulhauser

ILLUSTRATED

FREDERICK UNGAR PUBLISHING CO.
NEW YORK

Translated by Katharine P. Wormeley

Library of Congress Catalog Card No. 64-15699

INTRODUCTION

The essays in this collection seem to have been chosen by the translator according to two criteria: They focus on eighteenth-century personages and they come under the definition of a *portrait*. Sainte-Beuve himself made a careful distinction between the critical essay and the portrait. He joined the latter to the category of his elegiac and novelistic talent rather than to his critical work. Some of his twentieth-century detractors, who have perhaps read him too infrequently, tend to dismiss him as one who "used what he knew about a man's life to aid and corroborate his judgment of what the man wrote." Such critics seem to forget that one of the attractive qualities in the Homeric poems, for Sainte-Beuve, was exactly the fact that the work must stand alone, that we know almost nothing certain about the poet. It would, however, be an analogous misreading to attempt to maintain that Sainte-Beuve was not interested in the author of a given work. There is some importance, therefore, in stating quite plainly that Sainte-Beuve did not confuse literary criticism with literary biography. Their relationship is very close indeed, and they are certainly mutually enriching, but they are not identical. Sainte-Beuve's keen mind was well aware of when he was functioning as critic, when as literary biographer and when as literary historian.

Professor A. G. Lehmann, in an illuminating article on "Sainte-Beuve and the Historic Movement"[1] wrote cogently that Sainte-Beuve escaped "from the ubiquitous temptations of Romantic history with its conjoined lures of transcendental schematism and hero-worship." The reasons for this escape are not completely clear but Sainte-Beuve suggested in retrospect: "The surest way of getting away from reasoning according to a system, and from an aesthetic is *to do*, to apply oneself to a particular work; one starts with the system that one wants to verify and illustrate; but if one has any personal talent, this talent quickly comes to the fore in the work and before the end, it is walking alone, it has triumphed." [P.C. (1870 edit.) II, 535]* Professor Lehmann is not content, however, with the critic's explanation and adds, "A man whose freedom from self-deception went as far as is humanly feasible could still not plausibly claim the slogan 'le vrai, le vrai seul' without a comparative independence of standards. . . . From them [i.e., his unhappy formative years] he acquired not only the tinge of bitterness, but also detachment, the condition of insight."

The usual example of Sainte-Beuve's work as a literary historian is *Port-Royal*, tracing the vicissitudes of the great seventeenth-century Jansenist controversy to the destruction of their convent in Paris in 1710. *Port-Royal* is not, however, a document of analytic intellectual and political history; it is the *portrait* of an institution. The author's avowed purpose was to draw

---

1. *The French Mind. Studies in Honour of Gustave Rudler* Oxford, Clarendon, 1952. p. 256-273. p. 270-271.
* See Collation of Texts at end of each volume for abbreviations.

such a portrait: "I am not writing the history of Port-Royal. . . . It is the *portrait* of Port-Royal that I am making, the spirit of it caught in the most notable events of persons that make it up." For many readers today it is a moot point whether the portrait technique can be effective in such a long work, but there is no disagreement, on the other hand, that along with certain strikingly dramatic scenes some portraits stand out, and even detached from the total work, stand with individual unity to attest to the critic's delicate power of understanding and creating a likeness.

Sainte-Beuve describes his procedures in creating a portrait in charming fashion in the essay on Diderot in Volume II. A fortnight of seclusion in the country with the writings of an illustrious man, and diligent attention to each feature that comes forward leads to the birth and growth of the likeness until "analysis vanishes in creation, the portrait speaks and lives, you have found the man." The portrait then may well be viewed as a literary creation somewhat analogous to that done by a novelist who works from a prototype to bring alive a well-defined and complete character. The salient difference, however, is that the portrait painter must create without distorting in any manner the factual evidence from which he started. His creative imagination is not allowed full freedom to take flight from its own strength: rather it must fly like some large caged bird within the confines of historic fact. At least twice in this collection, in the essays on Buffon and Bernardin de Saint-Pierre, Sainte-Beuve warns against idolatrous biographers. The most apt literary parallel would be that of poetic translation, in which the successful translator must create poetry in his own language, but not poetry of his own free inspiration. He is strictly limited to re-creating the original poetry in a new language. Similarly Sainte-Beuve's portraits re-created life, personality, historic fact in the language of the essay. In 1850, reflecting on his own technique, Sainte-Beuve wrote: "In my youth I mingled much affection and enthusiasm into the portraits of poets I did; I am not sorry I did—I even collaborated a bit. Today I add nothing, I confess, except a sincere desire to see and portray things and people as they are or at least as they appear to me at this moment." [C.L.II, 287]

This collection then, has brought together a series of individual portraits. To some extent at least, the people portrayed here belonged to the same society; somewhat in the manner of Balzac, whom Sainte-Beuve neither appreciated fully nor liked personally but with whom he shared a mode of thinking in terms of the natural sciences and zoology in particular, these personages reappear in various essays like recurrent characters in novels. The research for the portrait of Frederick the Great obviously led Sainte-Beuve to an appreciation and desire to portray the Margravine of Baireuth, Frederick's sister. The Margravine's personality is not fully intelligible, however, without her brother's presence and their correspondence.

But although the majority of the persons portrayed here did leave some sort of literary document, literary merit is not the focal point of Sainte-Beuve's interest. He was, rather, very evidently interested in understanding and describing the social phenomenon of the *Ancien Régime,* not solely for the purpose of understanding more completely eighteenth-century literature, but also in order to understand better the stresses and picture of his own contemporary world. In the essay on the Duchesse de Maine, he points out tho "from '89 to 1850 the equilibrium between what remains of the essence of the old society and the increasing claims of the new society is still being sought." He also points out in the essay on Madame de Staal Delaunay that despite its industrial activity and scientific invention, the nineteenth century was retrospective. And any history of ideas and public opinion before the French Revolution, he says, would be incomplete without Benjamin Franklin who, with his democratic, middle-class ideals, must take his place in eighteenth-century Paris between Louis XV and Madame Du Deffand. Again in the essay on the Duchesse de Maine, however, Sainte-Beuve comments that the court of Sceaux had no beneficial influence on letters, that its only memorable facet was that which "affords food for human observation of prejudices, eccentricities, and absurdities." The interest in this society for Sainte-Beuve is then not solely either literary nor historic: it is also moral. This last preoccupation with the observation of society is evident in many essays, e.g., Chesterfield, Barthélemy, Louis XV, Madame d'Epinay and even in the essay on Marie-Antoinette where the queen is portrayed for the nineteenth-century audience as a very human woman and mother characterized by a high degree of personal heroism and dignity rather than as a political or even historic figure.

Sainte-Beuve's importance as observer and as commentator on society has not gone unnoticed, though its magnitude in his written work has remained ill defined. His penchant for short maxim-like thoughts in the tradition of the great French maxim writers, like Pascal whom Sainte-Beuve "re-discovered," La Rochefoucauld, and La Bruyère, resulted in sections of such commentary in the *Vie Poésies et Pensées de Joseph Delorme*, the *Causeries du Lundi* and the *Nouveaux Lundis* as well as in four or five notebooks left unpublished at his death. It is not surprising, moreover, that Sainte-Beuve seemed to see no necessity for rigid choice between literary criticism and observations on society, even on his particular contemporaries. They follow each other without logic in his notes as his mind ranged over literature and life, but always as a sharp, subtle observer and judge. The evolution of the critic's thought and self-definition resulted finally in his statement that the *Causeries du Lundi* were a campaign of literary criticism undertaken within the general aims of the moralist to remedy two decades of drift and deterioration. This monumental campaign resulted from a theory and ideal of functional criticism which, in turn, was most clearly defined in an important early essay on Pierre Bayle, philosopher and critic at the turn of the eighteenth century, who lived quietly in exile in Holland and hence played no active role in the society which the translator has chosen to represent.

In the 1835 essay, Sainte-Beuve undertook to define the critical *genius* of Pierre Bayle. The very concept of genius in criticism was not as generally accepted at that time as it is today, and Sainte-Beuve's assumption gave a new kind of dignity to the genre, if indeed it had even been conceived of as a separate literary genre. Bayle was not a philosophic rhetorician, nor even a systematic literary critic; he was the journalist critic who depended more on his own instinct and experience than on preconceived systems for his daily "battle of the eye." According to Sainte-Beuve, this kind of genius is quite opposite to the better-known creative and poetic genius, for it has no hard core of its own to

protect and express. The critical genius does not fear
misalliances, it goes forth eagerly to receive all new
ideas, curiosity is its mainspring. But infidelity is an
equally important quality, for such a man "sees all
sides of the question and does not hesitate to refute
even himself." Bayle's apparent inability to reach a
permanent conviction was one of the outstanding qualities of his critical genius, says Sainte-Beuve. A second
quality which distinguishes Bayle from Montaigne,
that other great critical mind comparable in its tolerance and curiosity, is the absence of a characteristic
Bayle style. The preoccupation with a personal style
implies a personal system and moreover, detracts from
the focal point in the work being studied. Voltaire,
with his "philosophic fanaticism and his passion which
falsified his criticism" is, though very great, less of a
critic than Bayle. Much of this article on Bayle may
easily be interpreted as the expression of Sainte-
Beuve's own ideal critic in 1835. One sentence in particular seems to apply to its author not only as an ideal
principle, but in fact also. He wrote: "This ideal of
universal tolerance, peaceful and in some fashion har-
monious anarchy in a state divided into a dozen re-
ligions like a city divided into divers classes of artisans
. . . he [Bayle] brought it about in his republic of
books, and although it is easier to make books be
mutually tolerant of each other than men, it is no small
glory for [Bayle] as a critic to have known how to conciliate and appreciate so many."

Sainte-Beuve's admiration and partial identification
in 1835 with Pierre Bayle as a critic has the natural
pendant and necessary complement in the 1851 article
on Diderot, that other great eighteenth-century critic.
Recognizing the *Encyclopédie* as Diderot's "great

social work and his principal work," Sainte-Beuve adds
nevertheless, "His principal glory in our eyes today is
having been creator of earnest, impassioned, eloquent
criticism." To Bayle's exact, shrewd, inquisitive criticism, Diderot added a more positive quality: the
search for beauties rather than faults, a "lively, fruitful searching." Diderot is distinguished by his ability
to identify at will and for a while with another mind
and to arouse enthusiasm "not only of his own brain
but of his heart." In doing this in his critical writings,
Diderot became "the great modern journalist, the
Homer of the profession, intelligent, ardent, effusive,
eloquent." Much of this description of Diderot's critical
genius and procedure might well be applied to Sainte-
Beuve himself and indeed it has been applied by
scholars since his death.

Sainte-Beuve's affinity and enthusiasm for Diderot's
method did not impede his critical sense; he recog-
nized quite clearly Diderot's tendency to literary art
criticism. But, he maintains, "Diderot is a great critic,
and in that kind of general criticism which no art can
possibly escape on the pretext of technique." Diderot
was, furthermore, very well aware of "superior execution which is the hallmark of every great artist" and, as
a critic, he interprets it for the public, for "he was the
first great critic . . . who definitely belongs to a democratic society." The picture is the source of inspiration
for Diderot's own creative mind: "Diderot is the king
and the god of those half-poets who become and appear whole poets in criticism; all that they need is an
external fulcrum and a stimulus." It would be hard to
imagine a more limpid personal allusion, written at
almost the height of Sainte-Beuve's career.

The enthusiasm and identification with both Bayle

and Diderot is central to a full understanding of the great nineteenth-century critic, but they should not lead to the unwarranted assumption that he was merely a disciple and imitator. The very quality of sympathetic understanding without commitment common to all three men permitted Sainte-Beuve to recognize a common bond without being bound by it. His affinity, in both cases, is with the intellectual and human qualities of the man more than with the actual critical product.

One other point of positive contact with the eighteenth century deserves brief comment here; namely, Sainte-Beuve's philosophic affinity for the preceding century. Instructed in the church, attracted momentarily by Lamennais' Christian socialism, Sainte-Beuve undertook his work on *Port-Royal*, as he says, seeking to understand the Jansenist doctrines and psychology. His epilogue is famous for its sympathetic rejection, an almost nostalgic declaration of defeat. The exact nuance of Sainte-Beuve's metaphysical beliefs has been much discussed with interpretations ranging from orthodoxy to Lucretian materialism and atheism. Jules Levallois, once secretary to the critic, wrote with some personal regret that Sainte-Beuve "disciple of Helvetius, Boulanger, de la Mettrie and d'Holbach, returned after 1840 to his first philosophic orientation." Philosophic heir to eighteenth-century rationalism, Sainte-Beuve, however, was no crusader; he never carried on the overt battles of the *Philosophes*, for he belonged to the school of Bayle and Montaigne, gently tolerant, universally curious and nonproselytizing.

Elsewhere in literature, however, Sainte-Beuve felt no special affinity for the eighteenth century. He is caustic about Rousseau and his progeny; appreciative of Voltaire but not as a major figure in poetry and tragedy. Montesquieu belonged to another age and hence has a limited attraction. Neoclassicism might have charm, but it lacked vitality. On the other hand, Sainte-Beuve considered Beaumarchais as one of the most original, most characteristic and most revolutionary figures of the century. Chénier, too, received the critic's unreserved admiration, but Sainte-Beuve did not see in Chénier the eighteenth century. Chénier was the precursor of Romanticism who brought a regenerative force to poetry. It was Sainte-Beuve in large measure who charted the great vogue of Chénier in the early nineteenth century. The critic's own romanticism was much more profoundly affected by this admiration for Chénier than by his enthusiasm for Victor Hugo, for in poetry as in criticism, Sainte-Beuve was cerebral. Even his happiest poetic effects are more rational than spontaneous. Joseph Delorme is almost a pastiche of the Romantic hero because he is so very ordinary. Neither a descendant of the neoclassics nor a typical Romantic, Sainte-Beuve as heir to the philosophic rationalism of the eighteenth century, turned the search for scientific truths toward literature where it became a pregnant artistic concept and critical standard.

RUTH MULHAUSER

Cleveland, Ohio

CONTENTS

CONTENTS

ILLUSTRATIONS

TRANSLATOR'S NOTE

In the following essays—taken from the *Causeries du Lundi,* the *Portraits de Femmes,* and the *Portraits Littéraires* — certain passages have been omitted, which relate chiefly to editions that have long passed away, or to discussions on style. Also, where two or more essays on the same person have appeared in the different series, they are here put together, omitting repetitions. The article on Louis XV in this volume, for instance, is compiled from four of Saint-Beuve's articles.

The *Causeries du Lundi* are published in fifteen volumes; eleven of which contain the first series; the other four volumes contain the later, or *nouveaux Lundis.*

Sainte=Beuve.

M. Edmond Scherer.

THE death of a man like Sainte-Beuve produces two effects. The first is, to make him greater; he is no longer there, we have suddenly become his posterity: he appears to us a being slightly raised above this humanity with which he has henceforth nothing in common. The other effect is the impression of sadness that we always feel in beholding the end of something memorable.

Sainte-Beuve was one of the last representatives of an epoch. He made part of that assemblage of statesmen, orators, poets, artists, who appeared in France, as if by enchantment, after the fall of the Empire. He had his distinctive place in the front rank. Sainte-Beuve was not less decidedly the first of our modern critics than Serre and Berryer were our first orators, Lamartine and Victor Hugo our first poets, Ingres and Delacroix our greatest painters. So, in departing today, he seems to carry with him all that still remained of that memorable era, and to mark with a funeral

3

stone the end of a period gone henceforth into the number of the things that are no more.

But it is not only a choir of immortal artists who have passed from the scene, it is more than that; it is a manner of conceiving the things of the mind that ceases, a literature which departs. Sainte-Beuve was the last of the *littérateurs* in the former sense of the word. We shall never again see writers solely occupied with the things of the intellect, and writing of these with grace and good taste. I would I were mistaken, but it seems to me that the pen, in future, is to serve more especially two classes of men—the money-makers and the amusers; on the one hand, the language of business; on the other, that of violent effects and puerile surprises.

Sainte-Beuve began by poesy; and he clung to his claim to be accepted as a poet. It would, in fact, be unjust not to respect such claim. I have never opened his volumes of verse without forgetting myself in them, as we forget ourselves and stray in autumn through woodland paths; for there is, in those volumes, if not poesy itself, at least so keen a sentiment and so sincere an intention of poesy. In other respects, especially in his experiments, Sainte-Beuve undoubtedly failed in his verses. He attempted to give us a new style. After enjoying early in life the English descriptive poets, Cowper, Coleridge, Wordsworth, he desired to make us all seek the wholly simple and artless poesy of things, the poesy that exhales from all about us if we have but the eye to see and the soul to feel it. A walk, the reading of a book, a meeting in the street, seemed to him enough to stir the imagination. He dreamed of a middle region, if I may venture so to speak, between the grand poetic flights and the kindly, familiar style of daily life.

Foreigners, Schiller and Goethe, for instance, in their correspondence, have reproached French poesy with being nothing more than eloquence; now, Sainte-Beuve—as perhaps it has not been sufficiently noticed—was altogether a stranger to this oratorical bent of our nation. He was absolutely without that gift of rhetoric which is always the foundation of our best talent. He had neither eloquence, nor exaggeration, nor rhythm. When he spoke in public, his speeches were hardly more than newspaper articles. When he wrote in prose, he dislocated his sentences as he pleased: he seemed to avoid accepted methods of harmony and completeness. And the same in his poetry: breaks, clauses begun in one verse and ending in the next, nothing musical; it seems, if our language had allowed it, that he would rather have written in blank verse.

We have Sainte-Beuve's own judgment on his poetic work. "I have risen near to the summit," I heard him say, "but I have never gone beyond it, and in France we must go beyond." Subtile and true!

The poet, moreover,—and in this is the clearest of

his results in that line,—the poet, in Sainte-Beuve, benefited the critic. With what penetrating taste he judged our poet-authors! With what inward sympathy he welcomed the verses of our contemporaries, those of the young men especially! With what experience and what authority he spoke to them of their art! Sainte-Beuve is the only great critic of poesy that we have ever had. But I anticipate; we have not yet reached the critic.

Sainte-Beuve was, all his life, a journalist; he chose to be that only. His works, excepting two or three, are all collections of articles. It was his natural and favourite manner of working. He needed, if I am not mistaken, the stimulant of immediate publication. We must therefore not expect to find among his papers the sketched-out work that most writers have in their portfolios. But although, during the last twenty years of his life, Sainte-Beuve confined himself to literary articles in the newspapers, he had not always done so. In the *Globe,* at the beginning of his career, and later in the *National,* he wrote politics—the politics of a young man, liberal, ardent, aggressive, which are now easy enough to bring into contradiction with his attitude in after years. And this leads me to speak of the adherence that Sainte-Beuve gave to the Second Empire; the most illustrious, assuredly, that the *coup d' État* of 1851 obtained, and all the more signal because other men of Letters, generally and honourably, refused to give their approval to that deed of violence. For my part, I do not think it difficult to understand the choice made by Sainte-Beuve, however unfortunate and mistaken that choice may have been. The side he took touched certain profound instincts that were in him. His choice was not, as might be supposed, the effect of the temperament of a man of Letters, easily alarmed by public agitations. Nor do I think it necessary to put his passing Cæsarism to the score of scepticism; to that distrust of human nature which insinuates itself so readily into the minds of those who have seen much of men and have gone through several revolutions.

Liberalism is one of two things: either a sort of religious faith, all the more robust because it is a matter of youth, the result of an illimitable need of action; or else the effect of a reasoned belief, confidence in the immanent power of ideas, the conviction that truth being, in the long run, conformed to the nature of things, needs only full light and equal weapons to triumph. Let us add that truth *is* not, it makes itself; it ceaselessly frees itself from the struggle of opposing ideas; so that, in fact, that struggle is the essence of truth, contradiction is its life; the sole thing it asks from gods and men is the tussle of opinions—in other words, simply liberty. Sainte-Beuve evidently did not share either the blind faith of the liberal by temperament, or the reasoned faith of the speculative liberal. Far from it; he was afraid of liberty on account of certain liberties that were dear to him. He did not think that in French society, constituted as it is, the game could be always equal. For instance, he asked himself whether, with a powerful and organised clergy, *bourgeois* classes lacking deep culture, and, below, a populace that could not read—whether, with those conditions, obscurantism was not too strong to be dislodged by the Voltaires, or even by the Renans.

But that which dominated Sainte-Beuve in this line of ideas, and made him less fervent for liberty than became a man of thought, was, assuredly, one of the honourable feelings of his nature. He had, in the highest degree, *humanity*. He was touched by the sufferings of the multitude; and the lessening of those sufferings seemed to him the highest duty and also the greatest interest of society. Under the influence of these conceptions, he made short work of all other considerations, short work also of the difficulties offered by the nature of things. We see here how it was that he felt attraction for such thinkers as Proudhon; he was predisposed to believe they were right because they promised to cure evils over which his compassionate soul quivered. We can understand, also, how his mind was able to accept the vision of a strong power; a beneficent dictatorship, which, deriving its rights from the very grandeur of its task, would guide the nation strenuously towards its new social destinies. I have always smiled at the misconception, when I have seen the ultra-democratic party affect contempt for a writer who, more delicate certainly and less assertive, was nevertheless one with all its generous aspirations and its ideas on the duties of authority. Sainte-Beuve, moreover, as there is no need to recall here, was not long in comprehending how much illusion there was in his hopes. He saw that the saving genius had not appeared, and that the safe way was still to cling to the liberty of all, and to all the liberties. Toward the close of his life the conversion,—or, shall I say, the disenchantment?—was about complete.

After all, what remains, and will ever remain of Sainte-Beuve, is literary criticism. In that lie his originality, his claims, his incontestable supremacy. In that line he stands first, or, rather, alone; for the effect of his writings has been to cause all those who preceded him to be forgotten. To what a distance he has brought us from those vain theoretical discussions and sterile debates over the merits and defects of authors! I know not if some new critic may not come, in his turn, to take the place of Sainte-Beuve,— that is the law of things human,—but meanwhile, we can no longer make our judgment on works of the mind under any other form than that of which he has given us the model.

His vocation was early manifested. He tried his hand at criticism when he tried it in poesy. He did it in the *Globe;* he did it in his *Joseph Delorme;* he

began, as early as 1829, in the *Revue de Paris,* those
" literary portraits " which were soon after continued
in the *Revue des Deux Mondes,* and which constitute
his first manner.   But here we touch a delicate subject, and one to which Sainte-Beuve attached much
importance; we must therefore pause, for a moment,
over his early life.

He was, as we know, to have been a physician.   In
1826, when twenty-two years old, he lived with his
mother in the rue de Vaugirard, and followed his
medical studies as an *externe* in the hospital of Saint-
Louis.   He had a little room for study in the rue de
Lancry; he made up his bed himself, and was so alone
in those days of his youth, he used to say, that for
three months at a time no one entered his room.   His
mother clung to this study of medicine as to a certain
and solid thing; he himself took to it half-heartedly.
He was not satisfied with the instruction he received.
The best result of his work in this line was a certain
fund of practical physiological knowledge, memories
of Bichat, Lamarck, and Cabanis, which came back to
him after his mystical phase, and remained, thenceforth, as a sort of background to his thoughts of life
and the world.

It was in these years that he began to write verses.
In 1827 he stayed with friends in England, he " bathed
in the Thames," he read the poets, those whose style
he afterwards attempted to introduce into our language.
He was employed, about this time, on the *Globe,* for

which he wrote criticisms: "not bad," he said, "but dry." Daunou, however, encouraged him to work for an open competition on the poetic literature of the sixteenth century: he lent him books and the young man set to work. Can we not see him, at that early age of twenty-two, already studious and curious, interrogating his talent and his destiny?

Destiny replied to him. Meanwhile, he made the acquaintance of Victor Hugo. The second volume of *Odes et Ballades* had just appeared (1826); Sainte-Beuve was to write an article on it, and he went to see the poet, who lived near by, in fact, within two doors of the critic. The latter owned to the poet that he, too, made verses; he showed some, received good advice, and behold the two young men bound inseparably together, and Sainte-Beuve renouncing medicine for Letters; he used to say that he never even went to the hospital to get his instruments.

Some time later, Hugo having changed his lodgings, Sainte-Beuve followed him, and they ended by living in the same house. This intimacy exercised over this part of our friend's life an influence that he never sought to conceal. He gave himself up to poesy, to friendship, to zealous ardour for the dawning romantic creed. The years from 1827 to 1830 rolled by in a sort of enthusiastic devotion, of which the preface to *Consolations* has preserved to us the lyric note; it was something like the relations of master and disciple at the period of the Renaissance, a need on the part of the latter to make himself humble and small, and to defer in all things to the pontiff of the new faith. This preface should be read again ; and all the more because Sainte-Beuve, if I am not mistaken, found difficulty, later, in forgiving himself for it ; recovering from that fervour, as did others, he was angry with himself for having ceased for a period to belong to himself ; his literary and moral taste suffered from it.

From 1830, a little coolness came between the friends. To this politics contributed. Other sentiments had taken possession of Sainte-Beuve and thrown him into a crisis during which, agitated and distressed, he tried many things, took up the most conflicting ideas, addressed himself to the new prophets, frequented Lamennais, Lacordaire, etc. From this crisis came *Volupté* ("all the characters are portraits, very exactly painted") and much poetry, of which the *Pensées d'Août* contain some, and the old collections contain others, but which are for the most part unpublished. "There are thirty or so which I will give you to read," he said, "and then you can burn them."

Thus, from 1825 to 1830, devotion to romanticism in the person of its great leader, and, from 1830 to 1836, a period of passion and fever,—in short, a period of ten years, to which Sainte-Beuve often made allusion, saying that if he then alienated his will, it was through "the effect of a spell." He was very solicitous to make it understood that during that period he was not yet himself; that he followed romanticism farther than his later judgment approved; in a word, and according to his own expression, criticism was not yet awakened in him. It was, as it were, held in check by his affections. But the affections themselves, oh, sorrow! had their disenchantment and their end. Sainte-Beuve left Paris for Lausanne. This was the close of the poetic and passionate period of his life. At Lausanne he planned and sketched out *Port Royal*, the first fruits of his new literary activity.

The "History of Port-Royal" occupies a very important place in the life of Sainte-Beuve. He had already written articles in the *Revue des Deux Mondes* and elsewhere, but nothing very distinctive: "praises, complaisance, foregone conclusions." The subject that he now chose brought him for the first time to grapple with real historical study. In so doing he trained himself to research, to exactitude. He developed the qualities that he brought to this, his first important work — psychological intelligence, infinite suppleness, and facility. At every step he met great literary figures; he avoided none; on the contrary, he knew how to bring them powerfully into his picture. Thus it was that Sainte-Beuve, on this monastic subject, broke himself in, as it were, for his future work; the apprenticeship was thorough. He published at the same time many of his *Portraits,* contemporary

and other, which have long been his title to distinction
as a critic, and had then already made a place apart
for him, and a lofty place, before the *Lundis* came to
make him another, and a greater.

The *Causeries du Lundi* are, I do not hesitate to
say it, one of the most extraordinary works of which
literary history has preserved a memory. The work
is as amazing for its extent as for the variety of its
subjects, as vast in the toil that gave it birth as for the
talent that is shown in it. All subjects are there: the
ancients and the contemporaries; the gravest beside gayest; foreigners as well as Frenchmen; prose
and poesy, eloquence and history; Bourdaloue and
d'Aguesseau rubbing shoulders with Musset and
Parny; and with it all, endless original research, notes
made on documents, curious delvings into unexplored
domains. One needs to have known Sainte-Beuve
personally to comprehend the importance, the almost
morbid importance he attached to the spelling of a
name, to the correctness of a quotation or a date.
He wished to see everything with his own eyes, to
verify everything. He had truly the religion of
Letters.

From the time when the *Lundis* began, his whole
life was governed by the conditions of the task he
had undertaken. Those marvellous articles came from
the cell of a Benedictine monk. Sainte-Beuve's door
was closed, except on Monday, the day of publication,
which was made a day of rest and holiday. The

books he needed for his work were collected in advance in the public libraries by devoted friends. The readings from them made, the passages noted, he made a first sketch of his article; then he "built it," as he used to say. After which, he corrected every part of it, and began to write it, dictating to his secretary, snatching the pen himself now and then, interlining, modifying, bettering. The whole conscience of the scholar and artist was on the *qui vive* during this labour, and to the last moment. On Friday the article was finished: Sainte-Beuve drew breath; he went to read his work to Véron (I speak of the first *Lundis,* those of 1849 and the following years), whose *bourgeois* tact he valued; after which he stayed to dinner with Véron and a few friends. The task was not finished, however; after the printing came the correction of proofs, of which two, sometimes three, were needed to satisfy his requirements. Saturday and Sunday were passed thus, and then the next week was already there with its new article to sketch out. Such is the cost of perfect things, of lasting things!

Sainte-Beuve continued this task without interruption for five years; after which, the occasion arising, he started the work anew, and pursued it more persistently than ever. Later, there was, now and then, a little relaxing ; as, for instance, when he became Master of Conferences at the École Normale. Towards the last, illness stopped the work at times. But it is

mainly none the less true that he pursued it for
twenty years, and laid down the critic's pen only
with his life.

I have too often, on too many occasions, spoken
of Sainte-Beuve's talent to feel the need of dwelling
upon it to-day. I am only struck with one thing at
this moment when his career lies there, completed,
before us. Progress, in him, was continual, but it
was slow ; as it is, they say, in the development of
all superior life. He needed time to reach the full
possession of his genius. But then, how all things in
him ever tended to that end! What perseverance in
effort ! What incessant progression! What distance
from his first style to that which he attained in after
years! but already, in the first, what visible struggle
to conquer the language, to chain the Proteus! What
sincerity of intention ! What need to satisfy himself
and himself above all! Sainte-Beuve *grew* to the last;
and he had no falling back ; he is almost the only one
of our men of letters who sacrificed absolutely nothing to the requirements of trade, who gave way to
no mannerism, who assumed as he grew older neither
trick nor pose. To the last, he remained faithful to
an heroic work, to an artist's conscience, to respect
for his own talent : Sainte-Beuve is the model for
men of Letters.

I perceive that I have said nothing of what was,
perhaps, the most extraordinary feature of his works.
Here are twenty-five volumes of the *Lundis;* add to

those the *Portraits,* the *Port-Royal,* the *Chateaubriand,* and we have forty volumes of literary criticism. Well, the writer never repeated himself. He always had something fresh to say, and he always said it in a skilful and piquant manner. I know no writer who can give us such an appetite as he. We open him at random, we read him, and we cannot close the book. He disappears so completely behind his subject ; and when he does show himself it is with so many ideas, often with a stroke so happy, a word so apposite, so decisive !—a Montaigne turned critic, as one might say. Searching, sensible, judicious, without a shadow of charlatanism, returned from all misleadings ; more sceptical than indifferent ; occasionally with a biting sarcasm, with here and there a flower of poesy—such are the books of Sainte-Beuve.

He has been blamed for injustice. I am convinced, on the contrary, that never was a critic more equitable. He had his passions no doubt ; but passions are the man himself, the living expression of his moral nature ; and repugnances, in Sainte-Beuve, were usually only the revolt of his taste and his literary honesty against mediocrities, pretensions, and affectations. There are authors who count for much in our literature whom he never enjoyed ; some because they were not artists enough to suit him, others because he understood art in a different way from theirs, and he suffered too much from their defects to enjoy their beauties. Apart from that, he was possessed with the desire to be just, and he was so, by the natural effect of his literary conscience. He felt that all judgment was necessarily provisional and partial ; that the only means of rendering it less imperfect was to rectify it, fill it out, complete it, and for that purpose, to return to it, once, twice, constantly. He was convinced, in general, that "all saying has its counter-saying"; that men, in particular, have a right side and a wrong side, he felt himself obliged to show the one after showing the other. Hence these several portraits of the same personage, which he took up anew, changing the tone and the point of view ; hence the retouches, the notes, the correction so near to the assertion. Sainte-Beuve, contrary to what those who have not followed him closely suppose, was one of the critics whose judgments have been least influenced by considerations outside of literature itself.

And now we must take leave of him, of that lucid intellect, of that wonderful writer, that charming talker, that indulgent friend ; we must bid him again the last farewell with which we bowed before him yesterday, as we saw the grave close over him![1] Happy shall we be if the melancholy natural forebodings at such a moment are not realised! Happy if the death of a man who has held so high a place in our literature is not at the same time the end of a literary era ; if delicacy and taste, deprived of their

[1] Written in October, 1869, at the time of Sainte-Beuve's death.

last representative, do not vanish with him ; if the
royalty of letters is not fated to pass away like the
other royalties, and give place to general mediocrity
and violent methods. I have often had the impression that Sainte-Beuve, towards the end, felt himself
homeless in the midst of the new tendencies ; it is inevitable, perhaps, that when we lose a man like him,
we should imagine that all is ended, whereas it may
be only that all is being transformed.

The Duchesse du Maine.

The Duchesse du Maine.

THE DUCHESSE DU MAINE was a species of fairy, and one of the most singular: she deserves to be studied, she and her princely existence, in her little Court of Sceaux, where she comes before us as one of the extreme and most fantastic productions of the reign of Louis XIV, of the monarchical *régime* carried to excess.

Born in 1676, the Duchesse Du Maine died in 1753, not quite one hundred years ago. In those hundred years a great revolution has taken place in the order and governance of society, in the whole body of public manners and morals, so that the existence and life led by this fantastic little queen seems to us like an Arabian Night's tale, and we ask ourselves seriously: "Was it ever possible?" La Bruyère foresaw and foretold something of this fundamental change when he said: "While the grandees of the land neglect all knowledge of—I will not say the interests of princes and of public affairs only, but of their own affairs; while they ignore domestic economy and science of the father of the home, and boast of that ignorance, citizens are instructing themselves in and out of the

23

kingdom, becoming shrewd and politic, learning the strength and the weakness of all things in the State, they are thinking of bettering their position, they rise, they become powerful, they relieve the Prince of a part of his public cares. The grandees who disdained them now revere them, and think themselves fortunate to become their sons-in-law." This revolution, which La Bruyère thus foretold under a form of compromise and friendly agreement, was not, as we all know, so peaceable. La Bruyère, out of courtesy, said of the grandees what he would not have ventured to say of princes. The newcomers on the social stage have not always been as conciliating as the *parvenus* of La Bruyère's time. The new state of things did not end in a marriage, and, from '89 to 1850, the equilibrium between what remains of the essence of the old society and the increasing claims of the new society is still being sought.

The Duchesse du Maine, with all her wit and cleverness, had no suspicion of all this, and never put such questions before her mind; she believed in her birthrights, in her prerogatives of demigod, just as firmly as she believed in Descartes's system and her Catechism.

Louise Bénédicte de Bourbon was a granddaughter of the Great Condé. Her brother, M. le Duc, had La Bruyère for his tutor, and she may, in some respects, have profited thereby. In excellence of language, in wit, in eagerness for knowledge, she early showed that she had, like her brother, sparks of the intellect

DUCHESSE DU MAINE
From a portrait by N. *Mignard*

of her grandfather. But it is to be remarked that the soul of a hero, when it is shared and broken up among his descendants, sometimes produces very singular beings, and even strange, abnormal ones. Everything is on a great scale in great souls, vices as well as virtues. Defects which, in the hero, were balanced and held in check by lofty qualities, reveal themselves all of a sudden in his descendants, and seem excessive. The Great Condé, at the bottom of his soul, had none of that natural kindness—*bonté*—for which Bossuet lauded him; but his great mind and his valiant heart covered a multitude of things. He was not to be opposed at certain times; violent and despotic in temper, he was easily irritated by contradiction, even when the matter concerned only topics of the mind. Boileau perceived this one day when he differed from him in some discussion: "In future," he said, "I shall always be of the same opinion as M. le Prince, especially when he is wrong."

In general, the descendants of the Great Condé (history may say it to-day, for the race is extinct) were not kind. Brutality, carried to ferocity, characterised the one called M. le Duc (the grandson), and also that other M. le Duc, the first prime-minister of the Regency; it was startling in the Comte de Charolais. Violence, impossibility of bearing contradiction, were vehement, even frantic traits in all of them. But the mind of the great ancestor held its own with distinction, and was distributed as if in

brilliant portions among his posterity. The Duchesse du Maine was one of those who were best
supplied with it. It is noticeable that already, in the
grandchildren, the race was becoming physically im-
poverished; their forms showed it. The Duchesse
du Maine, as well her sisters, was almost a dwarf;
she was the tallest of the family, but did not look
to be more than ten years old. When the Duc du
Maine married her, having to choose among the
daughters of M. le Prince, he chose this one because
she was, perhaps, a fraction taller than her elder sisters. They were never called, in familiar talk, the
"princesses of the blood" but the "dolls of the
blood."

The Duc du Maine, who, in 1692, at twenty-two
years of age, married this granddaughter of the
Great Condé, aged sixteen, was the eldest of the bastards of Louis XIV and Mme. de Montespan. The
little prince, tenderly brought up by Mme. de Maintenon, who was a true mother to him, had been
formed and trained on the ideals of the foundress of
Saint-Cyr. He had intelligence, an excellent gift of
language, gentleness and charm in private life, and
the habit of discretion and submission; in a word,
he was one of those youths who are early perfected,
who never emancipate themselves, and who never
altogether become men. He was club-footed, a con-
stitutional blemish which increased his natural shyness in society. Well-educated, but without real

intelligence, he was destined never, in the region of ideas, to go beyond the narrow horizon by which he had been hemmed in from infancy. The duchess, eager, bold, imperious, and fantastic, was destined never to go beyond that horizon herself; and all her audacity, all her flights of fantasy, were confined within the artificial and magical sphere in which she kept herself excited, without a thought beyond it.

On the day when Louis XIV, yielding to his son's desire, gave him permission to marry, he could not restrain the remark, full of the common sense of his royal conviction: "*Such persons* ought never to marry." He foresaw the confusion and the conflicts which this equivocal race of "legitimatised bastards" might bring into the monarchical system, which was then the whole constitution of the State. He yielded, however, and toward the last he did his best to increase that confusion by the favours and prerogatives which he never ceased to heap upon these adulterous and parasitic offspring.

No sooner was she married, than the little duchess took her timid husband in hand, and subjected him in all things to her will. She dreamed of future glory, of political grandeur and power; meanwhile she chose to live as she pleased, and in as much sovereign state as she could compass; doing as little as possible for others, gratifying all her caprices, and setting up a Court of her own where no rival star could shine. This dream of her imagination was not

fully realised until the Duc du Maine purchased the
estate of Sceaux from the heirs of M. de Seïgnelay,
at a cost of 900,000 *livres*. There she made her
Chantilly, her Marly, her Versailles in miniature
(1700).

Among the tutors of the Duc du Maine there had
been a M. de Malezieu, a well-educated man, knowing mathematics, literature, Greek and Latin, im-
provising verses, planning theatricals, understanding
something of business, and "combining in his servile
position," says Lemontey, "the advantages of a universal mediocrity." This M. de Malezieu, who became the indispensable personage of the Court of the
duchess, its oracle in all matters, and of whom they
said at Sceaux, as, in the olden time, of Pythagoras,
"The Master says it," must certainly have had more
than one good quality, but it is difficult to-day to form
a just idea of his merits.   Member of two Academies,
that of the Sciences and also of the French Academy,
he was extolled by Fontenelle, who, however, did not
overdo the matter, and shows him to us, with his
"robust and fiery temperament," sufficing for all
petty employments.   Voltaire, more critical, speaks of
him as a man in whom great erudition had not extin-
guished genius : "He sometimes took up before your
Serene Highness " (Mme. du Maine) "a Sophocles, a
Euripides, and translated on the spot into French one
of their tragedies.   The admiration, the enthusiasm
that possessed him, inspired him with words and ex-

pressions which rendered well the manly and har-
monious vigour of the Greek verse, as much as it was
possible to approach it in the prose of a language lately
issued from barbarism. . . . Nevertheless, M. de
Malezieu, by efforts that called forth immediate enthusiasm, and by vehement recitation, seemed to make
up for the poverty of our language, and to put into
his declamation the very soul of the great men of
Athens."

That is a eulogy which ought to give a high idea
of the man; but we must not forget that Voltaire expresses himself thus in a Dedicatory Letter. The
Memoirs of Mme. de Staal (de Launay) show us M. de
Malezieu in a less favourable light, as ceremonious,
demonstrative, and dull, without much discernment
when discernment was not useful to him, and with a
mind that needed the help of a little heart. M. de
Malezieu was, to all appearance, one of those men
who derive activity from a robust temperament, combining shrewdness with energy; and who, having an
extensive and solid fund of early knowledge which
they never increase, devote themselves solely to putting that knowledge to use in society, and to getting
a profit out of it from the great. He was a man of
intelligence and education, who could appear a genius
only to a small coterie. That coterie he found at
Sceaux, and, by dint of constant activity and invention, he was able to fill it, for more than twenty-five
years, with the idea of his great attainments and

sublimity. At three leagues from Paris people called him, without laughing, the great Malezieu!

M. de Malezieu had been one of the principal causes of the purchase of Sceaux. Already rich through the bounty of the Court, he owned a pretty country-house at Châtenay, where he received the Duchesse du Maine, who honoured him with a visit in the summer of 1699, and to whom he gave a gallant hospitality. She stayed there, being pregnant, during the whole sojourn of the Court at Fontainebleau. Games, fêtes, fireworks in her honour, were continual, and all was managed with a certain air of innocence, as of the Golden Age. The populace of the neighbourhood took part in these pleasures by songs and dances ; the country was then tasting the first sweets of the Peace of Ryswick. The duchess then and there made her début into that life of fairyland and mythology in which she took such delight that soon she would have no other ; and then it was that the idea came into her head to take possession of the whole valley. The description of this first visit given by the Abbé Genest, a colleague of Malezieu, and addressed to Mlle. de Scudéry, is quite piquant, and shows us the origin of that long play at pastorals which soon after became the very existence of the duchess. Romantic "surprises" attended her every step ; innocent amusements at all hours : they played at nymphs and shepherdesses ; they prepared for future prodigality by playing at economy. "M. le Duc du Maine," says the narrative, "complained when he left off playing that he had lost ten *livres;* the princesses boasted of their luck in having won nearly as much." In these fêtes, and in others that followed in the same place in succeeding years, we see M. de Malezieu doing the honours charmingly, and giving life as universal manager to the whole of that little sphere. No wonder that he was thought worthy of being in himself the Molière, the Descartes, the Pythagoras, of that kingdom of Lilliput!

The Duchesse du Maine, said Fontenelle, insisted that even in amusements there should be an idea, an invention, and that "joy should have wit." When we read to-day the narrative of these fêtes in the collection entitled "The Diversions at Sceaux," we recognise, in the midst of the insipidity, that M. de Malezieu did supply the mental quality that the fairy demanded.

Soon the whole of the pretty valley of Sceaux became the park of the duchess, her pastoral kingdom, her vale of Tempe. She never appeared that the "Sylvain of Châtenay," and the "Nymph of Aulnay," did not come to pay homage in person ; there was not a spot, even as far as Plessis-Piquet, without its rural divinity. The Abbé Genest had selected his hermitage, whence he came to offer his devotions to "Our Lady of Sceaux."

But, who was this Abbé Genest ? Oh ! something **very singular and** very amusing, I assure you; **the**

least solemn of the French academicians (for he belonged to the Forty), and the most difficult to eulo-
gise at their public session.   D'Olivet supplemented
the official eulogy by a private letter.   The Abbé
Genest was, like Socrates, the son of a midwife; he
began life in business as a peddler, then he was a prisoner, then copyist, tutor, horse-jockey, secretary to
the Duc de Nevers ; witty and well-informed through
it all, and making verses with ease and natural gaiety.
He received first the second prize and then the first
prize for poesy in 1671 and 1673 ; that made him
known.   He curried favour with Pellisson, and,
through him, with the Dauphin's tutors, Bossuet and
others.   He took part in the conference on physics of
the famous Rohault, and, through some queer notion,
he set to work at putting Descartes's philosophy into
verse.   Finally he came to know M. de Malezieu,
who enjoyed him, utilised him, and made him his
confederate in the games and poetical diversions of
society.   The Abbé Genest was to princes what they
have liked in all ages (even our own), a mixture of
poet and buffoon.   He was laughed at, and gave
occasion for it ; he had a very remarkable disfigure-
ment, which did no harm to his fortunes : his nose
was immense, so immense that apparently we can
form no idea of it.   Many a time the Duc de Bourgogne and the Duc du Maine, when schoolboys, joked
about their tutor's nose.   Louis XIV himself gave
way once, and laughed a natural laugh at one of the

pranks played upon the abbé with that stupendous
nose. They even went so far as to find an anagram
in his name, Charles Genest—*Eh, c'est large nez.* I
skip, out of propriety, many jests relating to a totally
different matter—how shall I mention it ?—relating to
the too habitual and very incomplete manner in which
the Abbé Genest, in his absent-minded moments, was
accustomed to fasten the garment that the English
never name. Thanks to his merits so real and diverse,
the facetious abbé was in demand at Châtenay, Sceaux,
and Saint-Maur, for all the rural and bucolic fêtes :

> Among the sylvan gods, forget not
> Him who weareth bands and black coat
> .   .   .   .   .   .
> With that coat and with that nose,
> That nose that measures two feet long,
> He surely must be pedagogue of Fauns.

But this is nonsense. Let us resume our subject
without further frivolity. The Duchesse du Maine
studied the philosophy of Descartes with M. de Malezieu ; with him and by him she read Virgil, Terence,
Sophocles, Euripides ; and before long she was able
to read some of those authors, the Latins at least,
in the original. Moreover, she studied astronomy,
always with that font of universal knowledge, M. de
Malezieu, who knew more than was needed to explain
"The Plurality of Worlds" by Fontenelle. She
applied her eyes to the telescope, and also to the microscope ; in short, she studied everything, by fits and

starts, out of passion or caprice, but without becoming one whit more enlightened in general. Through it all she played shepherdess and pastorals by day and by night ; supplied ideas to be made into madrigals by her two scribblers, the eternal Malezieu and the Abbé Genest ; invited and gathered about her a crowd of elect, set them to work, wearied them to extinction, allowed no delay in carrying out her desires, and kept herself in movement with impish energy, for fear of having to reflect, or of being bored for a single instant. As for sleep in the midst of these vigils and distractions, there was no question of it ; the duchess was persuaded that it was necessary only for common mortals.

From the literary point of view, which, whether from far or near, must be ours, the mischief of this rush of tumultuous life was that of being incompatible with good taste. Good taste examines, discerns ; it has its periods of repose ; it selects. In this case, natural intelligence did all, but discerned nothing, selected nothing ; in her theatricals the duchess played indiscriminately "Athalie," "Iphigenia in Tauris" (faithfully translated from Euripides), or Azaneth, wife of Joseph, in the tragedy of "Joseph" written by the Abbé Genest.

What did it signify to her, provided she kept up a constant turmoil, gave way to all her emotions, and reigned supreme? People compared her to the great queens who have loved knowledge,—to Queen Christina, to Elizabeth, Princess Palatine, the friend of Descartes, and gave her the pre-eminence. President de Mesmes (premier-president of the Parliament) addressed to her with a new-year's gift, verses which he had caused to be written in the chivalric and Marotic style (the fashion of the moment), in which he styled himself "The very powerful Emperor of Hindustan," writing to the "more than perfect Princess Ludovisa, Empress of Sceaux." On both sides the masquerade was perfect. Even when she looked into her mirror the duchess thought herself beautiful; though she could not deny that she was short. At the time of her marriage an emblem and a motto had been devised for her : a honey-bee, with these words from Tasso : *Piccola si, ma fa pur gravi le ferite*—Small she is, but she gives cruel wounds. This gave rise, in the early days of Sceaux, to the formation of a society of the persons who most often had the honour of being invited there, under the name of the Order of the Honey-bee. Rules and regulations were drawn up, statutes were framed, a medal was struck for the occasion which those of the Order were to wear suspended to a lemon-coloured ribbon, whenever they went to Sceaux. This mark of distinction was much coveted. Thirty-nine persons were appointed and took the required oath, swearing "by Mount Hymettus." On this occasion they played at being Greek.

But now, Louis XIV's last war, the War of the

Spanish Succession, was lighted, and all Europe was
in a blaze; fortune was beginning to turn against
France; the people were exhausted by taxes and
bloodshed; the Duc du Maine failed to distinguish
himself by valour on the battlefield ; but at Sceaux
the duchess, radiant with hope and pride, played her
plays and continued to amuse herself.   " She swam,"
says Saint-Simon, " in the joy of her future grandeur."
The full glory, the splendour of what were called the
"Grand Nights of Sceaux," belong to these very
years of disaster. The scandal of such fêtes and
ruinous amusements became all the greater, or at
least more notorious, when the misfortunes of the
royal family were added to those of France.   But the
death of the chief direct heirs brought the Duc du
Maine nearer to power, and even to the throne;
every rung the less in the ladder of legitimate succession was one step higher on the ladder of his fortune.
We know now that Louis XIV's weakness, beset by
that of Mme. de Maintenon, the foster-mother more
than mother of the Duc du Maine, would in the end
equalise in all things the bastards with the legitimate
princes of the blood, and declare them, definitively,
capable of succeeding to the throne.   His last will,
had it been followed, would have given to the Duc du
Maine the highest influence in the future Regency.

   Curious readers can look into the Collection called
that of Maurepas (Bibliothèque Nationale), for the couplets and savage squibs with which the Duc and Du-

chesse du Maine were assailed on the occasion of these
odious favours; they are not very witty, and, in general,
are too indecent to be quoted here.   Many are the scur-
rilous comments on the duchess, whose own poets
always spoke of her as "the modern Penelope." I
shall only say two words on that delicate subject.   M.
le Duc (de Bourbon), own brother of the Duchesse du
Maine, had, at one time, a great fancy for her; such
fancies were not rare in the family of the Condés.
The brother and sister exchanged, from Saint-Maur to
Sceaux, gallant sentiments, which the duchess made
Malezieu and Genest put into rhyme, while Chaulieu
and La Fare did the same for M. le Duc.   At last,
however, the couple quarrelled, but much gossip and
many songs had already been spread abroad.

After these first attacks on the score of M. le Duc,
something was said, but rather mildly, about President
de Mesmes, whom the duchess desired to attach to
herself in order that she might rule the Parliament
through him.   But Cardinal de Polignac seems to
have been the favourite most in evidence, and some
have gone so far as to quote parts of letters that would
seem to be decisive proof.   That cardinal, so agreeable
in person and so much of a wit, appears to have been
made expressly for the little Court à la Rambouillet.
He was always busy with his great poem of "Anti-
Lucrèce," in which he maintained in Latin verse the
soundest principles of theology and morality.   He read
it, he explained it to the duchess, and M. du Maine

took pleasure in translating the songs.   One day when
the prince brought a song he had translated to his wife,
she said impatiently: " You will wake up some fine
morning and find yourself in the French Academy,
and M. d'Orléans Regent of the kingdom."

Ambition brooded in her, beneath this life of games
and comedies.   In that pigmy body, in that epitome of
the Great Condé, lay sparks of the same civic mad-
ness.   Of humane sentiment or of patriotism in these
superior beings, who think themselves of the lineage of
Jupiter, there is no question whatever; the nation and
the world were made for them; they believe this sincerely, and they act loftily in consequence.   On the
eve of the Regency (1714), Mme. du Maine made a
declaration to two dukes and peers, whom she had
summoned to Sceaux to talk over *eventualities*—as we
should say and as she did not say, for if she thought
wrong she at least spoke better than we do. She wanted
to secure for herself a party in the Parliament, and
obtain support there in the event of any quibbles being
raised against the rights which she believed the Duc
du Maine had now acquired under the king's will.
Seeing that those she addressed were reserved and on
their guard, she flew into a passion (as she always
did when she encountered the slightest opposition),
and told them that " when once the power of succeeding to the throne was obtained, rather than let it be
torn from them, they would, if need be, throw the
kingdom into a blaze from its centre to its four

corners." There is the Great Condé himself! Louis
XIV dead and his will broken, furious with anger,
she did not rest till she had tried to put those evil
words into execution.

All this interrupted somewhat the festivities of
Sceaux; and there are two periods, two epochs, in that
long, mythological life of pleasure, or, as I call it, that
life hemmed between two hedges: the first epoch,
that of hopes, of proud intoxication, of ambition concealed beneath the flowers; then the second, after
hope had failed, after disappointment and miscalcula-
tion—if we can employ those words; for, even after
such a fall, after the degradation of rank, after the
abortive conspiracy and imprisonment, her incorrigible
nature, returning to its accustomed scenes, displayed
anew the same pride, the same intoxication, the same
absorption in self, the same faculty of active and noisy
illusion, so that she actually felt herself still young at
seventy years of age, and as much of a shepherdess as
ever.   Never was any one more naïvely goddess and
shepherdess than the Duchesse du Maine.   She played
the comedy to the very last, never once suspecting
that it was comedy.

"Put me, as ever, at the feet of Mme. la Duchesse
du Maine," wrote Voltaire from Berlin, in 1752 (she
was then seventy-six years old); "hers is an elect
soul; she will love comedy to her latest moment, and
when she falls ill, I advise you to administer some fine
play to her instead of Extreme-unction.   People die as

they live. . . ." To these words we may add, to
complete the picture, that, loving comedy as she did,
and playing it incessantly, she played it ill, and was
none the less applauded.

And now, is there not a serious lesson to be drawn
from the picture of such an existence and such a nature, which to-day seem fabulous? It was said of
the Duchesse du Maine that "she never, in all her
life, came out of her house, nor *so much as put her
head out of the window."* Philosophers, at any rate
some philosophers, have imagined that if man, after
his birth and his first motions, did not experience
resistance by contact with the things about him, he
would never be able to distinguish himself from the
exterior world, and would come to believe that the
world was a part of himself and his own body wherever he extended his hand or his steps. He would, in
fact, end by persuading himself that the whole world
was only an appendage and an extension of his personal being; so that he would say, in all confidence:
"The Universe is I!" Mme. du Maine was such a
one; she embodied that dream of the philosophers.
She never met with any resistance to her wishes until
the period of the Regency. She early put herself into
a condition of never meeting with opposition, by
shutting herself up in that little Court of Sceaux, where
all was hers, and hers alone. Any will other than her
own would have seemed to her an impertinence and
a rebellion. When she did "come out of her house,"

however, and had to meet real difficulties, she struck against them, and was wrecked. In that mad conspiracy which she undertook out of spite against the Regent (1718), and into which she forced her timid husband, she was obliged to see that the world was larger, more real, more difficult to move than she had thought it. Any other than she would have learned a lesson, or at any rate would have felt some mortification or depression; but the force of her nature and of early impressions carried the day. Returning to Sceaux after a hard experience of humiliation and disgrace (1720), she placed herself again, little by little, in the same conditions in which she had formerly lived; again she found no resistance, and soon forgot there was any for her outside of her own valley. She remained as convinced as ever that the law of the world, when it worked properly, was that all things were for her, and solely for her. In a word, she was like a person who has tumbled by accident out of a first-story window, without much injury, but who, for that reason, never again looks out of a window.

It is possible to speak of Mme. du Maine with certainty and as if we had known her, for we have the most direct, intimate, and sure testimony about her. She took into her service in 1711, under the title of waiting-woman, a person of worth, who was not below any station, who was fitted to be the equal and who was the rival in intellect of the most distinguished persons of her day, uniting gravity to gaiety, and possessed of a heart that kept its full value, even when time had withered it. Mlle. de Launay remained with her mistress for more than forty years, and left behind her racy Memoirs, which have long been greatly admired for the quality of their language and the charm of the narrative. In reading Mlle. de Launay, and in following her through the various vicissitudes of her menial condition, we say with La Bruyère: "The advantage of Great persons over other men is immense in one particular. I concede to them their high living, their rich furniture, their horses, dogs, monkeys, fools, and flatterers; but I envy them the happiness of having in their service persons who equal them in heart and mind, and often surpass them." Mlle. de Launay herself, who has, perhaps, never yet been given her true rank as moralist, represents to my mind a female La Bruyère, placed in the alcove of her princess. She does not tell all, but she sees all; and by weighing her words, she gives to her observations a more concise and ineffaceable character.

She represents to us marvellously that talent for saying the right thing well which was peculiar to the Duchesse du Maine, and which was the first characteristic that attracted her attention: "I gave it to her wholly and without effort," says Mlle. de Launay; "for no one ever spoke with more correctness, clearness, and fluency, or in a nobler and more natural manner. Her mind employed neither trick

nor figure of speech, nor anything that could be
called invention. Forcibly struck by a subject, her
mind rendered it as the glass of a mirror reflects,
without adding, without omitting, or changing anything." No words could better depict all that was
natural, accomplished, and even, in a certain sense,
just and correct, in that quick mind and speech,
always itself in the midst of her artificial world. Expression, in the Duchesse du Maine, was equal,
neither more nor less, to impression; and both were
always clear and vivid. "Language is never so perfect as when you speak it, or when people speak of
you," Mme. de Lambert wrote to her. Take out the
compliment, and the praise is the same as that we
have just read.

All those who have written of the Duchesse du
Maine, note this "precision" of her mind and the
"accuracy" [*justesse*] felt in her brilliancy. In this
respect, she belonged to that school at the close of
the seventeenth century to which Mme. de Maintenon
had taught the lesson that long sentences are a defect.

Mlle. de Launay also initiates us into the long train
of caprices, ambitions, and fantastic games of this
clever and arbitrary spoilt child. She shows her to
us, and shows herself beside her, conspiring all night
with her pen, striving, by dint of memorials and
letters, to stir up against the Regent a Fronde which
should bear the stamp of wit and *bel-esprit*. After
the imprisonment of the princess and the waiting-

maid, an imprisonment which did not redound to
the honour of the one, but was the glory of the
other, Mlle. de Launay, ennobled in the eyes of the
world by her constancy, returned to Sceaux with her
mistress, who rewarded that constancy by putting
her (although with a shade of difference) on the footing of her ladies.   Little by little, the miniature Court
was repeopled and reanimated; the whirlwind began
again.   Dream and delirium were soon in full swing.
But a rather spicy episode must here find its place
when the history of the Queen of Sceaux is written.

Mlle. de Launay, whenever she stayed in Paris, saw
much of Mme. de Lambert, and went to her "Tuesdays "—that was the day on which Mme. de Lambert
gathered around her Fontenelle, La Motte, Mairan, the
Abbé Mongault, and several other academicians and
wits.   Now it happened that Mlle. de Launay and Mme.
de Lambert read, at one of these Tuesdays, letters which
they had received from the Duchesse du Maine, who,
being informed of the honour done to her letters, pretended to be frightened at their production before so
learned and formidable a company.   Out of this grew
a correspondence between herself and La Metto(1726).
The latter was fifty-four years old and blind; the
duchess was nearing fifty.   The blind wit took to
playing lover; Mme. du Maine played artless innocence and pastorals.   Presently it became a question
of how to make a Serene Highness understand that
the lover was in love with her, without pronouncing

the word love, and how to turn and twist that gallant
idea to every meaning, and simulate an ardour, still
restrained within terms of respect, in order to obtain
from her certain favours. The first of these favours was
that she should sign her name in full: Louise Bénédicte de Bourbon. La Motte's game was then to say
that this signature of Louise Bénédicte de Bourbon
could not *last;* giving it to be understood that he was
devouring it with kisses, and he begged, clamorously,
for another signature. "I have, with your permission,
almost worn out the first," he wrote.—O Molière!
Molière of *Les Précieuses,* where wert thou ? In reading this correspondence, refined to the quintessence of
absurdity, we understand the weariness of those who,
spending their lives at Sceaux in making wit by night
and by day, could not help calling the little Court "the
Galleys of Bel-Esprit" and crying for mercy.   The
charming Prince de Ligne used to say: "I think I
should have been bored by the Duchesse du Maine;
she had a twist to her mind as well as to her shoulders.   Sceaux was the country-house of the hôtel
de Rambouillet."

During this second epoch of Sceaux, the duchess
placed at the head of those she called her "swains"
the witty Marquis de Sainte-Aulaire, who wrote his
famous quatrain to her when he was ninety years old;
it was very rejuvenating to the duchess to give herself
so old a swain; she seemed like a child beside him.
She managed to combine, no one exactly knows how,

religion with her various gallant, bucolic, and mythological practices, and one day she requested M. de
Sainte-Aulaire to go to confession with her, to which
he replied,

> My Shepherdess, in vain I seek,
> Nothing is on my conscience.
> In pity suffer me to sin,
> Then I may feel penitence.

Voltaire was one of the guests, if not one of the
swains of Sceaux; and he made certain memorable
sojourns there.   In the autumn of 1746, having compromised his safety by one of those imprudences that
were so habitual with him, he arrived one evening to
ask the Duchesse du Maine for an asylum.   She hid
him in a remote apartment, where the shutters were
kept closed all day.   Voltaire worked by candle-light,
and during the two months he lived in this way he
composed a number of his pretty *Contes,* especially
"Zadig," and every night he went to read them to
the duchess, who, having lost the habit of sleeping,
slept less on those nights than ever.   Other appearances of Voltaire at the little Court of Sceaux are on
record, and all were singular.

In spite of this demand for wit and intellect and for
the persons who were best supplied with them, it
cannot be said that the influence of the Court of
Sceaux was of any benefit to Letters, or that it ever inspired anything.   Nothing was felt there of the life-
giving and fructifying action that comes from a true

centre. Nothing was seen there but a round of enchantments, planned and directed, to which minds already formed came to lay their homage at the feet of the divinity of the place, and to exert themselves in rivalry to amuse her. To me the most impressive side of the little Court, and the one for which alone it seems to be memorable, is the moral side, the side which affords food for human observation of prejudices, eccentricities, and absurdities. If you wish to study in a perfect specimen, and as if under the microscope, the dainty egotism, the fantastic and coquettish despotism of a princess of the blood in the olden time, and the artless impossibility in which she lives of conceiving any other existence in the world than her own, go to Sceaux; there you will see these gross defects in miniature, just as we see gold-fish moving in the sunshine in a transparent bowl. You will see that spoilt child of sixty and more, to whom experience has taught nothing,—for experience implies reflection and an inward study of self,—you will see her to the last assembling a crowd around her; and to those who wonder at her doing so, she will reply: "I am unfortunate enough not to be able to do without the things I do not care for." It was necessary that every room in that palace of Armida should be filled, no matter how or by whom; a vacuum was the one thing dreaded.

"The desire to be surrounded increases," writes Mme. de Staal (Mlle. de Launay) to Mme. Du Deffand, "and I foresee that if you have an apartment and do not fill it, there will be great regret for what you lose, no matter what it is.   Great people, by dint of expanding themselves, become so thin one can see daylight through them; it is a fine study to contemplate them; I know nothing that brings one more surely back to philosophy."

Thus did Mlle. de Launay, the La Bruyère of Sceaux, observe things; and she crowns her Memoirs by a portrait of the Duchesse du Maine, which ought to be here transcribed at full length, so complete and finished is it, and so well does she sum up an entire species in the person of its most singular individual. It is a piece of the finest and most delicate moral physiology.   I give its principal features:

"Mme. la Duchesse du Maine, at sixty years of age, has not yet learned anything from experience; she is a child of much intelligence; she has the defects and the charm of a child.   Inquiring and credulous, she has desired to acquire all kinds of knowledge; but is satisfied to get them superficially.   The conclusions of those who brought her up are to her principles and rules, about which her mind has never formed the slightest doubt; she submitted herself to them once for all. Her provision of ideas is made; she would reject the best-demonstrated truths, and resist the best arguments, if they conflicted with the first impressions she received.   All examination is impossible to her volatility of mind, and doubt is a condition that her weakness cannot endure.   Her Catechism and Descartes's Philosophy are two systems that she understands equally well.   .   .   .

"The idea she has of herself is a conviction she has accepted like all her other opinions.   She believes in herself just as she believes in God and in Descartes, without examination or discussion.   Her mirror has not been able to raise the slightest doubt in her mind as to the charms of her face; the testimony of her eyes has no weight with her against the judgment of those who decided that she was beautiful and well-formed.   Her vanity is of a singular kind ; but it seems less shocking because it is unreflecting ; though for that very reason it is more absurd.

"Intercourse with her is slavery ; her tyranny is undisguised ; she never deigns to colour it with an appearance of friendship. She says, ingenuously, that she ' has the misfortune not to be able to do without persons for whom she cares nothing at all.' And she proves it. She hears with indifference of the death of those who, if they kept her waiting a quarter of an hour for a walk or a game of cards, would make her weep."

This insensibility was proved to the letter upon the death of the Duchesse d'Estrées, which took place suddenly at Anet in 1747. It seemed that Mme. du Maine could not exist without that duchess, who became the manager of all her pleasures, the Malezieu of her last years. She was buried; "then the curtain was lowered, and no one ever spoke of her again." The author of the portrait goes on to show us in this way all the artless vices of her princess, all her good qualities without soul and without ties, her religion without piety, her profusion without generosity, much information and no real knowledge, "all the eagerness of friendship with none of its sentiments," not the slightest suspicion of human sympathy and reciprocity: "there is no such thing as conversation with her; she does not care to be understood; it suffices her to have listeners." Mlle. de Launay concludes by quoting the following saying, which expresses the result of her study, and which the little duchess might well have written of herself:

" She " (the Duchesse du Maine) " sent word to a person of much intelligence that ' Princes were in the moral world what monsters were in the physical : we see openly in them the vices that are unseen in other men.' "

That conclusion is true of all those who are worshipped and believe themselves born to be worshipped, from Nebuchadnezzar to the Duchesse du Maine. But, while contemplating them with a sort of amazement (for, under this more or less royal form, the species is now disappearing day by day), let us avoid our own reefs and endeavour not to overflow in self-complacency; let us remember that in them there was much of ourselves; that their defects are those that we might have to-morrow if we were not restrained and warned by the resistance of things. In place of these people born demigods, who were the monstrous product of the old *régime,* let us put, in idea, the *parvenus,* who are the habitual product of the new state of things. We know the *parvenu* on the morrow of a revolution, for we have seen him, that being, that *monster* characteristic of modern society. Man may turn and overturn situations, he will not change his defects or his perversities; we see them all reappear; only they reproduce themselves, according to their period, in forms more or less noble, polished, and agreeable; and the form that combined excess of egotism with delicacy of mind and politeness is rather that of the past.

Madame de Staal=Delaunay.

Madame de Staal=Delaunay.

CERTAINLY the nineteenth is the most retrospective of centuries. We are never weary of searching, stirring, disclosing the past. At the same time that industrial activity and scientific invention are going forward in all directions towards the new and towards the unknown, intellectual activity, which does not find sufficient food in the works or thoughts of the present day, and is often in danger of turning against itself, looks back in search of an object, and finds it among the things of an olden time, whether those of four thousand years ago, or those of yesterday: little we care what period, provided we can occupy and interest ourselves in it, and that our mind and our curiosity can lodge there, if only for the passing moment. To-day, a well-known man of Letters, M. Barrière, is publishing a Collection, made with taste, of the numerous Memoirs of the eighteenth century, from the Regency to the Directory; it is a fortunate idea, which will enable us to see again, in its daily existence, an epoch that has for many persons already passed into the condition of romance.

This, if I count correctly, is the third time since

1800, that fashion and publication have turned to
the Memoirs of that period. The first period of such
return was that of the rebirth of society, under the
Consulate and the first years of the Empire. Then it
was that the Vicomte de Ségur published his Memoir
of Bezenval ; that M. Craufurd published those of
Mme. du Hausset; and that the series of little volumes
from the publishing house of Léopold Colin made
their appearance. The second period was under
the Restoration ; here historical and political interests
had sway. Long series of complete Memoirs of the
eighteenth century and of the French Revolution appeared, in which M. Barrière played an important
part as editor. To-day, for the third time, under this
return of fashion, nothing more than an interest of
literary taste is concerned, and in our opinion this
indifference is not a very propitious condition for
judging rightly, or for correcting old impressions and
forming others new and definitive.

Madame de Staal deserved, by good right, to open
the series, for it is with her that the style and tone
characteristic of the women of the eighteenth century
properly begins. An eloquent writer, M. Cousin, in
the sketch, so full of ardour, which he made of the
women of the seventeenth century, loudly awarded
them the preference over the women of the succeeding age. I understand him : the moment we bring
forth grandeur, contrast of character, splendour of
circumstances, there can be no hesitation. Whom

MADAME DE STAAL-DELAUNAY
From the painting by Mignard

can we contrast with women some of whom carried into cloisters loftier souls than those of Corneille's heroines ; while others, after all the vicissitudes and tempests of their human lives, have had the signal honour to be lauded and proclaimed by Bossuet ? Nevertheless, as, in the matter of womankind, strength and grandeur are not everything, I cannot, for my part, extend preference to exclusion. Neither the women of the sixteenth century—though they suffered the wrong of being seared by Brautôme— nor those of the eighteenth, although it is the tone of the day to be all the more severe upon them be- cause they are supposed to have been more indulg- ent, are, in my opinion, to be thus despised. What is it, after all, that is in question, if not grace, intellect, and charm (I speak of the charm that survives and still is felt throughout the ages)? Now the *élite* of women, in all three of those centuries, were abund- antly and diversely gifted with those qualities. This diversity reminds me of the charming story of the "Three Manners," each of which, according to the Athenians of Voltaire, was successful in its turn; and had there been a fourth manner of pleasing, who would quarrel with it? I would even go so far as not to exclude from competition the women of the nine- teenth century—if the time had come to form a judg- ment upon them. But let us not question too much for the present half-hour, but keep to Mme. de Staal- Delaunay and my subject.

Inasmuch as, in connection with women, I have used that word "century," I must be still further allowed to insist on certain distinctions that I think necessary, and on classification—a villainous term which I cannot avoid. The women of the sixteenth century, I have elsewhere said, were too much put to one side in the studies that have lately been made of the beginnings of polite society in France. Rœderer sacrificed them to his idol, the hôtel de Rambouillet. We shall return, if I am not mistaken, to those women of the sixteenth century, to those contemporaries of the three Marguerites, who knew so well how to carry on, abreast with public matters, conversation and pleasures. "I have often heard women of the highest rank talk and discuss with ease, with elegance, the gravest matters of morals, of politics, of physics." This was a testimony given to French women by an astonished German, who wrote of his travels in Latin and at a date (1616) when the hôtel de Rambouillet could not as yet have produced its results.

However that may be, the seventeenth century certainly opens with Mme. de Rambouillet, and closes with Mme. de Maintenon. In like manner, the eighteenth begins with the Duchesse du Maine and Mme. de Staal, and ends with Mme. de Staël and Mme. Roland; I give that latter name purposely, for it marks an event—that of solid merit and grace introduced into the middle classes, and thenceforth making an increasing place therein. I know how

true taste and refinement were long the almost exclusive appanage of the aristocratic world; and how,
in some respects, and in spite of the changes that
have supervened, they are so still. But it is no less
evident that the farther we progress, the more true
courtesy, distinction of nature and tone are found
naturally compatible with a middle-class condition;
the name of Mme. Roland signifies all this. After
her, women of that station began to possess as of
right what was formerly considered an audacious
usurpation.

The women of the eighteenth century, usually so-
called, the primitive type of whom was transmitted
without alteration from the Duchesse du Maine,
through the well-known names of Mme. de Staal-
Delaunay, Mme. de Lambert, Mme. du Deffand, the
Maréchale de Luxembourg, Mme. de Coislin, Mme. de
Créquy, down to Mme. de Tessé and the Princesse de
Poix, divide themselves, nevertheless, into two distinct groups—those before Jean-Jacques, and those
after. All the latter, those after Jean-Jacques, that is
to say, those who came under his influence, were
kindled into passion for him, had a vein of *sentiment*
which their predecessors never sought and never
knew. The latter, the women of the eighteenth century before Rousseau (and Mme. de Staal-Delaunay
presents a perfect and most faithful image of these),
are purely the pupils of La Bruyère. They read him
in youth, they verified him by experience. To that

book of La Bruyère which seems to set its seal on
their minds, add, if you choose, that they had also
read in early years "The Plurality of Worlds" and
"The Search for Truth."   Mme. de Staal begins the series of the female
writers of the eighteenth century as distinctly as
Fontenelle initiated the work of his group.   She was
born much sooner than has been supposed, or than
her biographers have stated.   A scholar, to whom we
owe many rectifications of this kind, M. Ravenel, has
cleared up this point, which is not without importance
to an understanding of the life of Mlle. Delaunay.   I
call her Mlle. Delaunay from habit, for (another correction made by M. Ravenel) she was not so named.
Her father's name was Cordier; but, having been
obliged to leave the country for some cause not mentioned, he left in France a young and beautiful wife,
who resumed her family name, Delaunay, and the
daughter, in turn, took the name of her mother, which
has remained to her.

The young Cordier-Delaunay was born in Paris in
August, 1684, and not in 1693, as was generally believed.   She was therefore nine years older than has
been supposed; not that she conceals her age, for she
nowhere mentions it.   She does not give the precise
date of her birth in her Memoirs (dates, under a
woman's pen are always rather nebulous); but she
mentions, in the narrative of her youth, certain historical circumstances which might put us on the right

track. It results from these extra nine years of which we have been unaware, that she was fully twenty-seven years old when she entered the service of the Duchesse du Maine, consequently she was already a woman whose mind was formed, and who might suffer from her position, but would take no moulding other than that of restraint. It follows from this great advance in her age that she was thirty-five years old at the time of her love-affair in the Bastille with the Chevalier de Ménil, and that she did not marry the Baron de Staal until her fifty-first year. Hence, during the course of this existence of which the bloom was so short and so quickly gone, we see how matters came to no result, and we understand better the art of delicate irony in that firm and charming mind, and its tone of enjoyment without gaiety born of constant thwarting.

An oft-quoted saying of Mme. de Staal might give an idea that her Memoirs were not as sincere as they should be. "I have painted only a half-length portrait of myself," she replied one day to a friend who expressed surprise that she should have told everything. The saying was much repeated, and it has done injustice to the veracity of the writer. Mme. de Staal was a person of truth, and her book is a true book in the full acceptation of the word; that characteristic is imprinted on every page. It is true that on certain delicate and reserved points she may not have said all: for instance, it is possible that her love-passages

in the Bastille with the Chevalier de Ménil may have
gone a little farther than she admits; all that is very
likely, and no one could reasonably ask a woman to
be more sincere on such points. The reader, if he has
the desire, can go the rest of the way himself without
much effort. Lemontey thinks he finds much malice
in certain remarks of hers on the Abbé de Chaulieu,
when she went to see him on leaving the Bastille
and found him quite changed from what he had been
previously : " He was already very ill," she says,
" from the disease of which he died three weeks later.
I saw him, and I noticed how, in that condition, we
become *indifferent to all that is useless to us.*" Lemontey thinks he sees in those words a revelation
that escaped her—which is being shrewd indeed. Of
whatever utility this able woman may have been in
past times to the Abbé de Chaulieu, who was almost
an octogenarian, it is not upon avowals of this kind
that I rest the greater or less degree of sincerity of any
woman-author in the Memoirs that she writes. The
sincerity I mean is of another order; it exists in the
sentiments expressed, in the total of the judgments
and the views; in a person's not lauding him or herself directly or indirectly, not claiming too much, not
magnifying self, looking at self and others from a
just point of view, and daring to show it. And
what book succeeds better than the Memoirs of Mme.
de Staal in rendering exactly that perfect and often
cruel accuracy of observation, that inexorable senti-

ment of reality? It was she who said these lasting words: "Truth is as it can be; it has no merit but that of being what it is." Thus her Memoirs are the contrary of the romances that we dream; like life itself they grow sad and sadder.

A noble spirit, lofty and stoical even in its weaknesses, a firm and free mind, stamp themselves in clear-cut, delicate lines upon those Memoirs. We admire a sureness of ideas and tone that is sometimes rather alarming. There is so little of the superfluous that we are tempted to ask if the necessary is always there. The words *coldness, dryness,* enter our minds; but, on reflection, we come to think that we mean in most cases merely accuracy and decision. Never does her pen grope its way, never does she play with her thought; she catches it and carries it along firmly and promptly. And there is very much strength in this small display of effort. Pliny the Younger, in the eulogies he made on certain writers, was wont to put together in one word, as being closely united, two qualities, namely: *amaritudo, vigour,* born and steeped in a secret *bitterness.* Mlle. Delaunay (we may quote Latin about a woman who so nearly became Mme. Dacier) possessed that vigour. Fréron, giving account of her Memoirs in his *Année Littéraire* (1755), has well remarked that we may apply to her what she said of the Duchesse du Maine: "Her mind never makes use of turns of phrase, or figures, or anything at all that calls itself invention. Vividly impressed by

objects, it renders them as the glass of a mirror reflects,
without adding, without omitting, without changing
anything." In my opinion, however, the comparison with the reflection of a mirror does not go deep
enough for what was in Mlle. Delaunay; objects when
she reflects them have the more solid character of an
etching. Grimm, in his *Correspondance* (August 15,
1775), in praising the Memoirs, says: "The prose of
M. de Voltaire excepted, I know none more agreeable than that of Mme. de Staal." That is true, although that prose, of a clearness so charming and
novel, does not resemble that of Voltaire, which alone
was truly light and flowing. The simplicity of Mme.
de Staal's diction is otherwise contrived. But what am
I about? Why should I trouble myself with Grimm
and his opinions, when, in the most delicate and delightful literary volumes that French criticism has
produced, we possess the judgment and the definition given by M. Villemain of the manner and the
delicacies of Mme. de Staal's style?

In all that concerns the person herself, the illustrious critic is severe; he thinks he sees in the satirical
sketches of the witty woman what he calls "the *sou-
brette* bias." Did Mlle. Delaunay deserve this back-
handed blow? Was the "indelible character of the
waiting-maid," as she bitterly calls it herself, so indelible that it follows her even into the productions of
her thought? Nothing could be less founded, it seems
to me, than such a judgment, nothing more unjust.

We have seen that she was already advanced into womanhood when she entered the service of the Duchesse du Maine; she was no longer a young girl easy to remould. Her early education had been solid, choice, brilliant; the convent of Saint-Louis at Rouen, where she passed her youthful years, was "like a little State where she reigned as sovereign." She, too, had her little Court of Sceaux in that convent where M. Brunel, M. de Rey, and the Abbé de Vertot were at her feet, and where those good ladies, de Grieu, had eyes but for her. "What they did for me," she says, "cost me so little that it seemed to me only in the natural order of things. It is only our efforts to obtain things that teach us their value. In short, I acquired, though I was so little, the defects of great people; which has served me since then to excuse them."

Thus brought up, and thus treated, till she was twenty-six years of age, on the footing of a perfect and admirable being, when, later, she fell into servitude, she was like a dethroned little queen, and she kept those feelings: "convinced," she says, "that it is our own actions only that can degrade us." No act of her life contradicted that noble sentiment. The injury to her of this early education and exclusive training was rather, as she very truthfully points out, to give her a somewhat learned tone, a liking to teach, to pattern others by herself, which was natural in a young woman who had read the *History of the Academy of Sciences,* and had studied geometry.

And here we must observe, that in the majority
of the passages quoted in proof of this defect, it
is she herself who denounces it, and gaily does
the honours of her person.   More than one reader
has failed to detect the smile lurking behind the
words.

The beginning of the Memoirs is full of grace and
has something of the novel in it; it is thus that life
appeared to her "before the charm ceased," before
illusion vanished.   The stay at the Château de Silly
with a friend of her childhood, the arrival of the
young marquis, his natural indifference, the scene behind the hornbeam hedge between the two young
girls, which he hears without being seen, his curiosity awakened far more than his desire, her emotion in
thinking herself the object of his affection, her self-
control, nevertheless, the *tête-à-tête* walk in which
astronomy is so useful, and the young soul tastes the
austere sweetness of mastering itself—all this com-
poses a romance, very simple and touching; it is one
of those memories of which there is but one in a lifetime, a memory in which the wearied heart can always rest and be refreshed.   These may be nothings,
but how true they are! how they cling to secret
fibres—to those of every one!   "The feeling that engraved these little facts upon my memory," says the
author, "has remained a distinct recollection."   Even
in depicting them, see how her sobriety appears!
She permits herself only a discreet sketch, a delight-

ful but restrained touch, the faithful expression of feelings too repressed.

Nevertheless, M. de Silly is the man she most truly loved. With what passionate vivacity she describes his first departure! "Mlle. de Silly burst into tears when he bade us adieu. I hid mine from his eyes that were more inquisitive than tender; but after he had disappeared, I thought I should have ceased to live. My eyes that were wont to see him could see nothing more. I did not deign to speak, for he could not hear me; *I even felt that I thought no longer.*" Observe that last touch; it reminds me of Lamartine's line addressed to Nature:

"A single being lacks thee, and thou art depopulated."

But in Mlle. Delaunay the gradation ends with *thought.* This absence of thought is, in truth, the most violent symptom to the mind of a philosopher, to whoever has begun by saying: "I think, therefore I am." What she adds is no less noticeable: "His fixed image filled my soul. I felt, nevertheless, that every moment took him farther from me, and my grief grew in the same proportion as the distance that parted us." Here we come upon her defect; the grief that grew in direct proportion to the distance is more than philosophy, it is geometry; and we can understand why M. de Silly should write to his young friend, in a letter which she transcribes: "Use, I beg of you, the simplest expressions; above

all, make no use of those that belong to the Sciences.'
As a man of the world, and full of tact, he had laid
his finger at once on the slight defect.

This, however, was an early inclination, soon repressed, which scarcely affected an exquisite diction
and the best of language. When the marquis returned
shortly after to Silly, the flower of sentiment in her
heart was already slightly wilted; reflection had
spoken. These few moments of enchantment were,
therefore, a very short springtime in the life of Mlle.
Delaunay; but their perfume was lasting enough to fill
her soul during the most exposed years of her youth,
and to preserve her at that time from all other risks.
She was twenty-three or twenty-four years of age
when she first met M. de Silly, and he was thirty-six
or thirty-seven.   His cold, ambitious character seemed
more marked as he grew older; Grimm declares that
he was a pedant and not amiable; he tells us that disappointed ambition finally so disturbed his mind that
he flung himself from a window and was killed.
Mme. de Staal glides over that frightful detail.   She
found him agreeable in his last years, and, in spite of
the errors of the intervening ones, she never ceased
to remain under subjection to his old prestige.   She
even carried her friendship, during a violent attack of
passion which convulsed him, so far as to assist him
in the character of *doctor-moralist:* I can find no
other terms so appropriate; the letters that she wrote
him at this period are those of a confessor and a

physician combined. They show consummate experience, lofty wisdom, and are charming still, even under the supreme disillusion. Like all true doctors, she better knows the veritable condition of the patient than the means of curing it; she can offer only palliatives, and she herself directs him to ambition!

"I had hoped much," she writes to him, "from time and absence; but it seems they have produced nothing; on the contrary, the evil has grown worse. The sole resource that I can imagine would be an occupation, strong and satisfying from the dignity of its object; love has no such expedient. I wish that ambition could give it to you. You are not made to live without passions; frivolous amusements cannot nourish a heart as voracious as yours. Try to find an object more vast than its capacity, otherwise you will for ever feel the loathing that all that is mediocre inspires." M. de Silly died November 19, 1727; he was lieutenant-general of the armies of the king.

If M. de Silly is the hero of the first part of the Memoirs, the hero of the second part is undoubtedly M. de Maisonrouge, lieutenant of the king at the Bastille, that perfect model of a passionate and delicate lover. It is well that Mme. de Staal, who so cruelly sacrificed him to the sulky Chevalier de Ménil, should avenge him upon herself, by the interest she sheds upon him, and by the affectionate colouring with which she surrounds him. Alas! at the moment when she most appreciates the devotion and merits of the poor Maisonrouge, it is the other whom she regrets! With a soul so firm, a mind so superior, yet the miserable plaything of an unworthy passion, she flees from him who seeks her, and seeks the man who flees her, according to the eternal cross-purposes of the heart. Oh! how truly it gave her the right to say —as she did later, when the storm had passed, in a letter to M. de Silly—"With due deference to Mme. de . . ., who treats love so methodically, every one in love is for himself, and makes it as he pleases. I am surprised that so venerable a person does not see that passions are aberrations of mind which are not susceptible of the order she wants to put into them. I think precepts on this matter ridiculous; fixed rules might as well be made for the manner in which crazy people should rave."

I said of Mme. de Staal that she was like a first pupil of La Bruyère, but a pupil who became the equal of the master. No writer could furnish as many new, true, irrefutable thoughts to add to the chapter on "Women" as she; besides which, she spent thirty years of her life in practising and commenting on the chapter on "Grandees." She observed the latter at her ease, but also to her cost, in that little Court of Sceaux, exactly as we watch big fishes in a little pond. "The Great," she wrote to Mme. du Deffand, "by dint of stretching themselves out become so thin that you can see through them: it is a fine study to contemplate them. I know nothing that leads sooner to philosophy."

The scenes with the Duchesse de la Ferté and the adventures at Versailles are excellent comedy, and in the best of taste, frank and simple; they are well on a par as to pleasantry with the Grammont Memoirs. The first scenes as waiting-maid to the Duchesse du Maine are also very amusing. In the art of relating amusingly, Mme. de Staal is a *classic,* and if she could judge of herself to-day, she would not find much reason to complain of fate. She was not loved by those who she desired should love her ; her youth was not all that could be wished, and she suffered ; but years brought her the satisfactions of thought, the reflecting enjoyments of observation; she saw true ; and it was given her to render what she saw. If she missed more than one gift of fate, she at least had those of mind, language, and taste. Some of her least sayings have come into the circulation of society, and have added to the riches of the mind of France. More than that: by her noble conduct during a miserable conspiracy, she has won a place in all future history. How many statesmen, who think themselves great men, and who are striving all their lives, do not obtain as much!

This tardy satisfaction, this posthumous triumph, were bought very dear, no doubt. The correspondence of Mme. de Staal with Mme. du Deffand reveals the petty miseries at the bottom under an

always agreeable surface; we can follow her habit of
mind and ironical gaiety persisting ever throughout
an existence without pleasure and burdened with ennui. The satirical scenes in which Mme. du Châtelet
and Voltaire appear present a brilliant variety by the
way. This correspondence is the true conclusion
of the Memoirs. Whatever may be said by Fréron,
Mme. de Staal did well not to prolong them, and
not to enlarge upon the closing years. There is a degree of experience, of knowledge of the depths, past
which there is no longer interest in anything, not
even in recollection; we hasten when we reach that
period to bar the window and close the curtains for
ever. What is there to tell the world henceforth,
after we have said to ourselves: "How can we really
care for anything when we look at it closely? We
owe our tastes to our mistakes. If we always saw
things as they are, far from getting impassioned over
them, we should scarcely make use of them at all."
That is how Mme. de Staal, in her latter years, wrote
to intimate friends; and on her best days she added:
"My health is pretty good, my life easy, and, if it
were not for ennui, I should be well enough. That
ennui consists in seeing nothing that pleases me, and
doing nothing that amuses me; but when the body
does not suffer, and the mind is tranquil, we ought
to think ourselves happy."

One day, after leaving the Bastille, and before becoming entirely resigned to the yoke, Mlle. Delaunay

resolved to return and live in her little convent of
Saint-Louis, at Rouen, where she had passed her
only years of happiness. She made the journey, but
returned in haste. The women of the seventeenth
century gladly took refuge in convents from the
storms of the world, and died there; not so the women of the eighteenth: they could no longer bear that
sort of life.

After the letters to Mme. du Deffand, those of Mme.
de Staal to M. d'Héricourt, less studded with wit, give
a sadder and perhaps truer idea of her manner of existence towards the last. Her health diminished, her
sight failed, and though she lived on, she was in the
way of becoming totally blind like her friend, Mme.
du Deffand. Meanwhile, the subjection, the annoyances of her life with a princess whose caprices were
not more attractive as she grew older, rendered intolerable a tie which there was no possibility of break-
ing; the chain must be dragged to the end. "I see
the misery," she said, "but I no longer feel it." That
is her last pillow. But a terrible speech escapes her at
a return of the springtime: "As for me, I no longer
care for it [the spring]; I am so weary of seeing flowers and of hearing them talked about that I await frost
and snow with impatience." After such an utterance
there is nothing further to say.

She was sixty-six years old when she died, June 15,
1750. The Duchesse du Maine was scarcely dead,
three years later, before it was arranged to publish the

Memoirs; they appeared in 1755; even the death of the Baron de Staal was not awaited. In those days little consideration was shown when it was a question of securing pleasures of the mind. The book obtained at once an immense success. Fontenelle, however, who was still living, was much surprised on reading it: "I am sorry for her," he said; "I did not suspect her of such pettiness. It is written with agreeable elegance, but it was not worth the trouble of being written at all." Trublet replied that all the women were of that opinion, but that all the men were not. Trublet was right; Fontenelle was mistaken. He was too near to the things that he thought petty to judge them fairly.

These Memoirs are, in fact, a faithful picture of life. We may, none of us, have been trained in a convent: none of us, certainly, have lived the life of the little Court of Sceaux; but whoso has felt the keen impressions of youth, and has seen, almost immediately, that first charm lose its bloom, and its freshness fade under the breath of experience, and life become arid, and at the same time turbulent and passionate, until aridity is nothing else than ennui—that person, I say, reading these Memoirs will see himself and say, at every page: "It is true." It is the special quality of truth to live; above all, when it is clothed in clear and definite language. Huet, Bishop of Avranches, tells us that he was accustomed, every spring, to re-read Theocritus under the budding leafage of the woods, at the edge of a brook, and to the song of nightingales.   It seems to me that the Memoirs of Mme. de Staal should be re-read at the beginning of each winter, at the end of autumn, beneath the November trees, to the sound of the falling foliage.

Le Sage

(Alain-René).

Le Sage.

GIL BLAS, in spite of its Spanish costume and all the imitations that are said to be in it, is one of the most truly French books that we have. It matters very little to the quality of the work that the author took his canvas here or there, that he inserted such or such borrowed episode; the merit of the book is not in its general invention, but in the marshalling and management of each scene and each group, in the detail of the talk and the narrative, in the easy air and the sportive gaiety that unite the whole. In prose and under the form of a novel, it has a merit and an originality of the same kind as those of La Fontaine. The touch of Le Sage is wholly French; and if our literature possesses a book that is good to re-read, after an invasion, after each convulsion in the moral or the political order, or in the domain of taste, to calm the temper, restore the mind to its point of view, and refresh the language, it is *Gil Blas.*

Le Sage was born, trained, and began to be known in the reign of Louis XIV. Twenty-four years younger than La Bruyère, seventeen younger than

Fénelon, and six years older than Saint-Simon, he belongs to a generation of writers who were born to honour the succeeding era, but whose opening careers brightened the decline of the great reign. His most careful biographers date his birth in 1668, on the peninsula of Rhuys, in Lower Brittany, where Abélard was abbé. From the depth of that energetic and rugged province, whence great writers, innovators more or less revolutionary, have come to us—Lamennais, Broussais, a later René, and others—Alain-René Le Sage arrived, mature, shrewd, gay, cured of much in advance, and possessing the least obstinate of minds. We shall find nothing of the Breton in him but his pride of soul and his independence of character.

But how, and through what trials, what obstacles, came he so early to his knowledge of life, to that complete and perfect maturity to which Nature destined him? We know but few of the events of his life. He received his schooling at the college of Vannes, where he had, it is said, an excellent master. He lost his mother at nine years of age, and his father at fourteen; this father was a notary and clerk, like Boileau's father. He had for guardian a negligent uncle. Coming to Paris at twenty-two years of age to take his course of philosophy and law, he led the life of a young man, and had, no doubt, some of those bachelor adventures which he related and diversified later. Every one agrees in saying that he had an

LE SAGE

agreeable countenance, an imposing figure, and had been a very handsome man in his youth. There was talk of an early gallant intimacy with a woman of rank. In any case, this life of mere worldliness was short, for we find him, at twenty-six years of age, marrying the daughter of a Parisian *bourgeois*, who was herself only twenty-two. From this time forth he led a domestic life, and one of labour and restraint. It was from the rue du Cœur-Volant, faubourg Saint-Germain, later from the rue Montmartre, or from other obscure homes where he lived, that those charming writings, which seem the mirror of the world, came forth.

Yet it appears that immediately after his marriage he tried to support himself by regular employment, and that he was for a while in provincial finance, as clerk to some farmer-general. He stayed but a short time, and brought back a horror of and contempt for such contractors, whom he afterwards stigmatised on every occasion. The habitual character of Le Sage's satire is gay, light-hearted, and pungent without bitterness; but whenever any question of contractors, of Turcarets, comes up, he sharpens his blade and drives it in without pity, as if he had reprisals to make. I notice the same thing in whatever concerns actors, of whom he had had to complain. These are the only two classes whom the amiable satirist attacks vivaciously, and almost savagely—he whose satire is, in general, tempered by good-humour and kindliness.

On becoming a man of Letters, Le Sage met with a protector and useful counsellor in the Abbé de Lyonne, one of the sons of that able minister of State under Louis XIV, Hughes de Lyonne. The abbé knew the Spanish language and literature at a period when they were ceasing to be known in France; and he drew from them as from a mine, still rich, which was beginning to be forgotten. Let us here form a just idea of Le Sage, exaggerating nothing in order to better appreciate his charming genius. Le Sage proceeded much as do the authors of the present time, and of nearly all times. He wrote day by day, volume after volume; taking his subjects where he could and whenever they offered themselves fittingly. He worked his *trade*. But he did it naturally, with facility, with a gift for narrative and a dramatic sense (his essential talent), with a vein of satire and comedy running through it all, and with a lively, gay, and easy morality, which was his personal manner of feeling and thinking. After a few rather unfortunate attempts at translation and imitation, he gained his first two successes in the year 1707, with the pretty comedy of *Crispin, le rival de son maître,* and *Le Diable boiteux.*

Le Diable boiteux, so far as title, framework, and personages go, is taken from the Spanish, but Le Sage brought the whole into the Parisian point of view; he knew our measure; he handled his original as he pleased, easily, appropriately; he scattered allusions throughout to suit French taste; he fused what he borrowed and what he added into a most amusing picture of manners and morals, which seemed both new and easy, unexpected but recognisable. This book is one that Le Sage remade and made over again in a hundred ways in after years, under one form or another; it is a picture of the whole of human life, a lively review of all conditions, with the intrigues, the vices, and the absurdities, that characterise every one. We should picture to ourselves, the state of men's mind at the time *Le Diable boiteux* appeared—that gloomy, wearied, calamitous old age of Louis XIV, burdened with enforced reverence and devotion which weighed so heavily upon every one, and with that decorum which had now become a torment and a constraint. Suddenly, Asmodeus came and perched with his pupil on the roof of a tower, let us say it was a tower of Notre-Dame; thence, by a turn of his hand, he lifted all the roofs of the city, and men saw all hypocrisies, all shams laid bare, in short, the secret side of humanity. The panorama lay there in broad daylight. Asmodeus had a wild success; they did not give him time to clothe himself, said the critics of that day; people came post-haste to get the pamphlet. Two editions were issued in one year: "They are working at a third," announced the *Journal de Verdun* (December, 1707); "two seigneurs of the Court fought, sword in hand, in Barbin's shop, to get the last copy of the second edition."

–6.

Boileau, one day when Jean-Baptiste Rousseau was with him, detected *Le Diable boiteux* in the hands of his little lacquey, and threatened to dismiss him if the book remained in the house. There is a success indeed! consecrated and enlivened by the wrath of Boileau.

For a little lacquey the book may not be very moral; certainly it does not preach the morality of the Catechism; it is that of practical life, namely: to be the dupe of nothing and of no one. We may say of *Le Diable boiteux* as was said, so wisely, of *Gil Blas:* "This book is moral like experience." Dating from this first work, Le Sage's character is clearly exhibited; he is La Bruyère on the stage and in action, without a trace of effort. *Le Diable boiteux* is a good predecessor to the *Lettres Persanes,* but it precedes them with a light step, without the slightest pretention to laboured wit, and without fatigue. There is not the shadow of mannerism about Le Sage; his shafts are lively, pungent words that escape him as he flies along. Thus Asmodeus, speaking of a brother-demon with whom he had quarrelled, remarks: "We embraced, and since then we are mortal enemies."

Nothing could be gayer or more amusing than the little comedy of *Crispin, le rival de son maître.* One of the first scenes between the two valets, Crispin and La Branche, offers an example of that light-hearted volatility in the comic, which is the peculiar character of Le Sage, whether in his plays or in his novels.

The two valets, meeting again, tell each other their adventures: both had been utter rascals in earlier days, but they think they have cured themselves of that rascality by again taking service. La Branche, especially, flatters himself that he is in the right way; he serves a young man named Damis: "He is an amiable fellow," says La Branche, "he likes play, wine, and women; he is a man for everything. We keep up all sorts of debauchery together. It amuses me; and prevents me from doing wrong." "What an innocent life!" remarks Crispin. For my part, I say, what excellent and guileless comedy that shows us vice so artlessly! This play of *Crispin* begins the attack on financiers: we see *Turcaret* looming up in the distance. Crispin tells himself that he is tired of being a valet: "Ah! Crispin," he says, "it is your own fault! You have always gone after trifles—you ought to have shone in finance. . . . With my wit and cleverness, *morbleu!* I ought already to have gone more than once into bankruptcy." And the last touch of all seems like a transition to the coming comedy, when Oronte says to the two valets: "You have intelligence, but you ought to make better use of it, and, to make you honest men, I will put you both into business."

Le Sage had the luck of opportuneness; he divined and slightly preceded the moment when, at the death of Louis XIV, the orgy of financiers and *parvenus* began. *Turcaret* was played in 1709; the absurdities

and turpitudes that displayed themselves on the triumph of Law's system are scathed in advance in
that play. The comedy denounces and precedes the
explosion of vice and absurdity; it might then have
been preventive, if warnings ever can be. *Turcaret*
is both a comedy of character and a page in the history of morals, like *Tartuffe*. Molière wrote *Tartuffe*
several years before the real Tartuffe triumphed under
Louis XIV. Le Sage wrote *Turcaret* several years
before Turcaret was on a pinnacle during the Regency.
But, like many other vices of the Regency, the real
Turcaret came from beneath the surface of the last
years of Louis XIV. All sorts of difficulties were
raised against the representation; it required the king's
son to remove them. *Turcaret* was played "by order
of Monseigneur," to whom we ought to be grateful
for this mark of favour to literature, the only one he
ever gave.

Great as was the need of protectors against the
cabal of offended financiers and jealous authors, Le
Sage held firm, and did not permit himself to give way
to any base compliance. Here the Breton in his
nature asserts itself. Before the play was acted he
had promised the Duchesse de Bouillon to go and read
it to her. She expected that the reading would take
place before dinner; certain matters detained Le Sage,
and he was late in arriving. When he appeared, the
duchess told him stiffly that he had made her lose
more than an hour waiting for him. "Very well,

madame," he answered, coldly, "I will let you gain two." And, making his bow, he departed. Collé, who relates the anecdote, knew it on good authority, and applauds it like a man who was of a somewhat similar nature.

Aside from this comedy, which was of the nature of a pitched battle in which Le Sage, spurring to the charge, resolved to make vice hateful, satire in him and in all his other writings keeps its amiable as well as amusing character; and it is this combination that makes the charm and originality of his writings. Such, above all, is the character of his novel *Gil Blas,* that delightful and varied masterpiece, with which his name is for ever associated.

Gil Blas was published, successively, in four volumes, the last two of which followed the first after rather long intervals. The first two appeared in 1715, the year of the death of Louis XIV. A freshness of youth, a freedom of movement were in them that suited well with the beginnings of an emancipated epoch. What can I say of *Gil Blas* that has not already been said, already been felt and expressed by many clever panegyrists, many delicate and acute critics, and that all judicious readers have not thought for themselves? I must content myself by humbly saying and repeating it all once more.

The author, in this lengthy, developed, and easy narrative, intended to depict human life as it is; with its varieties and its adventures, with the whimsicalities

that the play of fate and fortune produce, and, above
all, with those introduced by the varieties of our
tempers, our tastes, and our defects. Gil Blas is a
man of very humble and common birth, of the lowest
bourgeoisie; he early shows himself a wide-awake,
clever, and good-natured lad; he has some education,
such as it is, and he leaves his home at seventeen years
of age to make his way in the world. He passes, in
turn, through all conditions, even the lowest and
most vulgar; he is not much displeased with any
of them, although he is always seeking to push
on and to advance himself. Gil Blas at bottom is
frank and fairly honest, credulous, vain, and easily
taken in. Deceived at first in all ways—by a parasite
whom he happens to meet who praises him, by a
valet who plays the saint, and by women—he is the
dupe of his bad and sometimes of his good qualities.
He gets his schooling in all directions, and we make
our apprenticeship with him. Excellent subject for
practical morals, it may be said of Gil Blas that he
lets himself be made by things; he never goes ahead
of experience; he receives it. He is not a man of
genius, of great talent; nor is he anything very extraordinary: his mind is healthy and shrewd, facile and
active, essentially teachable, having all sorts of apti-
tudes in it. The only question is to apply them properly; and that he ends by doing; he makes himself
capable of everything, and he deserves the praise
given him by his friend Fabrice: "You have the

universal tool." But he does not deserve it until near the end, and that encourages us; we feel, in reading him, that we, also, without too much effort or presumption, can succeed some day as well as he.

All forms of life and of human nature will be found in *Gil Blas* — all, except a certain ideal and moral elevation, which is rare, no doubt, and often simulated, but which is found too real in some instances to allow it to be wholly omitted in a complete picture of humanity. Le Sage, worthy man in other ways, had not that ideal within himself. He was of the opinion that "the most perfect productions of the mind are those in which there are but slight defects, just as the most honourable men are those who have fewest vices." There is nothing more true than that remark, and in *Gil Blas,* the author has amply made use of that method of looking at things that bestows some small vices on the best of men. Gil Blas himself, though he has no very clearly defined innate vice, is very capable of acquiring nearly all kinds at the first encounter. He is, as I have said, an honest man in himself, generally preferring good to evil, but readily letting himself go when occasion, vanity, or self-interest tempts him, and not blushing too much for his conduct, even when it is past. I know the allowance to be made in such a case for the gaiety of the novel, for the habits of the class, and also for the easy morality of a period when people pardoned the rascalities of the Chevalier Des Grieux, and laughed

at those of the Chevalier de Grammont. Nevertheless, we cannot conceal from ourselves that it is
doubtless in order to keep him on the level of
human nature that Gil Blas has not a loftier soul:
he is kind to all, moderately scrupulous according to
circumstances, valet before he was master, and more
or less of the race of the Figaros.

Le Sage had thoroughly observed one fact, which
other moralists have also noticed, namely: the qualities that are, perhaps, most characteristic of men
taken in the mass, and most fitted to astonish those
who think they know them best, are not their
wickedness and their folly (into which they only fall
by fits and starts): the qualities that are most amazing in men, and most inexhaustible, are their baseness and their dulness. The author of *Gil Blas*
knew this well : his personage, in order to remain a
natural and medium type, could not, in any degree,
be raised to the plane of a stoic or a hero. He represents nothing that is peculiar, or unique, or even
rare. Gil Blas is you, is I, is every one. To this
conformity of nature with us, to his happy frankness,
to his ingenuous sallies and confessions, he owes the
fact that he remains, in spite of his vices, ever interesting and amiable in the eyes of the reader. As to
respect, as some one has wittily said, that is the
last thing he asks of us.

The names of Panurge and Figaro are often mentioned in connection with that of Gil Blas. But

Panurge, that most subtle and sagacious creation of the genius of Rabelais, is peculiar in quite a different way from Gil Blas; he is an original of another quality, gifted with a fantasticality of his own, a vein both poetic and grotesque. In representing certain sides of human nature Panurge exaggerates and caricatures them intentionally in a laughable manner. Figaro, who is more of the lineage of Gil Blas, also has a warmth, a natural gaiety, a *brio* which has something of the lyric in it. Gil Blas is more even, more in the habitual tone of us all. He is we, ourselves, I say again, passing through all those diverse conditions and periods.

The most competent judge of such matters, Walter Scott, said of *Gil Blas:* "This work leaves the reader content with himself and with mankind." Certainly, that is a result which might seem difficult to obtain by a satirist who makes no pretence of embellishing humanity; but neither does he seek to calumniate nor disfigure it; he contents himself with showing it such as it is; and always with a natural air and a diverting tone. Irony, with Le Sage, has no acrimony, as it has with Voltaire. If it has not the air of the great world, and the supreme distinction which is Hamilton's sign-manual, neither has it the affected refinements of causticity and barren feeling. It is an irony that bears witness to a healthy soul, an irony which remains, if one may say so, *good-natured*. It speeds along, finds and flings its

mischievous shaft, and still flies on, not pressing it in
I insist on this absence of bitterness, which constitutes the originality of Le Sage and his distinction as
a satirist; that is why he consoles even while ridicul-
ing. In this characteristic, above all, he is different
from Voltaire, who laughs and bites in bitter fashion.
Remember *Candide*. Pangloss may be a cousin,
but he is not the brother of Gil Blas.

It is very noticeable how works that please and succeed the best in styles not classified are sometimes
slow in obtaining a just estimation; I mean the estimation that is written and published in serious works.
Le Sage's reputation with the public was made and established a quarter of a century ago, while the praise to
which he was entitled, and which filled every mouth,
was still dealt out to him with a sort of parsimony by
the principal authors of the period. It seemed that in
their dignity they chose to look twice before saying
all the good that they really thought of the best of our
novels. The Abbé des Fontaines, it is true, as a good
journalist, praised Le Sage for "so many ingenious
tales." Voltaire, in the list of writers which he gives
in his *Siècle de Louis XIV*, confines himself, under the
head of "Le Sage" to a few lines; as follows:

"Le Sage, born at Vannes, in Lower Brittany in
1668. His novel of *Gil Blas* still lives because there is
nature in it; it is taken entirely from a Spanish novel,
entitled: *La vida del escudero don Marcos de Obrego*.
Died in 1747."

Voltaire's assertion is incorrect, and his eulogy reduced to a minimum. We could scarcely understand this severity and malevolence, if we had not read the chapter in which Gil Blas, during his stay at Valence, sees acted a new tragedy by the "fashionable poet," Don Gabriel Triaquero. This incident, wholly satirical, is pointed at Voltaire, who is evidently Don Gabriel. Le Sage was a classic of the preceding century, and not favourable to innovations; probably he had met the young author of "Œdipus" in the first intoxication of success, and being, himself, the most simple of men of intellect, he may have thought him rather a coxcomb and not enough of a good fellow. Voltaire, in turn, finding Le Sage on his path, took his revenge for the satire by faint praise and a false assertion. By those who surrounded Voltaire little praise could be given to Le Sage. Marmontel, in his "Essay on Novels," speaks of him with a sort of regret, and incidentally, as it were; the passage is remarkable for its insufficiency:—

" The satirical novel such as I conceive it," he says, " requires sometimes the pen of Lucian, La Bruyère, or Hamilton, sometimes that of Juvenal, I dare not say that of Molière: that of Le Sage might have sufficed with a more learned study of manners and customs, and a more familiar and intimate knowledge of a certain class of society which the author of *Gil Blas* had not sufficiently observed, and only saw from a distance."

We may here remark the implied reproach to Le Sage of not seeing good company. To us, at this distance, that reproach disappears. Gil Blas to our eyes is not a man of society, he is *man himself.*

La Harpe, a good critic when he speaks of what he knows and does not let himself be confused by passion, is the first writer who adequately appreciated *Gil Blas.* The page he devotes to him is worthy of Le Sage himself for its ease and lightness of touch:—

"*Gil Blas,*" he says, "is a masterpiece ; it belongs to the small number of volumes that we re-read with pleasure ; it is a moral and living picture of human life; all conditions are brought into it to give or receive a lesson. But the instruction is never without charm. *Utile dulci* should be the motto of this excellent book, which is seasoned throughout with good jesting. Many of its witticisms have passed into proverbs. . . . We know the personages of *Gil Blas;* we have lived with them; we meet them at every moment. Why ? Because in the picture made of them there is not a line drawn without intention and without effect. Le Sage had much intellect, but he devotes so much talent to concealing it, he likes so much to hide behind his characters, he is so little concerned about himself, that we must have good eyes to see the author in his work and duly appreciate them both."

Justice at last was done to Le Sage. After this, critics were not even content merely to say of him with the Abbé de Voisenon and with the public: "He wrote *Gil Blas,* a novel which, for lightness and purity of style and the shrewdness of its moral, will for ever remain a precious monument in French literature." They began to explain why *Gil Blas* was a monument and a masterpiece. All tastes, of course, did not agree. They never do. Enthusiasts by nature, like Diderot, grew heated over Clarissa; the idealists

and the passionate lovers clung to the novels of Jean-
Jacques and Mme. de Staël. The French Academy,
however, which owed reparation to Le Sage for not
having had the honour to possess him, proposed his
Eulogy, and divided its prize, in 1822, between two
discourses upon him, remarkable in different ways,
one by M. Patin and the other by M. Malitourne. I
cite part of the first and, as I think, the more solid.
In it, *Gil Blas* is admirably characterised; criticism has
advanced a step since the days of La Harpe; it has
reached the point of delicate detail of analysis and
literary anatomy.

"*Le Diable boiteux* was succeeded by *Gil Blas* which is much superior. Between the two works there is almost as great a distance as
that which separates the paintings of moralists from those of romance
writers. The subject is the same in both, but it is differently presented ; in one, observation takes the form of lively and witty expression ; in the other it is wholly dramatic : the first gives us a gallery
of portraits ; the second, a stage and the actors thereon. It is in the
latter, above all, that Le Sage shows his power of animating his
figures, and of giving them the appearance of life. . . . I do
not know if Le Sage himself was tricked by his art ; but is there a single one of his readers who has not, at some time, taken for reality the
picture that he made for us in *Gil Blas ?* His personages were known
to us before he showed them to us; since then, we have met them
often in the world. We are tempted to say to him what a comic
poet said to a critic of antiquity : ' O life, and thou, Menander, which
of you two imitated the other ?' . . . Such is the history of
Gil Blas : is it not our own, and that of the majority ? Is it not life
itself, such as fate and human passions, in spite of reason, have made
it ? "

But the judgment of authority, that which ought to
count the most and will last, is that of Sir Walter Scott,

the reviver of *genre*. That lovable genius, so frank, so benevolent, so free from envy, having to speak of Le Sage in his "Biographical Memoirs of Eminent Novelists," does so with a fulness of heart, a sympathetic intelligence such as one might expect from his fraternal soul:

"Few have ever read this charming book," he says of *Gil Blas*, "without remembering, as one of the most delightful occupations of their life, the time which they first employed in the perusal; and there are few also who do not occasionally turn back to its pages with all the vivacity which attends the recollection of early love. It signifies nothing at what time we have first encountered the fascination, whether in boyhood, when we were chiefly captivated by the cavern of the robbers, and other scenes of romance; whether in more advanced youth, but while our ignorance of the world yet concealed from us the subtle and poignant satire which lurks in so many passages of the work; whether we were learned enough to apprehend the various allusions to history and public matters with which it abounds, or ignorant enough to rest contented with the more direct course of the narration. The power of the enchanter over us is alike absolute, under all these circumstances. . . .

The whole concoction of *Gil Blas* appears to me as original, in that which constitutes the essence of a composition, as it is inexpressibly delightful. . . . It is a work which renders the reader pleased with himself and with mankind, where faults are placed before him in the light of follies rather than vices, and where misfortunes are so interwoven with the ludicrous, that we laugh in the very act of sympathising with them. All is rendered diverting—both the crimes and the retribution which follows them. . . . In short, so strictly are the pages of *Gil Blas* confined to what is amusing that they might perhaps have been improved by some touches of a more masculine, stronger, and firmer line of morality."

The master has spoken. The judgment is given with length and fulness. The regret at the end for the absence of a sterner morality seems to me a slight

concession made by Sir Walter Scott to the English
public and to Anglican prejudice. Gil Blas could not
have introduced a sterner and more virile morality
without ceasing to be himself.

M. Villemain, in his *Tableau du XVIIIe Siècle,* speaks
of Le Sage as he well knows how, and places him in
the centre of the circle of writers of his literary day
and stripe. This clever chapter is more a compilation
of all that has been said upon Le Sage and *Gil Blas*
than a new testimony delivered by the elegant critic.
It is difficult to extract a complete judgment from this
series of charming and fleeting meanderings. Dwelling a moment on the accusation of plagiarism brought
against Le Sage, M. Villemain, after refuting it in his
way, adds:

" It is not that in this affair we pretend to deny altogether the debt
to Spain; but that debt is something other than has been said. Our
Gil Blas was not stolen, no matter what Pere Isla may say, and,
quite recently, Dr. Llorente. There was no mysterious manuscript
found by Le Sage and concealed from others. But there is no doubt
that Le Sage skilfully adopted the clever pleasantry, the grave and
gentle philosophy, malicious yet merry, which shines in Cervantes
and Cuevedo, and of which many charming examples will always be
found in the Spanish moralists and narrators. To this general and
free imitation, Le Sage adds the taste of the best antiquity; he is, as
to style, the pupil of Terence and Horace."

Le Sage borrowed many other things besides the
wit and the philosophy of the Spanish authors; he had
no scruple in making use of their ideas, stories, fragments, in fact, of anything that suited him, as Mr. Tick-
nor, the American historian of Spanish literature,

peremptorily demonstrates. There is no author who has had less scruple in this respect, or who has acted with less ceremony than Le Sage. He justifies the witty definition given one day by M. de Maurepas: "An author who takes out of books what passes through his head." All this detracts nothing from the merits of Le Sage; but we must, above all, tell the truth and speak frankly on this subject without national and patriotic commonplaces. Let us not be more proud for him than he was for himself. Gil Blas's sense of honour was not high.

Scenes of comedy are so numerous in *Gil Blas* that they leave the reader but little time to perceive what there is that is common and wearisome in certain episodes, certain sentimental tales that the author inserted, here and there, to swell his volumes, and which he gathered from heaven knows where. The first two volumes of the work, after presenting to us all sorts of classes and conditions of men, thieves, canons, doctors, authors, and actors, bring Gil Blas to be intendant, that is, steward of Don Alfonso, and deputed to make a restitution in his name. "This was beginning the business of intendant where it ought to end." The third volume, published in 1724, which is the most remarkable of all, shows us Gil Blas, mounting by degrees from stage to stage; and in proportion to his rise the lessons may seem to be sharper and bolder. But, even in their boldness, they still keep a sort of innocence. Le Sage, even when he jeers, is

never aggressive; he has no thought of making anything triumph.   He laughs to laugh, to show nature
bare; he never scoffs at the present for the sake of
an idea, nor for the profit of some future system.   He
knows that humanity, in changing its state, will
merely change the form of its folly.   Here he is
wholly out of touch with the eighteenth century, belonging rather to the good old jesters of former times.

This third volume abounds in excellent tales.   Gil
Blas, become secretary and favourite of the Archbishop
of Granada, loses his place in the end through telling
the truth.   All these scenes at the archbishop's palace
are admirably natural, and breathe a spirit of gentle
comedy insensibly mingled with all the actions of life.
The self-love of authorship is painted in the good old
man in full relief, and in all its beatific *naïveté,* yet
with a remnant of meekness.   The scenes with the
actress Laure, that follow immediately, are incomparably true.   Le Sage knew to its depths the comic
type.

When he goes to Court, and finds himself the
secretary and favourite of the Duc de Lerme, we
think for a moment that Gil Blas will raise himself
into becoming a man of honour in certain respects;
not at all: he has to do with dangers of another kind,
and he succumbs.   The stage alone is changed; the
motives, the self-interest, the passions are still the
same.   Far from improving, he sinks, at this moment
of intoxication, to the lowest degree of unworthiness

to which he has yet fallen—to insensibility of heart, to repudiation of his family and of his early friends. The highest point of his prosperity is precisely the moment when, if he does not take care, his real depravity begins. He needs disgrace to show him to himself, and to bring him back within the true line of his habits and his nature.

The fourth volume of *Gil Blas* did not appear till 1735, that is to say, twenty years after the first two, and eleven years after the third. This fourth volume, in which Gil Blas comes out of his retirement and returns for a time to Court, does not present either the same vicissitudes or the same rapidity of action as its predecessors; but it does not shame them. We find in it a sketch of the author's literary tastes, when he shows us his Gil Blas in the library of the Château de Lirias (a castle in Spain!) taking special pleasure in books of cheerful morality, and choosing as his favourite authors Horace, Lucian, and Erasmus.

The literary theory of Le Sage can be fully extracted from more than one page of *Gil Blas,* and particularly from the conversations of the latter with his friend, the poet Fabrice Nunez. Fabrice, in order to succeed, has consulted the taste of the times; he has indulged in the style of Gongora, that of far-fetched, involved expressions — the romanticism of those days. Gil Blas reproves him, and demands *clearness* first of all; he desires that even a sonnet should be perfectly intelligible. His friend jeers at his simplicity and explains the modern theory: "If the sonnet is not intelligible, so much the better, my friend. Sonnets, odes, and other works that need the sublime, can never get along with the simple and natural; obscurity is their whole merit; it is enough if the poet thinks he understands himself. . . . We are five or six bold innovators, who have undertaken to change the language from white to black; and we shall succeed, please God, in spite of Cervantes and Lope de Vega." In writing this, we may be sure that Le Sage had in mind Fontenelle, perhaps Montesquieu, certainly Voltaire, whom he thought much too super-elegant and always endeavouring to improve on the language of Racine, of Corneille, and their illustrious predecessors.

Boileau, as we know, did not smile upon the opening career of Le Sage. In his turn, Le Sage seems to have been little favourable to what is called the grand and lofty literature of his time, which he thought, stilted. This sort of dissenting opinion, carried sometimes to aversion, is visible in all the acts of his literary life. He quarrels early with the Comédie-Française, and makes open war upon it, and upon the actors of the king, who represent the grand style and tragic declamation. He devotes his attention to the little theatres, and himself, or with others, writes, a hundred little plays which represent in the germ, or even to the full, what to-day are vaudevilles, comic operas, and our pieces at the *Variétés* and on the boulevards.

He did not choose to belong to the French Academy He resisted Danchet, his friend, who tried to entice him there; he absolutely refused to solicit votes, which proceeding was at that time necessary for election. He had aversion to " bureaus of intellect," such as the salon of the Marquise de Lambert; and, without mentioning his deafness, which embarassed him, he gives his reasons for this dislike. " In those companies they consider the best comedy or the gayest and cleverest comedy," he remarks (not without a little thought of his own), " as a feeble production that deserves no praise; whereas the slightest ' serious ' work, an ode, an eclogue, a sonnet, is welcomed as the greatest effort of the human mind." He is positively opposed to makers of odes and tragedies, and to all solemn and official styles, those "crownèd" styles, which the public respects and honours from etiquette without seeing that there is often infinitely more talent and intellect dispensed elsewhere. The authors of odes and tragedies paid him back in the same coin; Jean-Baptiste Rousseau exceeded all limits when he wrote to Brossette: " The author of *Le Diable boiteux* would do well to go into partnership with rope-dancers; his genius would then be in its true sphere. Gilles and Fagotin would have a good master; Apollo has a bad scholar." Voltaire had better wit than to refuse praise to *Gil Blas,* but he praises the work as little as possible. Judging by the two lines he bestows reluctantly upon it, he seems never to have suspected that it would soon

be infinitely more glorious to have written that novel
than the poem of the *Henriade*.

Le Sage was a practical philosopher; he early preferred to follow his inclinations and obey his tastes
rather than constrain himself. Man of genius, but
independent by nature, he knew how, for the sake of
his liberty, to renounce one part of that "consideration" he might so easily have conciliated. "We are
valued in this world only at the value we choose to
put upon ourselves," says La Bruyère. Le Sage knew
that; but, in order to appear to every one just what he
was, he never consented to pose before their eyes.
He had too much contempt for the way men seek to
make others believe in them. In his hatred of the
solemn and the false he would have thrown himself,
rather, on the side of the vulgar and the common. He
prefers to haunt cafés rather than salons. He seems
to have applied to himself that saying of an old classic:
Plebeius moriar senex ! May I return in old age to the
obscure ranks from which, for a moment, I came! He
plunged back with pleasure into the crowd, always
finding new matter there for observation. He worked
for the open-air theatres, and strewed his wit by the
handful on the stages of the mountebanks; he had
many successes not reputed creditable. I have just
read his *Foire des Fées,* and his *Monde renversée,* and
very pretty farces they are, truly. This vein, and this
vogue of Le Sage as a vaudevillist deserve study, for,
let us remark, it was not the necessity of a livelihood,

only, that turned him in that direction: the attraction and the vocation for it were in him. He did not deem it derogatory to write a part for Harlequin; he even descended, on one occasion, from Harlequin to puppets. Harlequin, puppets, actors for actors, he was of opinion that all were alike and were played by the same string.

Though that may be practical wisdom, we cannot deny that talent always loses something in not having a high ideal in view. Le Sage felt the effects of this: after attaining to the height of observation in *Le Diable boiteux,* and in *Gil Blas,* and to the quick of comedy in *Crispin,* and in *Turcaret,* he relaxed, he repeated himself, he dropped a little; he even went so far down as to allow himself certain last publications like the *Valise trouvée* and *Le Mélange Amusant,* which are, indeed, the bottom of his bag or valise.

Let us imagine Molière without Boileau at his side to spur him on, scold him, advise him on the noble comedy of the *Misanthrope;* Molière making a series of Georges Dandins, Scapins, and Pourceaugnacs in diminutive. Here is the misfortune that Le Sage, a sort of modified Molière, had to bear: he had no Aristarchus at his side, and he abandoned himself without reserve to the inclinations of his nature, while, at the same time, under the necessity of making a livelihood.

Le Sage was sixty-seven years of age when the last volume of *Gil Blas* appeared. Three years later (1738) he published *Le Bachelier de Salamanque,* which he valued, he said, as the fruit of his old age.

In this composition he followed his usual custom. While stating that it was taken from a Spanish manuscript, he filled it with French manners and customs, especially those of our little abbés, a class unknown in Spain; also with a description (to be found in the second part of the *Bachelier*) of the manners and customs in Mexico, which he took, without acknowledgment, from the narrative of an Irishman, Thomas Gage, translated many years earlier into French. But all these borrowings, these reports of others, and the things he added of his own invention, are united and blended together, as usual, in the course of an easy and amusing narrative.

Another work of his, and by no means the least admirable, was the comedian Montménil, his son, an excellent actor, whom all who saw him act declared inimitable. Montménil, who was for a time an abbé, but who could not resist his vocation, played Turcaret and the Avocat Patelin admirably; he also played the marquis in *Turcaret,* the valet La Branche in *Crispin,* and, in general, excelled in the parts of valets and peasants. It can be said that he acted as his father wrote and narrated. Montménil merely translated into another form the same comic spirit, the same family talent. Le Sage would not, for some time, forgive his son for becoming an actor, and, above all, an actor at the Comédie Française, with which he was perpetually at war in the interests of his Théâtre de la Foire. But one day friends dragged him to a representation of *Turcaret;* there he saw his son, recognised his double work, wept with joy, and became once more a father. And so much a father that the death of Montménil, which occurred suddenly in 1743, was the great affliction of his old age.

"Le Sage, having lost Montménil, and being too old to work, too proud to ask help, and too honest to borrow, retired with his wife and daughters to the house of his son, the canon, at Boulogne-sur-mer." It is the Abbé de Voisenon who speaks. Voisenon was then grand-vicar to the Bishop of Boulogne. The canon, son of Le Sage, to whose house the old father went to finish his days, was a joyous good-liver himself. "He knew imperturbably all the plays of La Foire, and could sing them even better than his Mass." Ecclesiastic, of about the same force as the Abbé de Voisenon, he would have made a capital actor. Le Sage had still another son, who became an actor, and travelled about Germany under the name of Pittence; he resembled the least good works of his father.

Le Sage was deaf, and became so at forty years of age. This affliction, which increased with years, must have contributed to keep him from the salons of the great world, but it did not check in the least his natural gaiety. He was obliged, in conversing, to use a trumpet, which he called his "benefactor," inasmuch, he said, as he used it to communicate with persons of intellect, and need only lay it down to avoid hearing bores and fools. Towards the end of his life, he did not have full use of his faculties, except in the middle of the day; those about him remarked that his mind seemed to rise and set with the sun. He died at Boulogne, November 17, 1747, in his eightieth year. The Comte de Tressan, then governor of the province, made it his duty to attend the funeral with his staff. Death placed Le Sage in his true rank; and he, who had never been of any consequence in his lifetime, and who was never mentioned without a little word of complaint and regret being mingled with his praise, is to-day classed in the memory of men after the Lucians and the Terences, beside the Fieldings and the Goldsmiths, and beneath the Cervantes and the Molières.

Montesquieu.

Montesquieu.

(Charles de Secondat, Baron de La Brède.)

"THE worst of journalists is that they speak only of new books, as if truth were never new. It seems to me that until a man has read all the old books he has no reason to prefer the new." It is Usbek, or rather Montesquieu, who says that in the *Lettres Persanes*, and it is fair to apply the words to himself. In looking over the field of the eighteenth century, in every direction, I have many times encountered the great name and the imposing figure of Montesquieu, without pausing over them. Why? For many reasons. The first is, that he is one of those men whom we approach with fear, because of the real respect they inspire and the sort of religion that has grown up around them. The second reason is that he has been so ably spoken of by masters that it seems useless to repeat feebly what has already been so well said. A final reason, and one which is peculiar to this order of sketches, is that in writing for journals one is always something of a journalist; we search for the timely, we await the occasion, and, without precisely binding ourselves to speak of none

but works "still hot from the forge" (another of
Montesquieu's expressions), we desire, at any rate,
that some natural circumstance should bring us back
to old books and direct attention to them.

I have always hoped to find something of the kind
in respect to Montesquieu. We have good and eloquent Eulogies upon him; but a complete History of
his life and works does not exist. We know many
details about him, but not as many as ought to have
been collected, and as we desire to know. He left
a great number of manuscripts; it was said at first
that his son, M. de Secondat, towards the close of
1793, when blood began to flow in Bordeaux, threw
all his father's papers and manuscripts into the fire,
from a fear that pretexts might be found in them to
trouble the family. It was a risk of death in those
days to be the son of Montesquieu or of Buffon; and
the only safety was to keep that fact out of sight.
One of the first acts of the mad-brained clubs in Paris
was to declare Montesquieu an aristocrat and an imbecile. But this news of the destruction of his manuscripts proved false; and M. Walckenaer, the great
biographical investigator, had the pleasure of thus in-
forming the lettered public. The greater part of these
manuscripts was brought to Paris about the year
1804, and M. Walckenaer, in acknowledgment of his
zeal, was allowed to examine them for several hours;
he wrote a letter on the subject which was inserted in
the *Archives littéraires de l'Europe,* accompanied by

MONTESQUIEU

a few extracts. Since then, M. Lainé, the former minister of the Interior, obtained permission of the Secondat family to make further researches among the precious papers, and he meditated a work on Montesquieu which remained a mere project. Let us hope that this family inheritance still exists, and that it may finally be put to use in the interests of all, and to the glory of the illustrious ancestor. Montesquieu is not one of the men who have anything to fear from close knowledge; he was a great man seen near by or far off; he had no recesses in his heart to conceal; all those who approached him have praised his goodness, his kindliness, as much as they have his genius. The few notes of his that have seen the light, and in which he draws his portrait, give a life and naturalness to his personality which are better than majesty. "Plutarch charms me always," he says: "there are circumstances attached to persons that give great pleasure."

Born on the 18th of January, 1689, at the château of La Brède, near Bordeaux, Montesquieu came of a family of the robe and the sword, belonging to the good nobility of Guienne: "Though my name is neither good nor bad," he said, "having little more than two hundred and fifty years of proved nobility, still I am attached to it." His father, who had been in the army, retired early and carefully superintended his son's education. Young Montesquieu was destined to the magistracy. Study was at all times his

great passion. Mention is made of precocious and
rather daring works which he produced, but had the
prudence to withhold. He read pen in hand, and
reflectingly. "On leaving school, they put books
on law into my hands; I looked for the spirit in them."
This spirit of the things of law and of history was
the object of his search through life; he never rested
till he thought he had found it. His genius was
essentially turned to this class of investigation. He
had, further, a gift of ready imagination, which easily
clothed both thought and maxim with a poetic form,
as did his compatriot Montaigne; but he was less easy
than Montaigne; he had not the same grace of style.

The classics were to him objects of worship. He
never knew much of that first simple, natural, artless
antiquity of which Fénelon, like an exiled contemporary
among us, was the exponent. Montesquieu's antiquity
went no farther back than the second period, which was
more reflective, more astir, and already Latin; or, to put
it more truly, perhaps, he confounded his classics
together, from Homer to Seneca and Marcus Aurelius,
obtaining from them all features or illusions to enhance
his modern thought. These he used like Corinthian
vases or bronze busts placed in conspicuous places as
glorious testimonials. A line of Homer, a verse of
Virgil, blended rapidly with his thought, seemed to
him to complete it, and consecrate it under a divine
form. Montesquieu's work is inlaid throughout with
these sacred fragments: " I confess my love for the

ancients," he exclaims; "antiquity enchants me, and
I am always ready to say with Pliny: ' It is to Athens
that you go; respect the gods!' "—And he, himself,
feeling thus, deserves to be treated as a classic: to
quote Montesquieu, to detach a saying of his and place
it in a writing, honours the writer.

Counsellor of the parliament at Bordeaux from 1714,
the death of an uncle left him the office of president
of the municipal court in 1716; he was then twenty-
seven years of age. Speaking of his friend the Maréchal de Berwick as being at the head of a regiment
and governor of a province while still adolescent,
Montesquieu said: "Thus, at seventeen years of age
he was in the situation, so auspicious for a man with
a lofty soul, of seeing the road to glory open before
him with every possibility of doing great things."
Without pretending to say the same of his office of
judge, obtained so early, Montesquieu was thenceforth on a footing where he could see all, where he
could judge men on their own level, without making
efforts to insinuate himself among them; he had only
to choose his relations with them as they offered. It
was thus that he knew Maréchal de Berwick, governor
of the province, so intimately. Born without ambition of great fortune, he found himself placed in a rank
which might seem mediocre compared with great
stations, but which was all the more suited to his
chosen rôle of political observer. He could apply his
whole youth to that rôle, without losing anything.

For ten years Montesquieu conscientiously filled this office of magistrate; then, finding himself, as his studies became more extended, too confined, he sold his charge in 1726. He recognised, himself, that he was not fitted for public employments, nor even for what is called a profession.

" What has always given me a rather bad opinion of myself," he said, " is that there are very few employments in the republic for which I should be truly fitted. As for my office of Judge, I have a very just heart, I readily comprehend questions in themselves; but as to legal procedure, I never understood it. Nevertheless, I applied myself to learn it ; but what disgusted me the most was to see stupid fellows possess the very talent that escaped me, so to speak."

From this we may infer that Montesquieu was not practical. Would he have been more in his right place as Chancellor of France than he was as judge of a municipal court ? Honest man like d'Aguesseau, man of Letters and philosopher like Bacon, would he have been more capable of business affairs than they ? A letter, written at the beginning of his travels, shows that he had a momentary idea of becoming an ambassador and being employed at foreign Courts; but what is certain is that he remained such as we know him and admire him—the great, the immortal investigator of the spirit of history, often venturesome, but always fruitful.

The first writings that we have of his are Discourses composed for the Academy of Bordeaux, of which he was a member after 1716; in them his talent shows itself; and we see, as its origin, the particular form which Montesquieu afterwards delighted in, namely: classic imagery or illusion applied to modern objects and ideas. But here we perceive affectation; the mythology is too profuse. Writing a report on the physical cause of the Echo, or a treatise on Anatomy, Montesquieu brings in too many nymphs and goddesses. At this period, he visibly imitated Fontenelle, whose clever Reports to the Academy of Sciences were made to charm. Was it Fontenelle or Montesquieu who wrote the following passage on the discoveries in physics which, after letting themselves be awaited for ages, burst forth suddenly, one after another, from Galileo to Newton: "One would say that Nature acted like those virgins who long preserved their most precious possession, and then allowed themselves to be ravished in a moment of that they had preserved with such care, and defended with such constancy."

And here is another thought that makes a singular appearance in a Report written by Montesquieu on the "Usage of the Renal Glands": "Truth seems sometimes as though it ran to meet those who seek it; often there is no interval between desire, hope, and enjoyment." Montesquieu, as academician of the Sciences of Bordeaux, certainly paid tribute to the style in vogue and to his admiration for Fontenelle.

What we like better to observe in these first essays of Montesquieu is the love of science, and of study applied to all objects. We have not only his

Reports on the work of others, but his own "Obser-vations" on natural history, read in 1721. He had studied under the microscope a little red insect, a plant of misletoe, and oak lichens; he had dissected a frog; he had made researches into the nutritive quali-ties of various vegetables. The author declared that he attached no greater importance to these observa-tions and experiments than they deserved: "They are the fruit of country idleness. They may die in the region that gave birth to them; but those who live in society have duties to fulfil; we owe it to ours to give account of even our amusements." In closing this report, he almost seems to be endeavouring to lessen the merit of an observer; whereas the latter has need of all his subtlety of mind and his skill of inven-tion to bring out the fact that is under his eyes:

"It does not need much intellect," says Montesquieu, "to see the Pantheon, the Coliseum, or the Pyramids; and it does not need much more to see a worm under a microscope, or a star through a telescope; it is in this that physics are so admirable: great geniuses, narrow minds, and second-rate people can all take a part. He who could not compose a system like Newton can make an observation which would put that great philosopher on the rack. Nevertheless, Newton is always Newton, that is to say, the successor of Descartes, and the other man is a common man, a worthless artist, who saw once, and perhaps never thought at all."

We ought to see in these words, not contempt of fact, but the subordination of fact to idea, which is a characteristic of Montesquieu. He does justice else-where to observation when he says: "It is the history of physics; **systems are its fable.**" Thus Montes-

quieu, at the beginning of his career, busied himself
with science, as Buffon did soon after, and as Goethe
did later; he furnished funds for a prize in Anatomy,
and seemed to aim only at serious results in keeping
with the gravity of his profession.

But during the time that he worked at these "Observations" on the objects of natural history, he gave
forth another work, by the way, for which he had
needed no microscope; his own eyes had served him
well enough. The *Lettres Persanes* appeared, without name of author, in 1721; and they instantly had a
success that marks a date and made it the book of
the epoch.

The *Lettres Persanes* is one of the three great books
of Montesquieu's life—for in truth he wrote but three:
these *Lettres* (1721); his admirable work, *Le Grandeur
et la Décadence des Romains* (1734), which is only a
detached episode in advance of his third and last great
book, *L'Esprit des Lois* (1748). The manner of these
three works differs, but not as much as one would
think. The basis of the ideas differs still less. The
book on the Romans is the one in which the writer
restrains himself most; he is master of himself from
first to last; his tone is firm, lofty, simple, and wholly
on the level of the majesty of the People-king. In
the *Esprit des Lois,* he often mingles, one hardly
knows how, epigram with grandeur. In the *Lettres
Persanes,* Montesquieu, then young, sports and takes
his pleasure; but gravity is found in his play; the

greater part of his ideas are there in the germ,—better, indeed, than in the germ, they are developing. He is more indiscreet than he is later; and it is in this sense principally that he is less mature. He will retain most of his ideas, but, in his future works, he will not produce them in the same way; he will reflect them differently, and will speak of them only with gravity, feeling more and more the grandeur of the social institution, and desiring the ennobling of human nature.

If we desire to estimate Montesquieu's nature and quality of mind, we must remember what he wrote himself, towards the close of his life, to d'Alembert, who asked of him (for *l'Encyclopédie*) certain articles on points he had already treated in the *Esprit des Lois:* "I have," he said, "drawn from my brain on those topics all that was in it. My mind is a mould; all that comes out of it looks alike; therefore I could only say for you what I have said, and perhaps say it worse than I did." This fundamental oneness of mould in Montesquieu is felt through all his great variety of productions, from his first to his last work.

That which gives the *Lettres Persanes* their date and the stamp of the Regency, is the touch of irreverence and libertinism, which comes in to lighten the background and season the book to the taste of the day. Where did Montesquieu get the idea of making Persians talk in that way, putting his own thoughts under that slender disguise? It is said that he owed the idea to Dufresny, who, in a book entitled *Amuse-*

ments sérieux et comiques, imagines, by way of variety, a Siamese in Paris, dropping from the clouds in the midst of the Rue Saint Honoré, and making reflections in his own way. Persons who have studied English literature prefer to think that Montesquieu had in mind a letter supposed to be written from London by an Indian of the island of Java, which can be read in Addison's "Spectator." But the idea, whether it belonged to the Siamese or the man from Java, became original in Montesquieu through the development that he gave to it, and the boldness with which he natural-ised it in Paris. The *Lettres Persanes,* with all their defects, is one of the books of genius which our literature has produced.

Usbek and Rica, two friends, two Persians of rank, leave their country and make a journey to Europe. Usbek, the principal personage, has a harem at Ispa-han, and on leaving Persia he commits it to the care of the Grand Eunuch, a black man, whom he reminds, from time to time, of his strict injunctions. In this harem are women whom he loves exceedingly, and the author would not be sorry to interest us in this romantic topic, very choice in its Asiatic taste and carefully studied. He succeeded, no doubt, in doing so at that date—1721; the libertine, or, to speak cor-rectly, the licentious part of the *Lettres Persànes,* the perpetual details of eunuchs, passions, practices, and almost of utensils, on which the imagination of readers could dwell with pleasure, required a society that enjoyed the novels of Crébillon *fils*. To-day, this part seems to us artificial, dead; and, if it were longer, intolerably wearisome. What pleases us, and what we seek in these *Lettres,* is Montesquieu himself, slightly disguised among his various personages, and judging, under that transparent mask, the manners and customs, the ideas—in short, the whole social life of his youth.

Rica is a satirist, Parisian from the first day, and painting with a jest the eccentricities and absurdities of the queer characters who pass before his eyes, and with whom he gets along very well. Usbek, more serious, resists and reasons; he takes up questions, he propounds and discusses them in letters which he addresses to the theologians of his own country. The art of the work, and what, through the apparent mixture, shows the talent of composition, is that, side by side with a harem letter, there will be one on free-will. An ambassador from Persia to Muscovy writes a half-page to Usbek about the Tartars, which might be a chapter in the *Esprit des Lois*. Rica, on the one hand, writes the cleverest criticism on the chatter of Frenchmen and on the talkers with nothing to say in society; on the other, Usbek discusses God and justice in a very noble and far-reaching letter. The idea of justice, independent in itself, is therein explained under the true principles of the social institution. Montesquieu (for it is he who speaks here, as he spoke in his own name to the end of his life), tries to establish in what respect that idea of justice does not depend on human conventions: "If it did so depend," he adds, "it would be a terrible truth that we should have to conceal from ourselves."

Montesquieu goes farther. He tries to render the idea and the worship of justice independent of all existence higher than man; he goes so far as to say, through the mouth of Usbek: "If there were no God, we ought always to love justice; that is to say, we should make efforts to resemble that Being, of whom we have so lofty an idea, and who, if he existed, would necessarily be just. Free as we may be from the yoke of religion, we cannot be free from that of equity."

Here we touch the very foundation of Montesquieu's thought, and of all his habitual mental procedure; let us not be weak or wavering, let us not hesitate to expose the truth in its nudity. He says still further:

"Even if the immortality of the soul is an error, I should be sorry not to believe it: I own that I am not so humble as the atheists. I do not know what they think, but, for my part, I do not choose to barter the idea of my immortality for that of the beatitude of to-day. I am glad to believe myself as immortal as God himself. Independently of revealed ideas, metaphysical ideas give me a very strong hope of my eternal happiness which I do not choose to renounce."

In these words we have the measure of Montesquieu's belief and his noble desire: even in the expression of that desire, the supposition glides in that "even if the thing did not exist" it would be best to believe in it. I do not blame that homage rendered, in any case, to the elevation and the idealisation of human nature; but I cannot help remarking that it is taking and accepting the ideas of justice and of religion on the political and social side and not potentially in themselves. Montesquieu, when, by degrees, he freed himself from the irony of the *Lettres Persanes,* came more and more to respect the objects of human veneration and conscience. Not that I think he entered into them with more personal feeling, for in the midst of his most majestic parts a sort of barrenness is felt. He has ideas, but he has not, it has been remarked, civic feelings. A sort of life is lacking, a tie that binds: we feel the powerful brain, but not the heart. I think it incumbent on me to note, if not this weak side, at least this cold side of a great man.

One of his thoughts has always impressed me:— "Fontenelle," he said, "is as much above other men by his heart as he is above all men of Letters by his mind." I have read and re-read those words and, recalling what Fontenelle was, I thought they ought to read: "Fontenelle as much *below* other men in heart."—But no, it seems really to be eulogy that Montesquieu desired to make of Fontenelle; and he adds an excellent quality in such a man: "He praises others without reluctance." What Montesquieu really admired in Fontenelle was equanimity, absence of envy, breadth, prudence, and, perhaps, indifference. The only conclusion that I seek to draw from this is, that, very superior to Fontenelle in talent and as a writer, he was, more or less, of the same religion in morals.

The following memorable confessions of Montesquieu are often quoted:

" Study has been to me a sovereign remedy against the vexations of life, having never had an annoyance that one hour's reading did not dissipate."

" I wake in the morning with an inward joy at seeing the light; I see the light with a sort of transport, and all the rest of the day I am content. I pass the night without waking; in the evening, when I go to bed, a species of torpor prevents me from making reflections."

" I am nearly always as content with fools as with men of intellect . . . etc."

Man of study and of thought, detached rather early from passions, and having at no time been led away by them, he lived and dwelt in the steadiness of intellect. Very kind in private life, natural and simple, he deserved to be loved by all around him as a man of genius can be; but even in his most human aspects we still find this stiff, indifferent side; a benevolent and lofty equity rather than tenderness of soul.

Who does not know that fine act in his life when at Marseilles, where he often went to visit his sister. Wishing one day to go out in a boat, he met a young man named Robert who, with none of the manners or tone of a sailor, offered to take him. The young man, while rowing the boat, told him he did that sort of work only on Sundays and fête-days, in order to earn all he could for the purpose of buying his father, who had been taken prisoner by a corsair, and was then a slave in Tetuan. Montesquieu informed himself carefully on the facts of the matter before parting from the young man at the wharf. Some months later, the father, freed from slavery, returned to his family, not knowing whence the unhoped-for succour had come. You weep; but wait! — admire, but do not shed tears. Two or three years later, the young man, who feels sure it was his unknown passenger to whom he owed the deliverance of his father, meets him on the quay and flings himself at his feet in gratitude, entreating him to come and see the family he has rendered so happy. Montesquieu brusquely draws back, denies everything, refuses to go with the young man, and tears himself without pity from a legitimate gratitude. It was not until his death that the benefaction was revealed. Here I seem to see in Montesquieu one of those gods who are benefactors of humanity without human tenderness. It is thus that in the "Hippolytus" of Euripides, Diana, at the moment the young hero is about to die, moves away, though she seemed to have loved him: but however friendly to mortals were these gods of antiquity, tears were forbidden to their eyes — the God-Man had not yet come.

In this view which I have allowed myself to express on the moral nature of Montesquieu, and which his *Lettres Persanes* called forth, far be it from me to diminish the severe yet human beauty of his character. I content myself by defining it, and by describing that stoical humanity in so far as it was apart from charity as shown by Pascal and Bossuet.

All the questions of the day under the Regency are touched upon in the *Lettres Persanes* — the dispute of the ancients and moderns, the revocation of the Edict of Nantes and its effects, the quarrel concerning the Bull *Unigenitus,* and so forth; the author serves the spirit of the day by mingling his views with it; the reign of Louis XIV is sharply attacked with a backward thrust. In the famous episode of the Troglodytes, Montesquieu relates, after his manner, his dream of Salente. In the portraits of the Farmer-general, the Director, the Casuist, the Man *à bonnes fortunes,* the Gambling Wife, Montesquieu equals La Bruyère in recollection. He resembles him also in language, but without intending it. His own language, while it is quite as new, is perhaps less complicated; it has a clearness and a singularly picturesque quality. The Casuist wishes to show that a man of his profession is necessary to certain persons, who, without aiming at perfection, wish to secure their salvation: "As they have no ambition," he says, "they do not care for the chief places; thus they enter Paradise as righteous as they can. Provided they get there, that is enough for them." Elsewhere, speaking of men whose conversation is only a mirror in which they exhibit nothing but their own impertinent faces: "Oh! how insipid praise is," he exclaims, "when it reflects back to the place whence it came!" The

whole style is clear, pungent, full of wit, a little thin
and sharp, and occasionally incorrect.

But Montesquieu has certain free and easy ideas as
to style. "A man who writes well," he thinks,
"does not write as other people write, but as *he*
writes; and often it is when he speaks ill that he
speaks well." He writes, therefore, in his own manner; and that manner, always refined and lively, becomes strong and proud and rises higher with his
topics. I have said that he liked and even delighted
in a style of imagery or of picturesque comparisons
to elucidate his thought: for example, wishing to
make Rica say that the husband of a pretty woman in
France, if he is worsted at home, takes his revenge
on the wives of others:

> "This title of husband of a pretty woman," he writes, "which is
> so carefully concealed in Asia, is borne in France without uneasiness.
> Men feel they have opportunity to find compensation everywhere.
> A prince consoles himself for the loss of a fortress by capturing an-
> other; when the Turks took Bagdad from us did we not take the
> fortress of Kandahar in Mongol-Tartary from them?"

Exactly in the same manner Montesquieu, in the
Esprit des Lois, describing an English Utopian who,
having under his eyes the image of true liberty, goes
about imagining quite another liberty in his book,
says: "He built Chalcedonia, having the shores of
Byzantium before his eyes." In Montesquieu's
thought, at the moment when we least expect it,
suddenly the summits glow.

Amid the audacity and the irreverence of the *Lettres*

Persanes, a spirit of prudence is observable in Usbek's pen. While discussing questions so well and occasionally letting daylight into them, Usbek (and here, perhaps, is a contradiction that Montesquieu failed to avoid), continues to remain faithful to the laws of his country and to his religion. "It is true," he says, "that, by a caprice that comes more from the nature than from the mind of men, it is sometimes necessary to change certain laws, but the case is rare; and when it does occur, it should be touched with a *trembling hand.*" Rica himself, light-hearted jester, remarking that in courts of justice when judgment is to be pronounced the votes of the majority are taken, adds, by way of epigram: "But they say they have found by experience that it would be better to take those of the minority; and that is natural enough, for there are very few just minds, and all the world agrees that there are quantities of unjust ones." This is enough to show that the mind that dictated the *Lettres Persanes* would never push things to extremity on the side of reform and popular revolution.

After touching upon questions which belong properly to the philosophy of history, after expressing astonishment that Frenchmen should have abandoned the old laws made by their first kings in the assemblies of the nation, and, having thus reached the threshold of the great work he no doubt foresaw in the future, Montesquieu resumes his laughter over many subjects, and when he has laughed enough he stops short. The *Lettres Persanes,* having exhausted the picture and the satire of present manners and morals, turns to the romantic: Usbek receives news that his harem, profiting by his absence, has made a revolution; all are in rebellion, flying at each other's throats, and killing one another. It is a voluptuous and delirious conclusion, a "fire and blood" end, that has nothing relating to us in it. All this sensual part is dry and hard, showing that Montesquieu's imagination lay solely in the direction of historical and moral observation. Once more I remark that there is in the *Lettres Persanes,* from beginning to end, and viewed as a whole, a resemblance to the novels of Crébillon *fils.*

Le Temple de Gnide, published in 1725, was an error of taste and a misconception of talent. Montesquieu thought he was imitating the Greeks in making this little prose poem out of complaisance to a princess of the Condé blood, Mademoiselle de Clermont. He was thirty-five years old at that time, and he wrote: " At thirty-five years of age, I still loved." But Montesquieu's loves seem never to have troubled or touched him much. In vain he paints his Thémire: he still seems to us more sensual in love than sentimental: "In my youth," he says, "I was fortunate in attaching myself to women who I thought loved me; as soon as I ceased to think so I detached myself from them suddenly." And he adds: "I liked fairly well to talk insipidities to women and to do them services that cost me little." *Le Temple de Gnide* is one of those insipidities, but it must have cost him some labour. M. Lainé relates that when he obtained permission from the Secondat family to make researches among Montesquieu's papers, he found in the secretary, which no one had opened since the death of the great writer, a mass of rough drafts of all his love-letters. The author of the *Temple de Gnide* worked over and made erasures even in his *billets-doux*, and we feel it in reading that tale. What in Montesquieu is vigour and nervous energy in great things, is stiffness in little ones. He has no grace.

About this time, Montesquieu was much more in his true line when he delivered, before the Academy of Bordeaux in 1725, a short Discourse in praise of Study and the Sciences. He avenges the Sciences, having questioned their utility in one part of the *Lettres Persanes;* he asserts, in a witty and original manner, that knowledge being gained, the intellectual result thereof is often the indirect and distant cause of the salvation of society. For instance, if the Mexicans had had a Descartes before the landing of the Spaniards, Fernando Cortez would not have conquered them; for the awe they had of the Spaniards under the idea that these strangers were gods, was "only a simple effect of their ignorance of a principle of philosophy." Courage was never lacked by either the Mexicans or the Peruvians, "only hope of success. Thus a false principle of philosophy, ignorance of a physical cause, enervated in a moment all the forces of two great empires."

In this little Discourse, Montesquieu speaks magnificently of study, and of the motives that ought to lead us to it. "The first is the inward satisfaction we feel when we see the excellence of our own being increase, and know that we render an intelligent being more intelligent." Another motive, which he did not go far from himself to find,

"is," he says, "our own happiness. The love of a lady is almost the only eternal passion in us; all others quit us as, little by little, this miserable machine which gives them to us nears its ruin. . . . We should make ourselves a happiness that can follow us through the ages; life is so short that we ought to count as nothing all felicity that does not last as long as ourselves."

Finally, he gives another motive, and one which he feels equally, usefulness to the public and to the world: "Is it not a noble purpose to work that we may leave behind us men more fortunate and happier than we have been?" Montesquieu, through integrity of heart and guidance of his intellect, was naturally a citizen of the race of the Vaubans, the Catinats, the Turennes, the L'Hôpitals, of all those who sincerely desire the welfare and honour of their country and of mankind: "I have always felt an inward joy," he says, "when a law has been made which served the common welfare."

The *Lettres Persanes* ranked him, whether he would or no, among literary men. He felt the advantages to

his reputation, and the hindrances to his career. A
powerful impulsion moved him henceforth to fulfil his
destiny as a writer, and he acted upon it. He freed
himself from his bonds, sold his office, was received, in
1726, into the French Academy (although, like the rest
of the world, he laughed at it before he belonged to it),
and undertook his travels in the spring of 1728, beginning with Germany and Hungary. In Vienna he saw
much of Prince Eugène; arriving in Venice, he had
the pleasure of meeting Bonneval, who had not yet
passed over to the Turks; he visited Turin, Rome,
Italy, returning by way of Switzerland, the Rhine,
and Holland, concluding his course of observations in
England (October, 1729). He was introduced to the
latter country by Lord Chesterfield, the most enlightened of guides; he saw all, and he saw well. Before
arriving there, he had travelled on the continent with
an Englishman, Lord Waldegrave, and had said already: "There are no men of true common-sense but
those who are born in England."

A few *Notes* from his journal have been published,
which relate to his stay in London. He remarks that,
in his time, ambassadors and foreign ministers knew
no more of England than a babe of six months; the
freedom of the press misled them: "As they see the
devil in the periodical press they are led to believe that
the people are on the verge of rebellion; but they should
bear in mind that in England, as elsewhere, the people
are dissatisfied with the ministers, and that the people

write openly what is only thought elsewhere." Montesquieu appreciates this liberty "which every man demands and enjoys over there—a slater has the newspaper brought to him on the roof and reads it there." But he has no illusions on the state of the country and its institutions; he rightly judges the corruption of political morals, the venality of consciences and of votes, the practical and calculating side of things, the fear of being duped which leads to hardness. He seems almost to have believed that a revolution was at hand; but we know how the political condition, very debased in those days of Sir Robert Walpole, improved and gained new vigour under Pitt. Though he saw these evils, Montesquieu thoroughly appreciated the advantages that compensated for them; he expresses his appreciation thus: "England is at present the freest country that there is in the world; I except no republic. . . . If a man in England had as many enemies as he has hairs upon his head, no harm could come to him: that is a great thing, for health of soul is as necessary as health of body."

A prophetic glance darts like a flash of lightning through the following sentence, thrown out in passing, and certainly predicts the emancipation of English America: "I do not know what will happen to the many inhabitants sent from Europe and Africa to the West Indies; but I think that if any nation is abandoned by her colonies, England will be the first."

I confess, in all humility, even if I do a wrong to

my sentiment of the ideal, that if we could have, in its consecutive entirety, Montesquieu's *Journal de Voyage,* the whole of these *Notes* so simple, so natural in their sincere and primitive setting forth, I should prefer the reading of them to that of the *Esprit des Lois,* and I should believe them to be more useful.

In Montesquieu's great work the artist counts for much; many things are said in it which are open to doubt. The author-artist is there in presence of his subject, of his vast study; he wants a law, he searches for it, and sometimes he creates it. From the accumulation of texts and notes which he has brought before him, and which press upon him and almost overwhelm him, he frees himself, he chooses his course; his work springs up. Boldly, sometimes painfully, he begins his *Considérations* and his perspective; he fashions them to suit himself. Was it not he who, in the privacy of his own study, said: "Histories are false facts composed on true facts."

And did he not say, still further: "In history we see men painted in noble portraits, but we do not find them to be what we see them." How is it, then, when the spirit of history alone is sought? Men are seen at too great a distance; the human stuff which the statesman should consider too often disappears in Montesquieu.

I spoke just now of the *useful:* Montesquieu joined to it an idea of the beautiful. He had a sacred pattern within him; he raised a temple, and the crowd flocked to it. But did he not set up in it certain idols ?

Let us lay aside regrets, and accept respectfully the unique and regal form of his *Considérations,* which is peculiarly his own; a form born of a mind so lofty and so firm, and bearing the imprint of a mould which, with all the fine accessories that characterised it, will not be met with again.

On his return to France, Montesquieu retired to his château of La Brède, far from the suppers of Paris, in order to collect and arrange his thoughts; he remained there two years, seeing only his books and his trees. He was full of England when he arrived, and had to repress and postpone the idea of writing a book on that original Government, so unlike our own, which tempted him much. He gave the preference to his *Considérations sur les Causes de la Grandeur des Romains et de leur Décadence* (1734), which has remained the most classic and perfect of his works; the only one, indeed, that seems to have been cast in a single mould like a statue.

The works of Montesquieu are nothing else than the philosophic summing up and the ideal review of his studies; no one reasons better than he on history when he has closed the book that contains the narrative. He expresses the thought in it; he gives it continuity, connectedness, counsel; and that which makes the beauty of what he says is the manner in which it is put forth. He advances with a firm step, by a series of vivid and compact reflections, which, as a whole, have the grand air; his wit is also quick, brief, and is aimed high.

This style of seeing and speaking was marvellously well suited for application to the Romans. To judge of the book of *Considérations* which he gave to them, we should have to examine what had been said before him on that subject, and render to Machiavelli, Saint-Évremond, Saint Réal, that which is their due; and as for form we should have to place the historic discourses of Montesquieu side by side with those of Bossuet.

The nature of Montesquieu's mind is so completely that of reasoning upon history, that he does it where there is no call for it, and where the grounds are insufficient; as, for instance, on the beginnings of Rome. Before making reflections on what he had read, he ought to have asked himself whether the historians spoke the truth; there was criticism to be made on the books and on the traditions that were semi-fabulous. Montesquieu does not make it. From the statement that Romulus took the shield of the Sabines, which was large, in place of the small shield he had hitherto used, Montesquieu jumps to the conclusion that a certain custom and a certain policy was in practice among the Romans to borrow from the vanquished whatever they had that was better than their own.

It is not until the period of Hannibal and the Punic

wars, that Montesquieu's thought develops with ease, and that he commands his whole subject. Chapter VI, on the policy of the Romans, and on their conduct at the submission of other peoples, is a masterpiece, in which prudence and majesty are combined; the grand style begins here, never to cease again. In speaking of the Romans, Montesquieu's language becomes like Latin; it takes a character of firm conciseness that brings it near to the language of Tacitus or Sallust; there is study, profound combination, effort, as with Sallust, to attain to propriety of expression in words, and to conciseness; also to make the image, as in Tacitus, both magnificent and brief, and to imprint on the whole diction something grave and august.

No one has entered more fully than Montesquieu into the ideal of the Roman genius; he is, by inclination, favourable to the Senate, and something of a patrician of the ancient Republic. It should be remarked that he who spoke so admiringly of Alexander, Charlemagne, Trajan, and Marcus Aurelius is less generous on the subject of Cæsar; at any rate, he does not speak of him as if he were under a sort of enchantment, as he does of those other great mortals. He is angry with him for having been the potential instrument of the great transformation of the Roman world. Montesquieu (if we except the *Lettres Persanes*) always used noble words in relation to Christianity, and, as he advanced in life, he more and more accepted and, so to speak, espoused its benefits in all that concerned civilisation and humanity. Nevertheless, he had for pure Roman nature anterior to all Christian influence, for the stoical Roman nature, a predilection that he never concealed. The suicides of Cato and Brutus inspired him with reflections in which there is, perhaps, a sort of classic idolatry, and even some prestige: "It is certain," he exclaims, "that men have become less free, less courageous, less inclined to great enterprises than they were when, through that power which they possessed over themselves, they could, at any moment, escape from every other power." He says this again in the *Esprit des Lois,* apropos of what the ancients called *virtue:* "When they had that quality in full force," he says, "men did things we see no longer in these days, and which, if we saw them, would astound our little souls."

Montesquieu divined many things, ancient or modern; about those even of which he had seen the least in his day—free government, civil wars, imperial government. One might make a piquant extract of such predictions or allusions taken from his works. Let us beware of that method which draws to self a great mind and turns it from its broad and special path. In all that Montesquieu foresaw and divined, one thing is lacking to make him wholly himself, and to complete the education of his genius,—he did not foresee the revolution. He did not believe that, in our day, proscriptions or wholesale spoliations would be possible.

Speaking of those of the Romans, he says: "We can draw this advantage from the smallness of our fortunes —they are safer; we are not worth enough to have our property torn from us." Montesquieu did not conceive that there could be a day, a near day, when the Clergy in a body would be dispossessed, and the Nobles also, in a great measure; when the chief heads of the Parliament of Paris were to fall upon the scaffold; he did not divine a 1793.

I desired to read Machiavelli in comparison with Montesquieu; the latter is the true refutation, or, at any rate, the true corrective. With Machiavelli, we are always closer to natural corruption, to primitive cupidity; Machiavelli distrusts himself; Montesquieu does not. It was Machiavelli who said that there is in all men a hidden, vicious inclination, which awaits only the opportunity to show itself, and needs all civil laws, supported by force of arms, to repress it. Men, according to him, never do right unless they cannot do otherwise: "And when they have that choice, and the liberty to do evil with impunity, they never fail to cause confusion and disorder everywhere." Machiavelli is convinced that, although men may seem to change in the course of a given state of things, fundamentally they do not change, and, certain occasions returning, we find them absolutely the same. Montesquieu is not wholly convinced of that truth. At the opening of the *Esprit des Lois,* he goes so far as to say that the first men supposed to be savages and

children of nature, were, above all, timid, and wanted
peace: as if physical cupidity, want, and hunger, the
blind consciousness that all youth has of its own force,
and "that rage for domination innate in the human
heart," would not engender from the very first, conflict
and warfare. This criticism is fundamental, and bears,
as I think, on the whole of the *Esprit des Lois.*
Montesquieu grants too much, not only outwardly,
but secretly in his own mind, to the decorum of
human nature. This defect in Montesquieu is infinitely honourable, but a real defect, none the less.
Admirable explainer and classifier of the past and of
those accomplished things that have no present consequences, he is likely to lead into error those who
take him at his word about the future. Born under a
mild government, living in the midst of an enlightened
society, where the memory of factions was far distant,
and the despotism that repressed them was no longer
present, or, at any rate, not felt, he lightly adjusted
humanity to his desire. He forgot what Richelieu had
known, and what he had had to do, and Louis XIV also,
at the beginning of his reign. He had need, as I said
before, of a revolution (were it only such a Fronde
as Pascal saw) to refresh his idea of the reality of
human nature, that idea which is so easily covered up
in calm and civilised epochs.

Machiavelli, on the contrary (let us not forget this in
a comparison of the two geniuses), lived at an epoch
and in a country where there were daily, for individ-

uals as well as for cities, thirty ways of being destroyed and of perishing. Such a state of society naturally keeps men on the alert, and gives prudence to all.

I return to the *Considérations,* from which I have wandered. Divided between the old Romans of the resistance and the Roman who first passed the Rubicon, Montesquieu does not understand Cæsar to the same degree that he understands other great men; he follows him with a sort of regret. Montesquieu had so lived in idea among those old Romans, that he had an opinion upon them, a direct, personal impression, which he produces sometimes in quite a naïve manner. Speaking of the triumvir Lepidus, sacrificed by Octavius: "We are very glad," he exclaims, "to see the humiliation of this Lepidus. He was the most wicked citizen in the Republic."—*We are very glad:* Montesquieu, when writing, lets many of these familiar expressions escape him, showing his intimacy with his great subjects; there is something abrupt and unexpected, like his own conversation, in these chapters. He says of Alexander: "Let us talk about him at our ease." Elsewhere he says: "I request the reader to pay a little attention"—I see in this the sort of gesture of an eager man who is full of his subject, who fears in talking to let something escape him, and so grasps the arm of his listener.

Sometimes the gesture is grander, less familiar; the orator rises: "Here we must give ourselves the spectacle of things human " . . . and he goes on to enumerate in a manner worthy of Bossuet all that labour of the Roman people and their Senate—the wars undertaken, the blood shed, so many triumphs, so much wisdom and courage, all to serve finally "to glut the happiness of five or six monsters." The whole passage is pure Bossuet.

There is a main point, nevertheless, on which Montesquieu differed from Bossuet. Both believed in a sovereign counsel in human things; but Bossuet assigns that counsel to God and Providence, who has His secret purpose and object. Montesquieu assigns it elsewhere:

"It is not," he says, "fortune that rules the world; we can ask the Romans, who had a continual succession of prosperity so long as they governed themselves on a certain plan, and an uninterrupted succession of reverses when they conducted themselves on another plan. There are general causes, whether moral or physical, which act in each monarchy, raising it, maintaining it, or flinging it down. All events are subject to these causes; and, though the chances of a battle, which is a particular cause, may have ruined a State, there was a general cause, which brought about that this State should perish by a single battle. In a word: the main procedure sweeps along with it all special incidents."

Montesquieu's whole philosophy of history lies in those words; and we must agree that in what concerns the Romans, judging things after the event, he seems to be right. The Romans certainly do lend themselves wonderfully to the application of this linked system: we might even say, in truth, that they came

into the world expressly that Montesquieu might
"consider" them.

And yet, even if we do not assign directly to Providence itself, as Bossuet does, the counsel and law of
the world of history, it seems to me very difficult and
very perilous to find it in this succession and linking
together of events in which Montesquieu flatters himself he has discovered it. Machiavelli, on this point,
seems to me wiser and nearer the truth than Montesquieu when he reminds us, even in the midst of his
reflections, how much of chance—that is, of causes to
us unknown—there is in the origin and in the accom-
plishment of the facts of history and the life of empires.
Here, again, Montesquieu suffers from living in his
study and never seeing history make itself before him.
Otherwise, he would oftener have said to himself:
"On what small things do great things hinge!"
Cardinal Alberoni is reported to have made a criticism of this kind upon him: "There is temerity," he
said, "in seeking for the causes of the grandeur and
decadence of the Romans in the Constitution of their
State. Events in which human wisdom had the
smallest part make epochs rather than consequences."

Montesquieu was sixty years of age when he published his *Esprit des Lois* (end of 1748). During the
preceding years, when he was not at his château of
La Brède, he lived in Paris, where he was much in the
great world, especially in the circle of the Duchesse
d'Aiguillon and of Mme. du Deffand, and was greatly

desired everywhere; a simple, kindly man, never seeking to shine. "I had the good fortune to frequent the same companies that he did," says Maupertuis; "I have seen and shared in the eagerness with which he was always awaited, and the joy with which we saw him arrive." "Who would not love this man," wrote the Chevalier d'Aydie to Mme. du Deffand, "this good man, this great man, original in his works, in his nature, in his manners, and always worthy of admiration, or else adorable." A contemporary of Montesquieu, whom I scarcely dare quote in connection with him, the frivolous Abbé de Voisenon, gives, nevertheless, a few pleasant anecdotes of him, and tells them well:

"He was such a good father," he says, "that he really believed in good faith that his son was worth more than he. He was a kind and firm friend; his conversation was varied, like his writings. He had both gaiety and reflection; he knew how to argue and at the same time he conversed well. He was extremely absent-minded; he started one day from Fontainebleau, telling his carriage to follow, so that he might go on foot for an hour, to get some exercise; he went as far as Villejuif, supposing he was not yet at Chailly (a distance of 48 kilometres)."

Garat, in his life of Suard, shows us Montesquieu in his domain of La Brède:

"among the lawns, the fountains, the woods, laid out in the English fashion, walking about from morning till night, a white cotton cap upon his head and a vine-prop over his shoulder. Persons who came to present to him the homage of Europe have been known to ask him more than once, taking him for a vine-dresser, if that were Montesquieu's château."

The Marquis d'Argenson, who judges him very truly, says:

" As he has immense intelligence he makes a charming use of what he knows; but he puts more intellect into his books than into his conversation, because he does not seek to shine and will not take the trouble to do so. He keeps the Gascon accent which he brought from his native region, and thinks it in some way beneath him to correct it. He takes no care of his style, which is much wittier and sometimes more vigorous than it is pure."

Speaking of the great work that Montesquieu had had in preparation for twenty years, M. d'Argenson goes on to say:

" I know some portions of it, which can only sustain the reputation of the author; but I foresee that, as a whole, it may fail, and that we shall find more agreeable single chapters to read, more clever and seductive ideas, than really true and useful instruction on the way that laws should be drawn up and put in force. . . . I know the author to have all possible intelligence; he has acquired vast knowledge, during his travels and also during his retirement in the country; but I again predict that he will not give us the book we are needing; although we shall surely find in the one he is preparing many profound ideas, new thoughts, striking images, sallies of wit and genius, and a multitude of curious facts—the collecting of which supposes even more taste than study."

M. d'Argenson was not mistaken in one direction, but much mistaken in another. Montesquieu's book, with all its defects, was destined to quell the fears and surpass the hopes of his friends. There are works at which we must not look too closely; they stand as monuments. Mme. du Deffand's remark, *"Ce n'est pas l'Esprit des Lois, c'est de l'esprit sur les lois "* ["It is not the Spirit of the Laws, it is wit and humour, about

the laws"], is a saying which might be true in the
private society of Montesquieu, but ceases to be so
from the point of view of the public and of the world.
The public sees things more as a whole, and when
there is a breath from above and a lofty imprint on a
work it takes for granted that the author is right on
all points, and yields to its influence.

It was of this same *Esprit des Lois* that the studious
Gibbon said, speaking of his studies: "I read Grotius
and Puffendorf; I read Barbeyrac; I read Locke and
his treatises; but my delight is to read and reread
Montesquieu, whose vigour of style and boldness of
hypothesis are so potent to rouse and stimulate the
genius of the age." And Horace Walpole, speaking
of the work on its appearance, wrote: "I consider it
the best book that was ever written—at least I never
learned half as much from all the books I ever read.
There is as much wit in it as there is practical knowledge." This last point has become doubtful in the
present day. "There is no book," says, on the contrary, a recent English critic, "that can be cited as
having done more for the human race at the time
when it appeared, and from which a reader in these
days can draw so few practical ideas." But that is
the fate of nearly every work that has made the human
mind progress.

Montesquieu, at the period of its publication, appears to us, in his correspondence, in all the suffering and extreme fatigue of childbirth. He had spent

the three preceding years on his estate (1743–1746), working without intermission. His eyes gave out; he saw but little; his better eye was afflicted with cataract. His secretary and his daughter read to him, for he could no longer read for himself. "I am crushed down by weariness," he wrote (March 31, 1747); "I hope to rest for the remainder of my days." The idea of adding to his work a digression on the origin and revolutions of civil Laws in France (which forms the last four volumes of the *Esprit des Lois*), came to him only toward the last. "I thought I should kill myself these three months," he said (March, 1748), "trying to finish a piece I wished to add, which will be a book on the origin and revolutions of our civil Laws in France. It will take three hours to read; but I assure you it has cost me such labour that my hair is whitened by it." The book finished, and published in Geneva, he cries out: "But I confess the work has nearly killed me; I shall rest; I shall toil no more."

Something of this effort, thus vividly described, has crept into his work. The first book, which treats of laws in general, taking them in their broadest acceptation and in relation to all beings in the universe, is very vague; and, if I may dare to say so, we feel in the first book an embarrassed man, just as we feel a wearied and rather breathless man in the last. At the head of his second volume (that is, half-way, the edition of Geneva being printed in two volumes), he intended to place an "Invocation to the Muses" in the classic style:

"O Virgins of Mount Pierus! list to the name I give you! Inspire me! I have run a long course; I am crushed beneath sadness and weariness. Put into my spirit the charm and the sweetness I felt in other days, which desert me now. Never are you so divine as when you lead wisdom and truth by pleasurable ways.

"But, if you will not soften the rigour of my toil, hide the toil itself! Let men be taught, and I not teach! Let me reflect, let me feel, and then, when I proclaim new things, make men believe that I knew nothing; that it was you who told me all . . ."

The whole "Invocation" is full of beauty; and the sentiment of the delights of reason, which is defined as "the most perfect, the most noble, the most exquisite of our senses," rises into poesy. The friend in Geneva, who was charged with printing the work and of revising the proofs, objected to this hymn as being too antique for a modern work, and begged leave to suppress it; which request Montesquieu, after some opposition, granted.

No one will expect me to assume the airs of a critic in speaking of the *Esprit des Lois:* many volumes would be needed for such criticism, and the work would have to be taken book by book, chapter by chapter. I know three attempts of this kind: that of M. de Tracy, which, in spite of its title, is a logical refutation, or rectification, rather than a *Commentaire;* that of the farmer-general Dupin, which is not to be despised; and I have seen still a third refutation in manuscript, written by Cardinal de Boisgelin, former

Archbishop of Aix. Montesquieu can be stopped at every step on his general divisions of government, on the principle he assigns to each of them, on climates and the influence he attributes to them, on the quotations with which he strews his work. It often happens that he quotes incorrectly and for effect, as Chateaubriand has done later; that happens to men of imagination who make use of erudition without binding themselves down to it or mastering it. They take note, as they read, of witty or salient passages, and later, when composing, they take infinite pains to turn their royal road past their illustrative note, which may sometimes be merely a lively anecdote. Montesquieu makes too much use of classic incidents and the petty equivocal examples they afford him. What is it to us, I ask, how Arribas, King of the Molossians, modified an absolute government? Why should we know whether such or such police measures were adopted by the Epidamnians, and what conclusions could we reasonably draw from them?

The frequent breaks in the *Esprit des Lois,* the cutting up into chapters—composed, sometimes, of a single sentence—also show either a certain hesitation in arrangement, or a certain pretension to authority. Buffon, himself the very opposite to this style of writing, explained it in Montesquieu by physical causes: "The president," he said, "was nearly blind, and he was so eager, that half the time he forgot what he wanted to dictate, so that he was obliged in the end

to restrict himself to the smallest possible space."
Montesquieu himself states that if, when talking, he
felt he was simply listened to, the whole subject
seemed to vanish from before him. He needed an
interlocutor to keep him going. "As for conversations of reasoning," he continued, "where the subjects are argued, give and take, back and forth, I get
on pretty well." The *Esprit des Lois* gives us very
often the "cut and thrust" [*coupé et recoupé*] of
which Montesquieu speaks. All said, however, the
book remains a work of genius; chapters like those
on Alexander and on Charlemagne compensate us for
everything; chapters like those on the Constitution
and, especially, on the political morals of England
(book xix., ch. 27), are discoveries in the world of
history. We feel at every turn in Montesquieu one
of those rapid, penetrating minds which are the first
to stir a mass, and then enlighten it.

I have stated the radical defect that I believe is in
Montesquieu's statesmanship: he puts the average of
humanity, considered in its natural data, rather higher
than it is. It is not ill that a legislator should impel
men, even by means of a little illusion, to the use of
all their faculties and all their virtue; but he ought to
know under what inward conditions that is possible,
and take his precautions in consequence. Montesquieu not only does not acquaint his reader with this,
he does not acquaint himself. In picturing the government of England as so noble (which he had, never-

theless, seen closely with all its shadows), he seems never to have asked himself what effect his pictures might have in France. He certainly did not wish for the ruin of the monarchy, even that of Louis XV; he considered it tempered by the parliaments, and reformable in itself: "I have not, by nature," he said, "a disapproving spirit"; and he was far indeed from having a revolutionary one. Very different from Jean-Jacques, he desired that every man, after reading him, should have "new reasons to love his duty, his prince, his country, and the laws"; and yet he shows nowhere the slightest anxiety as to the result of the comparison he presents to the imagination of his compatriots. In the *Esprit des Lois,* Montesquieu seems to forget that Frenchmen remain what he saw and described them to be in the *Lettres Persanes;* and, though he speaks continually, with virtuous conviction, of moderate government, he does not sufficiently tell himself under his breath that such moderation is not one of the qualities that can be transplanted.

No doubt a certain chapter can be quoted in which he warns the French legislator that he must not correct too much, and that he must be careful not to change the general spirit of the nation (book xix., ch. 5); he compares the French and the Athenians, and makes it understood that Frenchmen, with all their good qualities and all their defects, ought to remain what they are. But here, again, Montesquieu is like a certain Athenian, who, unintentionally, spoke so highly of the Lacedæmonians that afterwards he cried in vain to his compatriots, "Do not imitate them!" they all rushed in rivalry to the ways of Lycurgus.

Being Frenchmen, when we have read much of Montesquieu, temptation seizes us:

> "He seems," says a sagacious critic, M. Joubert, "to teach the art of making empires; we think we are learning it as we listen to him; and every time we read him, we are tempted to construct one. Montesquieu does not sufficiently tell his readers: ' You are not statesmen enough, neither am I, to consider history with any such reflection, or to reason on it so easily and loftily '—The first and last word of the *Esprit des Lois* ought to be:—Statesmanship cannot be taught by books."

That we all—minds which form the commonalty of the world—should fall into such errors from which we are freed in after years by experience, is natural and simple,—nothing more so; but that the legislator and the genius who arises as our guide should, to a certain point, fall into the same errors and seem not to suspect that they can be fallen into, *there* is the weak side, and a sort of imprudence. Jean-Jacques Rousseau, who feared no revolution, might be bold and foolhardy; but Montesquieu, who does not desire one, was he sufficiently foresighted?

Let us take the *Esprit des Lois* for what it is: a work of thought and civilisation. What is finest in it is the man behind the book. We must not ask of that book more method, more continuity, more precision, and more practicality in detail, more sobriety in imagination and in erudition, more practical counsels than are actually in it; we should see the characteristics of moderation, patriotism, and humanity that the writer wrought into all his noble words and into many of his magnanimous utterances. It is in this sense that he has reason to speak of the "majesty" of his topic, and to add: "I do not think I have totally lacked genius." Everywhere, and in those noble portions so often quoted, we feel the man who desires true liberty, the true virtue of the citizen; things of which he had seen no perfect pattern among moderns, the idea of which he had formed for himself in his study and before the busts of the ancients.

The *Esprit des Lois* is a book which now is of no other use than that noble, perpetual use of carrying the mind into high historic regions, and giving birth to a vast array of fine discussions. In the order and practice of free and moderate governments men will continue to find in it general inspiration and memorable texts. As for its oracles, those who want them may seek them. The circle of things human, which has so many turns and twists, and of which we can never say that it is closed for ever, seems many a time to have given both right and wrong to Montesquieu. Very clever and very confident would he be who could see the confirmation of any certain order announced by him, and not eternal vicissitude.

The great work was scarcely published before it excited clamours which were only the signal of the revolution it was about to produce in ideas. At first, its success was decided solely among the *élite* of minds. " I hear," said the illustrious author, " a few hornets buzzing around me; but if the bees only gather a little honey that suffices me." Montesquieu lived six years longer; he was old before his time. He said one day to young Suard and others who were listening: "I am at an end; I have fired all my cart-ridges; all my candles are burnt out." About the same time, he wrote this melancholy yet serene and lofty thought: "I had conceived the design of giving greater breadth and depth to certain portions of my *Esprit,* but I have become incapable; my eyes are weakened by reading, and it seems to me that all that remains for me of light is the dawn of the day when they will close for ever."

We are able to form some idea of Montesquieu's conversation. In a *Defense* which he deigned to make of the *Esprit des Lois,* in reply to a Jansenist Gazette (for he was very sensitive to criticism), there is, towards the end, a very lively page which, accord-ing to d'Alembert, represents fairly well what he was as a conversationalist. His manner of talking was eager, rapid, abrupt, and full of metaphor. Marmontel remarks that he always " waited till the ball came to him, when he took it on the bound; he was naturally witty." Speaking in the *Defense* of narrow-minded critics who attacked a great work by School sophistries and sect scruples, Montesquieu adds:

" That style of criticism is the one thing in the world most capable of limiting the extent and diminishing the sum of national genius. . . . Nothing stifles knowledge more than to put upon all things a professor's robe. . . You cannot have your mind occupied in speaking well when you are terrified by the fear of speaking ill. . . Such critics come and clap a child's cap on our heads, and tell us at each word we utter: ' Take care, now; you want to speak your way, but I choose you to speak like me.' . . . Just as we begin to soar they pull us by the sleeve. Have we life and vigour?—they will take them away with pin-pricks. . . . Are we rising to any height? here come those men with their foot-rule or their tape-line, calling out to us to come down that they may take our measure."

Add to this picture a slight Gascon accent, and you might think it was Montesquieu himself who was speaking. Sometimes, in his rolling fire of imagery we fancy that we are reading Montaigne.

" His modest, free demeanour," says a contemporary of Montesquieu (Maupertuis) " is like his conversation. His figure is well proportioned. Though he has lost the sight of one eye almost entirely, and the other is very weak, no one would perceive it; the expression of his countenance unites sweetness and sublimity." His long, thin, refined face was a type of the region where he was born, the Bordeaux type; his well-cut profile had a noble aspect, and seemed made to stamp a medal.

In society, Montesquieu did not allow himself to yield to coteries that inclined to be imperious; we have the judgments upon him of Mme. Geoffrin and the Duchesse de Chaulnes, that is to say, of two women who liked to get much out of those who surrounded them and to play with them as they pleased. Mme. Geoffrin paints Montesquieu as an absent-minded man, "not knowing the names of his servants, and having a carriage that makes as much noise as a hackney-coach, etc." Mme. de Chaulnes says: "That man came into society to make a book; he remembered all that was told to him; he spoke to no strangers unless he thought he could get something useful out of them." She says elsewhere: "What is he good for, that genius?" Montesquieu answers both when he says in his *Pensées:* "I like the houses where I can get along with my every-day intellect." That is for the Duchesse de Chaulnes. And here is for Mme. Geoffrin: "I am not sorry to pass for absent-minded; it enables me to risk many negligences which might have embarrassed me."

This superior spirit which, without his intending it, gave birth or pretext to a number of demi-Montesquieus both supercilious and self-sufficient, was in him modesty itself:

"Modest men," he exclaims in the *Lettres Persanes,* "come, that I may embrace you! you make the sweetness and charm of life. You think you have nothing, and I tell you you have all. You think you humiliate no one, and you humiliate every one. When I compare you in my mind with the arbitrary men I see everywhere, I fling them from their tribune and lay them at your feet."

He had the kind-heartedness to think that he had neglected to make the fortune of his family and the glory of the name. "I confess," he said, "that I have too much vanity to wish that my children should one day make themselves a great fortune; it would only be by force of reason that they could then support the idea of me; they would need all their virtue to own me." He thought, for example, that if one of his sons became minister, chancellor, or something of that kind, it would be an embarrassment to so important a personage to have a father or grandfather like him, who had made nothing but books. This is certainly an excess of modesty, or a remains of class prejudice which is difficult to comprehend.

Montesquieu died at Havre, February 10, 1755. The circumstances of his death, and the obsessions that accompanied it have often been related. What is less known is that his funeral was attended by almost no one. Diderot (so Grimm tells us) was the only man of Letters who followed him to the grave. The eighteenth century army of men of Letters which was soon to march as one man with unanimity and proselytising zeal, and to give itself a final rendezvous at the funeral of Buffon (April, 1788), was not yet enrolled, nor even astir when Montesquieu died.

Adrienne Le Couvreur.

Adrienne Le Couvreur.

THERE are names that live, and of which we speak at any moment as of something present. Utter the name of Heloise, of La Vallière, every one knows them, and yet is glad to hear them spoken of again. We desire, we hope to learn something more about them. Brilliancy, romance, a destiny of ardour, devotion, and tenderness, of pathetic misfortune,—all this attaches to these poetic figures, and, transmitted and consecrated, procures for them in the imagination of the ages a perpetual youth. A sort of legend forms around them that never dies out If we knew where their graves were, we would gladly go each year piously to lay fresh wreaths upon them.

Somewhat similar is the case of Adrienne Le Couvreur. The reasons for this are confused; I shall try here to disentangle a few of them. She was the first actress in France who was renowned on the stage, and, at the same time, received with consideration in society. She was loved by the greatest soldier of his time; she inspired the greatest poet of the day with his most pathetic elegy. The public scandal caused by

the refusal of sepulture to her body, the tragic explanation and frightful suspicion that attended her
death, have, one and all, cast a mysterious interest over
her fate, and made her a victim whom we feel disposed both to love and avenge.   What further shall I
say? She is of those who, living, had *charm;* and
(what is given to very few) the mysterious essence
of that charm survives; it continues to operate in her
memory.

I have lately witnessed the drama, full of action, in
which two men of talent, Scribe and Legouvé (one of
them the most skilful dramatic engineer of our age),
have reconstructed and brought into play that memory.
They have conceived the rôle from the point of view
of a great actress, the Adrienne of our day [Rachel],
suiting it to her by many happy touches.   Nevertheless, this would not be a sufficient reason for me
to meddle in matters belonging to the stage, and to
encroach upon a domain which is not mine, if I had
not been informed of new documents, original writings, relating to the affair of the poisoning, and also
of certain unpublished letters that do honour to this
woman, as remarkable for her mind and her integrity
as for her talent.   One of my friends, an ardent bibliophile of choice tastes, feeling, in respect to Mlle. Le
Couvreur, that indefinable charm of which I have
spoken, determined to make careful search for all that
could be further learned of her, and, as he is lucky, he
found enough to add, on several points, to what was

ADRIENNE LE COUVREUR
From a portrait by Coypel

known already. While awaiting this coming publication, which M. Ravenel is preparing, I feel myself
permitted to pause for an instant on this subject of
Adrienne Le Couvreur, as not inappropriate at the
present moment.

Adrienne was born about the year 1690, at Fismes,
between Soissons and Reims. Her father, a hatter by
trade, moved his family to Paris in 1702, and lodged
in the faubourg St.-Germain, not far from the Comédie
Française. This neighbourhood offered the child
opportunities to strengthen a passion for the theatre
that was born in her: "Many of the bourgeois of
Fismes," relates the Abbé d'Allainval, whom I cannot
help quoting for these beginnings of her career, "told
me that, from childhood, she took pleasure in reciting
verses, and that they often enticed her into their houses
to listen to her. The Demoiselle Le Couvreur was
one of those extraordinary persons who are self-
made." When she was fifteen, she arranged with
some young people of the neighbourhood to act
Polyeucte and the little comedy of *Deuil* by Thomas
Corneille. These performances took place at a gro-
cery in the rue Férou. They were talked of in the
quarter. Adrienne played Pauline, and was not ill
seconded by her comrades; one of them distinguished
himself by the truth of his acting. Mme. Le Jay lent
the little troop her house, rue Garancière; society
rushed thither; it is said that the doors, guarded by
eight Swiss, were forced in. The tragedy was

scarcely over when the police entered and forbade
the performance. The afterpiece was not acted.

Thus ended these unlicensed performances. Adrienne played some time longer within the precincts of
the Temple, under the protection of the grand prior
of Vendôme; we know that she took lessons from the
comedian Le Grand; after that, we lose sight of her.
She travelled about the provinces and their adjoin-
ing countries, acting in the theatres of Lorraine and
Alsace. She must have returned more than once to
Paris, but she did not appear there in public till the
spring of 1717, when she made her début in the rôles
of Monime and Electra; from that first day she proved
herself an accomplished actress. It was loudly declared
that she began where other great actresses ended.
She was then about twenty-five years old, and continued on the stage for thirteen years longer.

In an art that leaves behind it so few traces, it is
difficult, when judging from the distance of years to
do more than repeat the testimony of contemporaries,
which we have almost no means of verifying. In this
case, praises were unanimous, all agreeing on the
same points: "To her is given the glory," said *Le
Mercure,* March, 1730, "of having introduced simple,
noble, natural declamation, and of having discarded
sing-song." She also sought more truth and correctness in costumes; she was the first, for instance, to
bring into use court dresses in the parts of queen and
princesses. She made this innovation when playing

Queen Elizabeth in the *Comte d'Essex*. In assuming
the queen's dress, she also assumed her tone—that is,
she spoke the part naturally, without ostentation, without feeling herself obliged, like other actresses, to make
up for what was, until then, lacking in the costume
by an affected solemnity. The audience seemed to
see "a princess acting for her pleasure." She also
played comedy, properly so-called, but with less
freedom and resourcefulness: she never shone except
in a few comic parts. Her true domain, her incomparable glory was in pathos. "She had the art of
entering into the greatest passions to the degree necessary to express them and make them felt in full
force."

It was said of Mlle. Champmeslé that she had so
sonorous a voice that if, when she declaimed, a door
were opened at the farther end of the theatre, she
could be heard in the Café Procope. I doubt if this
would have been the case with Mlle. Le Couvreur,
but her voice was penetrating, true in tone, and
subtle; she sustained weak verses, and gave their full
value to the finest. " She had not many tones in her
voice, but she knew how to vary them to infinity,
adding inflexions, some vehemence, and I know not
what that was expressive in her air, her face, and all
her person, which left nothing to be desired." She
excelled in gradation, in the passing from one tone
to another, which so fully expresses the vicissitudes
of passion. The memory still lasts of certain passages

in her rôles of Berenice, Elizabeth, Electra, in which she moved all hearts by these contrasted and affecting tones. No one ever understood so well the art of mute scenes, the art of listening well, and of continuing to act with her person and her expressive attitude while others spoke.

It does not appear that, off the stage, her beauty was very striking or extraordinary; but she had natural elegance and harmony. We know her portrait by Coypel, who painted her in mourning garments, holding her urn as Cornélie. *Le Mercure* shows her far more as she was naturally,

"perfectly well made, of medium height, with a noble and composed bearing; the head and shoulders well placed, the eyes full of fire, the mouth beautiful, the nose slightly aquiline, with much charm in her air and in her manners; no *embonpoint,* but the cheeks rather full, and with features all well fitted to express grief, joy, tenderness, terror, and pity."

Much soul, much tender feeling, constant study, a passionate love for her art, all contributed to make her that ideal of a great tragedian which, until then, seems never to have been fully realised. Mlle. Duclos was the representative of the declamatory school only; and though Mlle. Desmares and the Champmeslé had great and noble qualities, they certainly never attained to the full perfection of Adrienne Le Couvreur. When the latter came she had no other model than her own taste; she created.

In the various arts, but especially in that of the

stage, there have been, at all times, two manners opposing each other; the manner of the official school (Conservatoire or Academy), and that of original talent —the manner that declaims or chants, and that which speaks. We find these two schools already in opposition and at war at the dawn of our stage; the troop of Molière against that of the Hôtel de Bourgogne. Remember the *Impromptu de Versailles,* in which this conflict is so well defined. Molière wished, even in tragedy, that the parts should be spoken naturally, *humanly ;* the difficulty lay in harmonising perfect dignity and nobleness with this naturalness, which on the stage can be only a cultivated and conscious naturalness. Molière, when acting, succeeded imperfectly in doing this in tragic parts, for which nature had not fitted him. Baron, his pupil, formed wholly by his teaching, put those lessons into practice. Mlle. Le Couvreur had seen Baron when, old but still excellent, he returned to the stage in 1720; but she had not awaited that sight to realise, in her own way, Molière's poetic idea, and to unite in herself the lofty, pathetic, and natural qualities of a great tragic actress.

It is related that when she first appeared in Paris and was received with eager applause, a man, seated alone in the corner of a box, was not carried away by the universal enthusiasm, but merely said from time to time, at a few points: "That is good, *that,*" as if he meant it to be understood that the rest was not equally good. This incident was told to the actress, who desired to know the recalcitrant auditor, and invited him, in a charming note, to dine alone with her. The man was Du Marsais, the philosopher and grammarian, a simple, naïve man, little accustomed to society, frank, and inexorably accurate. Before sitting down at table, he asked Mlle. Le Couvreur to recite a few pieces; as he listened to her in attentive silence, he ejaculated now and then: "That is good, that." Urged to give the reasons for his criticism, he made no difficulty about telling them; and a long friendship ensued, in the course of which the modest philosopher spared no useful advice; advice which related to truth, naturalness, and propriety of expression. He desired that no more value should be given to words than was required by the situation. Such counsel found in Mlle. Le Couvreur's honest intelligence a ground prepared for it.

This relation of Du Marsais to Mlle. Le Couvreur is partly that which the authors of the new play ascribe to Michonnet; and this reminds me that the actor who plays that part so admirably, M. Regnier, is preparing for publication a study on the talent and dramatic invention of Mlle. Le Couvreur. I shall therefore not dwell upon them here. Michonnet's part is a double one: he is a true, sincere, disinterested counsellor, as Du Marsais was in real life; but he is, besides, the lover, equally true, sincere, devoted to the point of sacrifice; and that half of the rôle we find

no less filled by another friend of Mlle. Le Couvreur,
M. d'Argental.

Mlle. Le Couvreur, in her early youth, had many
adorers, of whom we have the right to name a few,
Voltaire, for instance. Speaking to Thieriot of the
touching verses forced from him by his indignation
over the burial of the celebrated actress, Voltaire says
that his anger, too keen perhaps, is " pardonable in a
man who was her admirer, her friend, her lover, and
who is, besides, a poet." This is sufficiently clear.
Mlle. Le Couvreur had two daughters who survived
her. One, born in Strasburg, daughter of M. Kinglin,
at that time chief magistrate or, as they say there, præ-
tor of that city; she is often mentioned in Voltaire's
letters. The other daughter was born in Paris, and
was baptised at Saint-Eustache, September 7, 1710, as
the "daughter of Philippe Le Roy, officer of Monseigneur le Duc de Lorraine, and Adrienne Le Couvreur"; she married, in 1730, Francœur, musician at
the Opera. The learned mathematician, of that name,
was of this family.

But the great passion of Mlle. Le Couvreur, that
which put an end to the levities of her early life, was
her love for the Comte de Saxe, who came to Paris for
the first time in 1720, and fixed his residence there in
1722. From the moment when she first loved him,
and in spite of his infidelities, which he never denied
himself, it is plain that Mlle. Le Couvreur never afterwards considered herself free. Passionately beloved

by young d'Argental, she did all she could to cure
him. She did not take half-measures, which are more
fitted to excite and allure that which they are supposed to repel; her action was straightforward, loyal,
without *arrière-pensée;* it was that of an honest man.
She wrote to him:

"You wish, against all sorts of reasons, that I should write to you.
How is it that with so much intelligence you are so little master of
yourself? What can you gain but the pleasure of exposing me to
disagreeable annoyances, not to say worse? I am ashamed to quarrel with you when you fill me with pity, but you compel me to do so.
Be, I beg of you, more reasonable; and say to him whom you have
commissioned to torment me, that he must give me a respite; for the
last four days he has hardly left me in peace for a moment. I will
show you clearly the impropriety of this conduct the first time that
accident brings us together, and I shall have no difficulty in making
you agree that you do wrong. Adieu, unhappy child—you fill me
with despair."

Hearing that d'Argental's mother, Mme. de Ferriol,
thought of sending her son away even as far as St.
Domingo, for fear that he might be induced to make
her an offer of marriage, Mlle. Le Couvreur attempted
to reassure her. She went to see Mme. de Ferriol,
and as the reception she met with did not encourage
her to speak freely, she wrote her a letter, noble in
tone, admirable in feeling, the letter of a woman who
seeks to reconcile natural duties with the conventions
of social life. In writing this letter, dictated by her
heart, she did not suspect the moral height on which
it placed her ; that height is great, especially when we

think of the sort of woman (worthy sister of Mme. de Tencin, and that is enough to say) to whom it is addressed:

(Paris, March 22, 1721). "Madame, I cannot hear without being keenly grieved, of the uneasiness that you feel, and the plans which that uneasiness has caused you to form. I might add that I have no less pain in hearing that you blame my conduct. But I write to you less to justify that conduct than to assure you that in future it will be, in the matter that interests you, whatever you may prescribe to me. On Tuesday last I asked permission to see you, that I might speak with you in private and ask your orders. Your greeting destroyed my zeal, and I found I had nothing left but timidity and sadness. It is necessary that you should know my true sentiments, and, if I may be permitted to say something further, that you should not disdain to listen to my very humble remonstrances if you do not wish to injure Monsieur your son. He is the most respectful child and the most honest man I have ever seen in my life. You would admire him, if he did not belong to you. Once more, madame, deign to join with me in destroying a weakness which irritates you, and of which I am not the accomplice, whatever you may think. Do not show him either contempt or bitterness; I would rather take upon myself all his hatred, in spite of the tender friendship and reverence that I feel for him, than expose him to the slightest temptation to displease you. You are too interested in his cure not to work for it anxiously, but you are too much so to succeed alone, and, above all, by combating his inclination with authority, and by painting me to him in disadvantageous colours, however true they may be. Surely this passion is extraordinary, since it has lasted so long a time without the slightest hope, in the midst of rebuffs, and in spite of the journeys you have made him undertake and of eight months in Paris without seeing me, and without knowing whether I would ever receive him again in my life. I believed him cured; and in that belief I consented to see him during my late illness. It is easy to believe that his friendship would please me better than this unhappy passion, which surprises as much as it flatters me, but of which I do not wish to take advantage. You fear that in seeing me he will neglect his duties; and you carry that fear so far as to take these violent resolutions against him. In truth, madame, it is not right that he should be made unhappy in so many ways. Do not add to my unkindnesses to him; seek rather to compensate him for them; let all your resentment fall upon me, and let your kindness give him compensation.

" I will write to him whatever you wish ; I will never see him again if you desire it ; but do not threaten to send him to the end of the world. He can be useful to his country ; he can be the delight of his friends ; he will crown you with satisfaction and fame ; you have only to guide his talents, and let his virtues act. Forget for a time that you are his mother, if that quality is opposed to the kindness that I ask you on my knees to give him. In short, madame, you will see me retire from the world, or love him with love, rather than suffer him in future to be tormented about me, and by me."

M. d'Argental had no knowledge of this letter at the time it was written. It was not until sixty years later, when he was over eighty, that one day, looking over some old papers relating to his mother, he found it. It was read to him, and then, for the first time, did he truly know the heart of his early love.

Mlle. Le Couvreur, as everything we know of her proves to us, was not only a person of talent, she was a woman distinguished by intellect, by heart, and by all the solid qualities. She had need of them to raise her from the inferior social position in which actresses were still held at the beginning of the eighteenth century. Molière, by force of genius and wit, Baron by his talent aided by his self-conceit, had raised the profession of actors in the social world, in which they now maintained themselves on a footing of respectability. But the women, even those of talent like the Champmeslé, had never been able to win any degree of consideration; they remained in the very lowest position socially. People went to the Champmeslé's

house; they lauded her in gallant verses, like those of
La Fontaine; they lived with her on familiar terms,
but she had nothing that could be called a salon.
She never succeeded in gaining that social esteem
which is marked by such nicety of shade, the esteem
that Ninon secured.   Racine, the tender and once
lover-like Racine, speaks of Champmeslé, on hearing
of her death, as "that poor unfortunate," in a tone
that the most austere devotion would not have dictated to any honourable man of the world in after
years.   The century that was soon to be that of Voltaire did not long permit such inequalities among the
different interpreters of art, and Mlle. Le Couvreur
was the first, not to protest but (what was far better)
gently to work a revolution by the charm of her
influence.

She had much to do, as we can well believe.   An
actress was at the beck and call of the whole privi-
leged class.   It was in speaking to Mlle. Le Couvreur
that Lord Peterborough said: "Come! show me much
love and much wit."   What he said crudely, like the
queer original that he was, many others felt they had
the right to think, if they had the politeness not to say
it.   By intelligence, good sense, a sentiment of propriety and modesty, Mlle. Le Couvreur obtained a
position in society which, at that epoch, no other actress had any right to claim.   She was the first to win
for actresses in France the position of Ninon; that is
to say, the position, as a woman, of an honourable

man, receiving the best company of men, and even
of women, when the latter were prompted by curiosity and possessed a little courage. "It is an established fashion to dine or sup with me," she writes,
"because it has pleased a few duchesses to do me
that honour." That honour had its burdens, and entailed subjection, as she herself wrote:

"If my poor health, which is feeble, as you know, causes me to refuse or miss a party of ladies whom I should otherwise have met, but
who only think of me out of curiosity, or, if I may dare to say so, out
of vogue (which enters into everything), one says : 'Just see how she
affects importance.' Another adds : 'It is because we are not titled!'
If I am serious, for one cannot always be gay among a quantity of
people whom one scarcely knows, they say : 'So that is the woman
who has so much intellect! Don't you see how she disdains us ; we
ought to know Greek to satisfy her.' 'She goes to Mme. Lambert's,'
says another; 'does n't that solve the enigma for you?'"

Mme. de Lambert was the friend of Fontenelle, of
La Motte, and of Mairan. People accused her of keeping an office for intellect, because her house was
"nearly the only one," says Fontenelle, "that was
preserved from the epidemic disease of card-playing;
the only one where persons could meet to converse
together reasonably, and even wittily on occasion."

The salon of Mlle. Le Couvreur was among the
few where, on certain days, wit and reason had a
chance to meet. She lived in a little house in the rue
des Marais-Saint-Germain, in which it was said that
Racine had once lived, and which was afterwards
occupied by Mlle. Clairon. A considerable fortune

for those times, amounting, some said, to more than three hundred thousand *livres,* gave her an honourable independence. The days on which she was not too much invaded by duchesses and persons of fashion, Mlle. Le Couvreur took pleasure in receiving her friends.

" My vanity," she said, " does not find that great numbers are any compensation for real merit in people. I do not care to shine; I have a hundred times more pleasure in saying nothing and listening to good things; I like better to find myself in a society of wise and virtuous persons than to be made giddy with insipid praises that are showered upon me at random. It is not that I lack gratitude, or the desire to please; but I find that the approbation of a fool is not flattering, except in a general way, and that it becomes a burden when it must be paid for by special and perpetual affability."

So she deprived herself, as much as she could, of the approbation of fools, and clung to that of her friends. These friends, honest men, whom she preferred to all, were Fontenelle, Du Marsais, Voltaire, d'Argental, the Comte de Caylus, the Abbé d'Anfreville, the Comte de Saxe, and certain intimate friends of the latter, such as the Marquis de Rochemore. To these we may add a few clever women, of good social position but not fine ladies overmuch, such as Mme. Berthier, for instance. This I imagine to have been, on certain days, the *personnel* of a supper at Mlle. Le Couvreur's, and there was surely a less well-assorted one in high places. The tone that prevailed in this company could not have resembled that which we see established towards the middle of the century, at the suppers of Mlle.

Quinault. The Memoirs of Mme. d'Épinay make us
spectators of the latter. The conversation there is racy,
but free to licentiousness, which fact does not prevent
it from becoming at times declamatory. That was
not the habitual tone of a house where, it is true,
Voltaire had free entry and permitted himself, no
doubt, his usual sallies, but where Fontenelle was
enjoyed and welcomed; it was not the tone of Mlle.
Le Couvreur's suppers. She has left us a charming
portrait of Fontenelle, which paints herself as fully
as it does the philosopher she knew so well how to
appreciate.

" Persons of no account," writes Mlle. Le Couvreur, " do too little
honour to those of whom they speak for me to dare to say publicly
what I think of M. de Fontenelle; but I cannot deny myself the pleasure of privately painting him such as he appears to me.

" His countenance proclaims at once his intellect: an air of society,
pervading his whole person, makes him agreeable in all his actions.

" Charms of mind sometimes exclude essential things. Unique in
his own line, he also combines all that can make him loved and
respected—integrity, uprightness, equity, compose his character. A
lively and brilliant imagination, subtle and delicate turns of mind,
novel and always happy expressions, are its ornaments. A pure heart,
straightforward proceedings, uniform conduct, principle in all things;
exacting little, justifying others, seizing always the good, abandoning
evil so quickly that one might doubt if he perceived it. Difficult to
acquire, but more difficult to lose. Firm in friendship, scrupulous in
love; the man of honour is nowhere neglected. Fit for the most delicate occupations, those that delight learned men; modest in his speech,
simple in his actions, the superiority of his merit shows itself, but he
never makes it felt. . . ."

Here we find that excellent and restrained language
which I have, more than once, tried to characterise,

the language of the beginning of the eighteenth century, remarkable especially for its turns of phrase, its clearness, and its accuracy; a language formed on that of Mme. de Maintenon, which all intelligent Frenchwomen—Mme. de Caylus, Mme. de Staal, Mlle. Aïssé—were henceforth to write. The personal taste of Mlle. Le Couvreur comes to light, without her knowledge, in this portrait ; we feel what qualities she prized above all others and desired in the men who formed her circle. "Difficult to acquire, more difficult to lose": that is the true motto of friendship; and it is a merit that Mlle. Le Couvreur's noble heart places it far above hasty caprices and passing passions. I find, in one of the unpublished letters written by her to a friend of whose name we are ignorant, words which confirm this sincere and habitual sentiment of her heart. This friend had departed suddenly, without telling her, and without writing to her. She complains, with grace :

"I wish," she writes, "to inform you of my principles. When it is a question of writing to my friends, I never think that I need wit or intellect to reply to them ; my heart suffices me for all. I listen to it, then I act ; and I have always found it well for me. People take me such as I am, or leave me. All the art I know is that of not throwing myself at their head for whatever sentiments there may be. I seek honesty first even in my slightest intimacies. When the graces are added I know how to feel them, nature having given me an admirable instinct to perceive them. Experience of the world, time, and a little reason have convinced me that great indulgence is necessary n life ; but those who need it the least lose nothing with me. I give them, on the spot, all the esteem and admiration that they seem to me to deserve. And when they honour me with some kindness, you

can readily see that gratitude is added to those sentiments, and
assuredly I have never been ungrateful. . . ."

While she desires friendship, she rather dreads enthusiasms ; she is always afraid that another sentiment may slip in, and she speaks of it in a tone fitted
to convince her friend that she wishes to remain as
she is :

"I am," she writes, "of a sex and a profession in which this honourable sentiment is not expected ; it is the only one I desire, the
only one that flatters me ; and I dare to think myself worthy of it by
the manner in which I feel it; I will even add, by that in which I
have inspired it more than once. . . ."

Though at an age when women are still, if they
choose, able to appear young, she did not hesitate to
speak of advancing years, and what they would
bring with them " of attentions and duties which ten
years hence friends may have to pay to an *old* friend."
She wishes they should consider all that in advance,
and grow accustomed to the idea ; she is the first to
propose it frankly : "Let us go honestly," she said,
"towards friendship." The great preservative that
she had against all fresh weakness was that her heart
was filled ; she loved ; she trembled for an absent one
in the midst of dangers, whose return she was awaiting with impatience :

"A person long expected," she writes, October 23, 1728, "arrives,
at last, to-night, and, according to appearances, in pretty good health.
A courier has come on before him, because his carriage broke down
thirty leagues from Paris.   A post-chaise has been sent down, and to-
night he will be here."

It is not difficult to imagine who that person thus awaited was : Maurice de Saxe was returning, at that date, from Courlande to Paris.

The last year of Mlle. Le Couvreur's life was disturbed by a strange incident, which gave rise to a rumour of poisoning. I shall try to disentangle the story from the popular tales that were mixed up with it, which can be read in the *Lettres* of Mlle. Aïssé, and in the *Journal* of the lawyer, Barbier. About the month of July, 1729, a little humpbacked man, a painter of miniatures, the Abbé Bouret, son of a treasurer of France at Metz, went twice to the house of Mlle. Le Couvreur, and, not finding her, left a letter in which he said that he had very important things to reveal to her ; and that if she wished to hear them, she had only to come on the morrow to a certain solitary alley in the Luxembourg, which he described ; when there, she would recognise him by three taps he would give on his hat, and she could then hear all. Mlle. Le Couvreur, after taking the advice of friends, went to the place indicated with a companion. There she found the little humpback, who told her in substance, that a Court lady, whose miniature he was painting, had proposed to him to gain access to Mlle. Le Couvreur as a painter, and so give her a philter that would drive the Comte de Saxe from her ; that two masked persons, to whom he was referred for the details of the plan, told him that the drug to be given was not a philter, but a poison ; and with that object poisoned tablets would be deposited, on a certain day, in a yew-tree in the Tuileries gardens ; that the abbé was to take them from there, and if he gave them to Mlle. Le Couvreur, he should be guaranteed a pension of 600 *livres* and a payment down of 6000 *livres*. The abbé added that he had pretended to consent to everything, and now came to ask what he should do.

Mlle. Le Couvreur did not at first think this story as improbable as it now seems to us. The Comte de Saxe was not faithful by nature, though sincerely attached to Mlle. Le Couvreur. He had tried for some time to make advances to the Duchesse de Bouillon, but without success. He had also taken a fancy to an Opera singer. Mlle. Le Couvreur thought vaguely that she might have something to fear either from the hôtel de Bouillon or from the Opera. The abbé saw her thought, and indicated the hôtel de Bouillon as the quarter whence the danger came. She gave him a second appointment, consulted her friends, and the Comte de Saxe himself. It was decided that the abbé should seem to lend himself to the affair, and take the tablets from the Tuileries. All was done as proposed. The abbé found the tablets, and took them to Mlle. Le Couvreur ; they were then taken to M. Hérault, lieutenant-general of police. The Abbé Bouret was arrested at once, and the tablets were analysed. The analysis, made by Geoffroy, of the Academy of Sciences, showed nothing decisive.   I have before my eyes the *procès-verbal,* dated July 20, 1729.   Some of the tablets seemed doubtful; but the quantity was not sufficient, says the chemist, to decide the experiments and base a judgment.

Meantime, the affair became known, and it was openly said in public that the Duchesse de Bouillon had attempted to poison Mlle. Le Couvreur. The Abbé Aunillon du Gué de Launay, a friend of the Bouillons, in Memoirs more interesting than known, which he left behind him, tells us that he was the first to inform the duchess of the odious rumour, in order that she might take steps to refute it.   He describes to us in natural language the astonishment and pain she showed at the news.   This Duchesse de Bouillon, I may remark in passing, was not the princess of that name, born Sobieska, who appears in the drama of the Théâtre Français, but her young mother-in-law, born in Lorraine.   The Duc de Bouillon was at once informed ; and the whole family were roused to indignation.   The lieutenant of police was summoned and lectured for not having at once pushed the affair to an end, and for having allowed the Abbé Bouret to go at large.   The latter was re-arrested and put in Saint-Lazare.   Being questioned, he maintained his statement.   Mlle. Le Couvreur, touched by the imprisonment of a man who, though he might have intended to dupe her and insinuate himself into her house, might also have sincerely desired to serve her, wrote a letter full of dignity and humanity to the lieutenant of police :

"I have talked with him, and made him talk often and for a long time," she said of the young man, " and he always answered connectedly and intelligently. It is not that I wish what he said to be true; I have a hundred times more reason to wish he may be crazy. Ah ! would to God I had only to solicit his pardon ! But if he is innocent, think, monsieur, what an interest I ought to take in his fate, and how cruel this uncertainty is to me. Do not consider my profession or my birth, deign to see my soul, which is sincere and laid bare in this letter. . . ."

Matters remained thus for some months The abbé, still a prisoner in Saint-Lazare, persisted in his statement. The Bouillon family urged, or seemed to urge, an investigation of the affair, when suddenly Mlle. Le Couvreur, whose health had failed very much during the past year, was carried off by violent inflammation of the bowels on Monday, March 20, 1730, after playing Jocaste in *Œdipe* and Hortense in *Le Florentin* three days earlier. This sudden death renewed all the reports of poison; though it was certainly most improbable that persons suspected for several months should have chosen this time to renew their attempt —supposing them capable of so doing. The cause of the death was explained more naturally by a dose of ipecacuanha taken by mistake. We have the *procès-verbal* of the post-mortem examination ; it indicates nothing but a most acute inflammation. Voltaire, who was present, and in whose arms Mlle. Le Couvreur died, says that all the rumours then current

were without foundation ; and his testimony would
be decisive did we not know that he was systematic-
ally opposed to all ideas of poisoning.

To finish on this obscure and delicate point,—after
Mlle. Le Couvreur's death, a retraction of his first
statement, and a species of exoneration of the Duchesse
de Bouillon, were obtained from the Abbé Bouret,
still a prisoner at Saint-Lazare. But this document,
dictated evidently by the need of the unfortunate man
who, in ending it, puts the whole blame on his
"distracted brain," would be of little real value if a
friend of the duchess, an honourable man, the Abbé
Aunillon, whom I have already mentioned, had not
given us still another and quite different explanation.
He thinks that a Court lady, whom he has in his eye
but does not name, a person of consideration, jealous,
and no doubt a rival of the Duchesse de Bouillon, and
fully as powerful as she, contrived the whole plot, not
to poison Mlle. Le Couvreur, but to throw suspicion
on the unfortunate duchess, whose name she used,
and thus ruin her reputation. The abbé adds that the
duchess, being on her death-bed, seven years later,
made, in presence of her friends and her whole household, a general confession of her faults and her trans-
gressions (of which there were many), but that she
firmly protested her entire innocence in the matter of
Mlle. Le Couvreur.

All things combined at one and the same moment to
excite and inflame the public interest around the coffin

of the beloved actress. The rector of Saint-Sulpice, Languet, refused to allow her body to be buried in consecrated ground. She had made a considerable bequest in her will to the poor of his parish. On the day of her death she said to a vicar who came to see her: "Do not be uneasy, monsieur l'abbé; I know what brings you here; I have not forgotten your poor in my will." True, it is added, that, turning towards a bust of the Comte de Saxe, she exclaimed: "There is my universe, my hope, my gods!"

M. de Maurepas wrote to the lieutenant of police that it was not Cardinal de Fleury's intention to enter into any question of ecclesiastical sepulture, but to leave the affair to the Archbishop of Paris, and to the rector of Saint-Sulpice. "If they persist in refusing it to her, as seems likely," he wrote, "she must be carried away at night and buried with the least possible scandal." The body was therefore taken by night, in a hackney-coach; and two street porters, guided by a single friend, M. de Laubinière, buried her in a deserted wood-yard, in the faubourg Saint-Germain, near the present south-east corner of the rue de Grenelle and the rue de Bourgogne. The faithful d'Argental, whom she had made her residuary legatee, did not think that he compromised his character as a magistrate by accepting that confidential mission, and he thereby honoured himself in public opinion. The legacy was in reality a trust, for Mlle. Le Couvreur left two daughters to be thus provided for.

Voltaire had one of those spasms of sorrow and sensibility of which he was so capable, and it was then that he wrote those touching lines which every one knows by heart:

" She is no more—and now she is criminal !
She charmed the world—for that you punish her.   .   .   ."

But here I will not expatiate, lest I seem to fall into declamation in speaking of one whose chief merit, on the stage and in her life, was to be truth itself and nature, the very opposite of declamation.   Those two simple words sum up the character of Adrienne Le Couvreur.

Voltaire.

Voltaire.

THE truth about men, as about things, is difficult to discover, and when discovered it is no less difficult to preserve. What is our present judgment of Voltaire? We are still disputing, still contradicting, still flinging that name at one another like a weapon of war ; making it, as ever, a rallying signal or a rock of offence. I ask permission, having now to speak of him, to hold to my own impressions, gained long before recent debates, and to restate the rather complex judgment which I have tried, for the last twenty years, to form upon him, maturing and rectifying it constantly ; wishing to detract in no wise from a great mind, so essentially French in its fine qualities and in its defects ; but still less wishing to make of one who respected nothing, or nearly nothing, a personage of moral and philosophical authority, a religion in himself, or an idol.

There is no originality or singularity in this. Three generations have now succeeded one another in which a rather considerable number of minds, starting from very different points of view, have formed a fairly just idea of Voltaire, but an idea which has remained among them behind closed doors, and has always been questioned by the oncoming youth—for young men, at the moment when they enter active life, seek, unconsciously, in the celebrated men of the past and in the great names in vogue, precedents for their own passions or systems, vehicles for their own train of ideas and ardour. Whether they espouse or exalt them, whether they accept them in part or insult them, it is themselves whom they see through those noted men ; it is their own idea they bow to and extol; it is the idea that opposes theirs which they flout and depreciate. To see things as they are, and men as they have been, is the part of an intellect that has grown unbiased—an effect, I fear, of refrigeration.

I have said that for three generations Voltaire has been soundly appreciated by certain minds, although their judgments came to no purpose, and were never consolidated or established among us. Let us consider. In his lifetime, he was perfectly known and judged, for his good qualities as well as for his defects, for his fine and charming gifts as well as for his follies and his detestable perversities, by the persons of his society, and, up to a certain point, by his friends. Whosoever will gather from the correspondences of that day the sayings and judgments upon him of Mme. Du Deffand, President Hénault and others of that set, Frederick the Great, President de Brosses, Mme. de Créquy, will gain an idea of the true Voltaire, not a man indorsed, idealised, and ennobled by the

VOLTAIRE
From the sculpture by Houdon

VOLTAIRE

spirit of party, but one to whom the full glory of his talents is given. But this opinion of certain clear-sighted and well-informed witnesses has been little known. The remote distance at which Voltaire kept himself in his last years, the reverence he inspired from afar in his precincts of Ferney to the new genera-tions who had seen nothing of his petulant youth, the concert of praises which his clever and indefatigable old age excited in France and in Europe—all this pre-pared the apotheosis in which he himself was extin-guished, and against which very few protestations were then raised.

Nevertheless, he had against him, at bottom, even in the philosophical party then triumphant, the dis-ciples and votaries of Rousseau, whom he had mis-conceived and insulted. After the Revolution had completed its work of ruin, many of Voltaire's former adorers detached themselves more than half-way from that worship; they felt the value of the institutions he had rashly sapped; they told themselves that he, too, would have regretted them as they did; they took better account of his inconsistencies and, while pre-serving their admiration for an inimitable and seduc-tive intellect, they came at last to judge him with a moral severity justified by experience. Marie-Joseph Chénier continued to admire everything in Voltaire, and the "Epistle" which he addressed to him might be made the brilliant programme of the Voltaireans. But men of taste, whose minds had opened to

perceptions of a higher order, men, for instance, like M
de Fontanes, knew better how to distinguish what Voltaire merited as a charming author from what was due
to him as an indecent satirist, an imprudent and inex-
cusable philosopher. In this second generation Voltaire found, therefore, enlightened judges, very just in
their estimates, and well able to distinguish between
his merits and demerits.

As for those I call the third generation, in which I
take the liberty of placing the men of my own age
after those who are a dozen years older, it is less an
excessive admiration they have had to recover from
than a sentiment more or less the reverse. The influence of M. de Chateaubriand (in some respects a fairly
impartial judge of Voltaire), that of Mme. de Staël, in
other words, Rousseau still, the awakening of a spiritual philosophy respectful to human nature, the action
also of the religious Renascence which touched imaginations if not hearts, the literary influence that
breathed from the land of Schiller and Goethe, and
from that of Shakespeare, Byron, and Walter Scott
—all these diverse general causes acted strongly
upon many among us at our first reading of Voltaire.
Some were inclined to deny him too much. But in
time, and by losing their juvenile haughtiness and ri-
gidity, men were led to do more justice to this natural
human being, to this language that seeks to be only
the swift medium of agreeable good sense, and to
which, after so many adventurous flights and fatiguing

varieties of style, they are glad to return to refresh themselves as if from the material source. They have been brought to recognise those many qualities of quick precision, of sarcastic reason, and grace. I say, therefore, without thinking that I grant to ourselves too much, that in this third generation, more than one mind has, without wavering on essential points, come to see in Voltaire what ought to be seen when considered for himself, and for the immediate consequences that resulted from his works.

But those consequences (and here is the misfortune) were not only immediate and related to his time : they will still flow on and influence for generations; they are far from being exhausted. The man and the writer in Voltaire may be thoroughly known and defined, at any rate they can be; but the combatant and the leader of a Voltaire party will still continue. Like a dead general, whose name is the pledge of victory, his followers have tied him on his horse, and the battle rages round him as round a mighty warrior. He is the champion of immortal quarrels. In vain may we look for impartiality in that *mêlée!* Sorry effort of a posterity that continually turns tail and retreats! What pains it takes to attain to righteousness, to see the right, and when it has all but reached that point, in a moment here are new-comers, who convulse everything, put all at stake once more, and in the name of their passions or their convictions choose to see but one side, are excessive in their

enthusiasms as they are in their invectives, and compel the whole work to be done over again.

The various volumes of Voltaire's " Letters " enable
us to make a rapid survey of his life. At twenty-four
years of age we find him in Paris spending his time
among the Villars, Sullys, Richelieus, etc. ; he floated
on the top wave of the great world, at his ease and
as if he belonged there, but with a slight touch of inso-
lence that denotes conquest. These were the days
of the Regency, when ranks were becoming mixed.
Voltaire, conscious of intellect, sees no limit to his
upward flight; from the first, he makes his way on a
footing of equality with great people. The latter
caress and spoil him, until the day comes when one
of them makes him feel that all is not won, that
favour is not claim, and that tolerance is not right.
Meantime, in the midst of his social successes, and
while working at his tragedies and his epic poem,
Voltaire bethinks him of making his fortune. By a
sure channel which he has to the Regent (he was
in the way of having several through his friends) he
obtains the promise of a licence for the formation of
a company of some sort, for which he finds the
capitalists.

Admire who will this faculty of Voltaire at twenty-
four years of age for writing tragedies, epic poems,
and attending to *business !* He foresaw, he said, that
he must be rich in order to be independent. I think
his foresight was less than his obedience to a natural

inclination, to a need in his nature very strongly marked, which was noted by all who knew him; but he combined it well with an air of fashion and of the great world. That great world and its salons made him, in some respects, an accomplished man, a poet with the easiest and liveliest turn of phrase, a man of Letters with a taste that was naturally elegant. When we think only of the ideal of pleasure, of the charm of delicate raillery and urbanity, we like to picture to ourselves Voltaire in that enjoyment of society into which, at various times in his life, he entered, but from which he was always fleeing.

"*Mon Dieu*, my dear Cideville," he writes to a friend of those days, " what a delightful life it would be to lodge with three or four men of Letters with talents and no jealousy, to love one another, live quietly, cultivate one's art, talk of it, enlighten ourselves mutually! I picture to myself that I shall some day live in this little Paradise, of which I desire you shall be the god."

This letter was written in 1732, that is to say, after his life in England. The personages of this ideal intimacy, which he saw from afar, were to be such as Formont, Cideville, Des Alleurs, Mme. Du Deffand, President de Maisons, Genonville, the élite of the friends of his first or his second youth: persons of intelligence and safe intercourse, judging everything, laughing at all, but among themselves, not letting the public share their laughter; persons who knew everything, or thought they did, taking the world handsomely and ironically, and chiefly concerned in making themselves happy together by the pleasures of conversation and communicative study without constraint.

But Voltaire, in being the divinity of such a society, in moderating himself sufficiently to be contented in it, and in condemning himself to lead the life of a perfectly polished man, would have been no more than a very accomplished Voiture and a superior Hamilton: he had in him other stuff, other faculties, which were at once an honour and a danger to him. Often in life he made part of those delightful coteries (*suavissimam gentem,* he said) which were formed for a moment around him, rallying to his light, coteries of which he was the genius and the soul, and from which he soon departed through some accident. He was usually the cause of that accident; and this resulted from a defect and from a good quality. The defect was the need of action at any cost, the need of fame and renown, which did not deny itself intrigues and manœuvres, and worked with doubtful tools; hence a whole series of indiscretions, concealments, retractations, disavowals, falsehoods; in short, an infinity of miserable things. The good quality was a passion, often sincere, and a conviction on points that concerned humanity. But even after he became what, in any case, he could not have hindered himself from being,—the king of the poets of his day and the leader of the philosophic party,—even then Voltaire had regrets; he had the habits of a man of society, of the author of society, and he would fain have remained such. To

hear him, the man of incessant publicity, who wearied
fame, one would think he never, or scarcely ever,
published a book by his own will but always reluctantly: he had a secretary who stole his manuscripts;
an indiscreet friend who hawked his writings about;
a piratical publisher had got possession of his property and was spoiling it, falsifying it, and thus he was
forced to print his productions himself that the public
might have them in their integrity. Such were his
apologies. "How is it that they have printed my
letter to the Abbé Dubois?" he wrote to Thieriot in
1739; "I am much mortified; it is very hard to be
always a public man." All his life it was his pretension to lead the existence of a literary nobleman, who
lives on his own fortune, amuses himself, plays tragedy
in society, is gay with his friends, and laughs at all the
world. "I am very sorry," he wrote to d'Argental
from Ferney in 1764, "that they have printed *Ce qui
plait aux dames* and *l'Éducation des filles;* this is
withering little flowers that are charming only when
they are not sold in the market." It is, however,
certain that Voltaire, from his earliest entrance into
society, before the buffoon's laugh and the fleshless
grin, Voltaire, in the bloom of his gaiety and malice,
was, by temperament as well as by principle, the poet
and the artist of an epoch whose avowed end and
inspiration was pleasure—pleasure before all else.

But the most agreeable circles did not suffice Voltaire, and could not hold him; he left them, at all

moments, as I have said, partly from his own fault, and partly for reasons more serious and laudable. He left them because he had *le diable au corps*—the devil was in him; and also because there were some sparks of a god there too. To sccff is very amusing; but it is only a slight pleasure if we cannot scoff at people to their faces; if the " silly foes " we deride are not informed of our derision; hence many sallies and imprudent skirmishes, which soon became war to the death between those foes and himself.

The stage, the drama, which Voltaire adored and in which he excelled, according to the taste of his day, presented him to the public on a nobler side. History, in which he also excelled,— showing himself especially superior when it was contemporaneous, or nearly so,—invited him to become a serious author in the most respectable meaning of the word, the painter of his own and of the preceding century. Voltaire was interested in all that happened in the world near him, or distant from him; he took part in it, he was fired by it; he busied himself about the affairs of others, and if they stirred his affections, he made them his own. He carried movement, bustle, and confusion wherever he was, becoming either a charm or a torment. That *devil of a man* (it is the name that we give him involuntarily) could not, in any case, in spite of his visions of a quiet retreat and smiling wisdom, confine himself to the gentle and brilliant existence of an Atticus, or even of a Horace, or con-

tent himself with the motto of his life which he politely
wrote to Maréchal de Richelieu: " I limit myself to
amusing you."

His *Correspondance* gives few details concerning
his departure from France in 1726 [caused by his quarrel with the Chevalier de Rohan] and his three years'
retirement in England, which was so decisive for his
intellectual education. He was doubtless prepared
for it by his conversations with Bolingbroke, of whom
he had seen much in Paris and at his country-house
of La Source, near Orléans; but the impression he received of that new spectacle, less perhaps for its political side and for the working of the Constitution than
for the philosophical and liberal-thinking group of men
whom he met in England seems to have surpassed
his expectations; it made a profound and indelible impression on him. This period of Voltaire's life, these
three years of study and of silence, which he began as
nothing more than a Sceptic of the Temple and a
charming figure in society, and from which he issued
a man and a philosopher, still remain obscure and
somewhat mysterious, precisely because he passed
them in silence. We see by his letters to Sir William
Faulkner what strong and tenderly serious ties he
there contracted, and how closely and durably he kept
their memory. This period seems to me the only one
in Voltaire's life that makes us desire fuller details.
There is a moment and an environment when talents
and minds, until then young and adolescent, complete

that first condition and become adult. England was the place of that change in Voltaire. He returned from there definitively formed, with a fund of ideas that he did not much increase, and with an inward stamp that he never lost.

On his return from England, he seems to have thought of realising his dream of a quiet retreat, where he could shelter his life and embellish it, giving to the world the overflowings only of his mind. It was then that he began his close intimacy with the Marquise du Châtelet, and had his period of Cirey. He lived for her, and through her. If we consider his temper and petulance, and Mme. du Châtelet's character, we may wonder that this *liaison* lasted more than fifteen years and was severed only by death. He was happy in it, save for a few brief storms, domestic squabbles that transpired, the particulars of which were collected by malignant curiosity. He was truly under a charm; he admired her, he proclaimed her sublime, he thought her beautiful; he took pleasure, when writing to Faulkner, in giving his address at her house, the château de Cirey: "Here," he says, "lives a young lady, the Marquise du Châtelet, to whom I have taught English." A shrewd observer said, however:

" Three things spoil Cirey for me—first, this mania for geometry and physics, which sits very ill on Voltaire, in whom it is only an imitation of the marquise ; it turns him from his true vocation and from the happy domains of which he is master ;—second, these stormy scenes, these sudden household quarrels, brief but burlesque, of which we are, willingly or not, informed ; making a critic remark that he had never

MADAME DU CHÂTELET

before supposed that the expression ' daggers drawn ' was anything more than a metaphor ;—and third, the impossibility that Voltaire, though he be now in love, master of the establishment, natural philosopher and geometrician at second hand, should ever really be anything but a man of Letters, from the tips of his fingers to the marrow of his bones. Hence his quarrels with publishers, his sleeplessness, his extraordinary agitation about the copies of *La Pucelle,* his fits of fury, his cries, as of one possessed, against Desfontaines and the Paris pamphlets. It is enough indeed to spoil an Eden."

As for the morality of the eighteenth century, there has been many a case which I have reprobated; but if some readers (as I have reason to know) would like me to condemn oftener and more sternly, I beg them to remark that I succeed much better by inciting them to give the condemnation themselves than if I took the initiative and seemed to impose upon them my judgment at every turn ; a course which, in the long run, is sure to weary and disgust a reader with the critic. The reader, moreover, likes to think himself more severe than the critic; I leave him that pleasure. It suffices me to relate and expound faithfully, so that every one may profit by matters pertaining to the intellect and to good language and be in a position to do justice upon the other and wholly moral sides, which I have not tried to conceal.

I continue now to speak of Voltaire and Mme. du Châtelet, who, for fifteen years, were inseparably united. Mme. du Châtelet was not an ordinary person; she occupied a rank in higher literature and philosophy which it was easier for the women of her time to laugh at than to emulate. The love, the friendship that Voltaire had for her was founded on admiration, an admiration that never failed at any period; and a man like Voltaire could not be so much in love that intellect in him would long be the dupe of his heart. Mme. du Châtelet must, therefore, have had real claims to the admiration of so excellent a judge, and the first of them is that she knew how to retain and charm him.

Her maiden name was Mlle. de Breteuil, and she was born in 1706, twelve years later than Voltaire. She had a fine education, and learned Latin in her childhood. Married to the Marquis du Châtelet, she lived, at first, the life of her period, the life of the Regency, and the Duc de Richelieu was inscribed on the list of her brilliant conquests. Voltaire, who had always known her, did not become intimate with her until after his return from England, about 1733. He was then thirty-nine years old, and Mme. du Châtelet twenty-seven. The mission of Voltaire, at that time, was to naturalise in France the English ideas, the philosophical principles which he had imbibed in reading Locke and in the society of Bolingbroke. But, more than that, having appreciated the soundness and the immensity of Newton's discovery, he blushed to see France still amused by worthless systems while full light reigned elsewhere, and he determined to propagate the true doctrine of knowledge of the universe, with which he mingled his ideas of philosophic deism. Mme. du Châtelet was a woman to second him—what am I saying ?—to precede him in that path.

She loved the exact sciences, and felt herself impelled to them by a true vocation. Beginning to study mathematics, first with Maupertuis, and then fundamentally with Clairaut, she made remarkable progress and soon outstripped Voltaire, who was content to admire without being able to follow her. Mme. du Châtelet wrote and published *Les Institutions de Physique,* in which she explained the particular ideas of Leibnitz; but her great title to distinction is that she translated into French Newton's immortal "Principia." To it she added an algebraic commentary, in which she was assisted by Clairaut. Thus, by inscribing, her name below that of Newton she seemed already to invoke Laplace's method of exposition. What an honour for a woman to have been able to slip her name between two such names!

That honour would have cost Mme. du Châtelet dear, during her lifetime, had she been sensitive to ridicule and to epigrams. In other days, the beautiful Hypatia, mathematician and astronomer, was stoned at Alexandria by the populace. Mme. du Châtelet, less beautiful, it appears, and without all the virtues of Hypatia, was not stoned, but she underwent the sharp mockery of the society in which she lived; the wittiest of all societies and the most malicious. I do not think there exists in the French language a more savage page, more bitterly, more cruelly satirical than the Portrait of the "divine Emilie," drawn by Mme. du Deffand (her intimate friend), which begins with these words: "Picture to yourself a tall, gaunt wo-man, without, etc., etc." It should be read in Grimm, having been mutilated and "softened" elsewhere. I dare not transcribe it, lest it burn this paper. It seems to have been written by a cold-blooded Fury, who knew how to write, and who steeped her pen in gall or vitriol. On every line is the pitiless word. The poor victim is denied, not only the natural use of her good qualities but even that of her defects. The final stroke is the most treacherous, the most humiliating of all; the writer shows her fastening, at any cost, on the celebrity of M. de Voltaire: "It is he who renders her an object of public attention, and the subject of special conversations; she will owe it to him in time to come that she lives; meantime she owes him that which *enables her to live now.*"

To this Portrait should be added, to complete the satire, passages from Mme. de Staal-Delaunay's letters to Mme. du Deffand, which describe graphically but in ugly colours, the entrance of Voltaire and Mme. du Châtelet one evening into the salon of the Duchesse du Maine. "They appeared at the stroke of midnight like two spectres, with an odour of em-balmed corpses." They diverted society with their airs and their absurdities, they irritated it with their singularities. Working all day, he at history, she at New-ton, they would neither play cards nor move about:

"They are absolute *non-values* in a society where their learned writings are of no account." Mme. du Châtelet, especially, could not find a spot sufficiently quiet, a room silent enough for her meditations:

" Mme. du Châtelet went yesterday to her third lodging," writes Mme. de Staal; " she could not endure the one she had last; there was noise, and smoke without fire (which seems to me her emblem). The noise does not trouble her at night, so she told me, but in the daytime, at her work; it disarranges her ideas. She is now making a revise of her " Principles "; this is an exercise she goes through every year, otherwise they might escape and get away so far she might never recover a single one of them. I think her head is a house of detention for them, and not the place of their birth, so she has to keep them carefully watched. She prefers the fine air of this occupation to all amusement, and persists in not showing herself till night-time. Voltaire makes gallant verses, which do in some sort repair the bad effect of their singular conduct."

The tone of this satire is that of the wittiest and most delicate of feminine pens. In reading the letters of Mme. de Staal to Mme. du Deffand, we cannot help noticing, in the midst of that society, apparently the most civilised and the most courteous, the melancholy character of this sneering gaiety in two women bored by their lives. What a moral and intellectual void is felt in such backbiting, more idle, perhaps, than malicious! what bitter and sterile hardness! It was time that the fire of heaven should fall and burn away those dried husks to renew the earth.

Mme. du Châtelet escaped, at any rate, from such miseries as these; her noble studies, her mental occupations, guarded her from the paltry topics on which the distinguished minds around her consumed themselves.

Voltaire was perhaps mistaken, and had a bandage over his eyes when he wrote: "No one was ever so learned as she, and no one ever deserved so little to have it said of her: 'That is a learned woman.' . . . The ladies who played cards with her in the queen's salon little thought they were seated beside the Commentator on Newton." But he was certainly right when he added: "All that occupied society was within her province, *except its slander.* No one ever heard her criticise an absurdity. She had neither the time nor the will to perceive such things; and when she was told that certain persons did not do her justice, she said she would rather not know it." If the mathematics of Mme. du Châtelet served only to give her this moral superiority, it was much.

We can judge her directly from her letters, and from certain writings in which she painted herself. In the early days of her *liaison* with Voltaire, in 1734, the latter, having taken alarm from information that came to him relating to one of his many imprudences, thought himself obliged to leave Cirey in the depth of winter, and go for safety to Holland. Mme. du Châtelet, in her intense anxiety, writes to the good friend of her friend, to M. d'Argental, begging him to clear up the affair, and bring about the return of him without whom she cannot live:

"I am," she says, "one hundred and fifty leagues from your friend; and it is twelve days since I have had any news of him. Forgive me, forgive me, but my state is dreadful. . . ."

"For fifteen days I was not two hours away from him ; and then

I wrote to him from my room to his ; and now it is fifteen days that I know not where he is, nor what he does. I have not even the consolation of sharing his misfortune. Forgive me for deafening you with my griefs—but I am so unhappy! "

They fear some danger, but they do not know what. Mme. du Châtelet suspects that the threat may have been a trick against her, to frighten Voltaire, and break up their happiness. In all her letters we see how she distrusts his wisdom when he is away from her, abandoned without advice to his irritability, to his hasty emotions and his petulance. "Believe me," she writes to d'Argental, " do not leave him long in Holland. He may be discreet for a time, but remember 'there is little virtue that resists for ever.' " She is constantly sending him word through d'Argental, to be wise and keep to an *incognito*—an *incognito* for Voltaire! that man, that child, with a passion for celebrity! She fears that he may accustom himself, over there, to do without her: liberty has great charms and so have Dutch publishers; those publishers who tempt you to print all, and say all. She has a fixed idea that he must be made to behave wisely "over there," and not put too much into those Dutch editions. "Above all, he must not put in *Le Mondain*" (this refers to an affair of State at that time, on which the life of a man depended). "It is necessary at every moment," she cries, "to save him from himself; and I use more policy to guide him than the Vatican employs to keep Christianity in its fetters." This last remark is at least solemn and may seem

disproportionate; but thus it is that passion reasons.
On the next page she will speak of him with tender
solicitude as a child: "We are sometimes very obstinate," she says; "this demon of reputation, which I
think very ill-understood, never quits us."

Voltaire remained in Holland to obey his nature and
commit imprudences. He sent to the Prince Royal of
Prussia (afterwards Frederick the Great) a manuscript
on *La Métaphysique;* and that *Métaphysique,* if printed,
is of such a nature that it would ruin its author for
ever. Mme. du Châtelet perceives the folly; she
complains to d'Argental sadly and eloquently:

"If any friend twenty years old asked him for a manuscript, he
ought to refuse it ; but to send it to an unknown youth, and a *prince !*
Why should he let his future tranquillity depend on another man ?
and that from no necessity, solely out of silly vanity (for I cannot falsify
the proper word) to show to a person, who is not a judge, a work in
which he will see nothing but the imprudence of it. He who confided
his secrets with such levity deserves to be betrayed. And I, what
have I done that he should make the happiness of my life hang upon
the prince-royal ? I own to you I feel outraged. . . ."

That is the complaint of a woman who feels her
rights; yet, at the same moment, she loves him; she
calls him "a creature so lovable at all points"; she
sees none but him in the universe, and proclaims him
"the finest ornament of France." Elsewhere, the
happy expression escapes her: "It is my belief that
the persons who persecute him have never read him."
She is evidently under the charm: love, for her, has
taken the path of intellect.

A reflection, however, presents itself, and she herself could not help making it: what temerity to go and confide her happiness, her fate, all her future as a woman, to a man of Letters such as Voltaire, to a poet so much of a poet, and to be at the mercy, every day, of his irritable temperament! The fate of these two united beings was always hanging on the chances of vanity or of petulance. Àpropos of the perpetual disturbances that Voltaire's thoughtless capers brought into the daily life of Mme. du Châtelet, the good souls of those days were never weary of talking; they pitied her openly; President Hénault, one of her best friends, wrote to Mme. du Deffand: "That poor du Châtelet ought to have put into the lease of every house she hires a clause about Voltaire's follies. Truly, it is incredible that a man should be so inconsiderate."

If you are a woman, if you are wise, and if your heart, though taking fire, will give itself time to choose, listen to a piece of advice: love neither a Voltaire, nor a Jean-Jacques, nor a Goethe, nor a Chateaubriand, if such great men should cross your path. Love—whom then? Love whoso fully and honestly returns you the same; love whoso has a whole heart to give you, though he bear no celebrated name and may even call himself the Chevalier Des Grieux. An honourable Des Grieux and a virtuous Manon—that is the ideal of those who know how to be happy in silence; fame as the third in a *tête-à-tête* spoils all.

But we moralists may talk as we please, the realities of life are not perfectly regulated by rule. Mme. du Châtelet loved Voltaire, and in rendering account of it to herself she passes over this point. At heart, he loves better (and she knows it) to publish his *Métaphysique* and to set it in the broadest light, than to sacrifice it without a word to love and good sense. There is the man of Letters, in the plain truth of his nature.

This was, nevertheless, the point at which the *liaison* between Mme. du Châtelet and Voltaire began to weaken. Three years later, in 1738, Voltaire was seized with one of his literary freaks which "entirely altered the charming sweetness of his manners." A libel of the Abbé Des Fontaines had so put him beside himself that he wanted, every time that the post brought him letters, to start for Paris to see the ministers, the lieutenant of police, to present a petition, to lay a complaint, and pursue his vengeance to extinction. Mme. du Châtelet could not succeed in calming him, nor in convincing him that the happiness of two choice beings cultivating together philosophy and Letters, ought not to depend on miserable insults coming from low sources. The terrestrial paradise of Cirey was now a hell of wrath and disquietude. "Truly, it is very hard," she writes, "to pass one's life battling in the bosom of retirement and happiness. Good God! if he would only believe us " (d'Argental and herself) "he would be happy !"

But things were much worse three or four years later, during a stay they made at Brussels, when Voltaire escaped her altogether for politics. He had taken it into his head to obtain a secret mission from the ministry of Foreign Affairs to the King of Prussia. I do not know whether it was diplomatic ambition, the temptation of another career, or merely the simple attraction of novelty, that seized him at this moment. He departed, rushed through the lesser principalities, and went from Berlin to Baireuth (October, 1743). "He is *drunk*, absolutely, he is *mad* about Courts and Germany." The King of Prussia is evidently Mme. du Châtelet's great rival at this time—"singular rival" she adds, bitterly. She remains whole weeks without hearing from him, and learns of his journeyings hither and thither from the newspapers; her heart is wounded:

"How many things to reproach him with! how far his heart is from mine! . . . To be forced to complain of him is a sort of torture that I never knew before. . . . All I have endured for a month past would, perhaps, alienate any woman but me; but, though he may make me unhappy, he cannot diminish my feelings. . . . His heart has much to make amends for if it is still to be worthy of mine."

Evidently, no matter what she says, she is becoming weaned from him. These painful impressions may have softened and concealed themselves when Voltaire, his caprice exhausted, returned to the magic circle of Cirey; but a sad conviction remained in the depths of Mme. du Châtelet's heart; we find traces of

it in a little treatise she wrote about this time on
"Happiness"; towards the close of which she says:

> "I was happy for ten years through the love of him who had sub-
> jugated my soul; and those ten years I spent alone with him, without
> one moment of distaste or of languour. When age and illness diminished
> his liking, I was long in perceiving it: I loved for the two; I spent
> my whole life with him, and my heart, exempt from suspicions, enjoyed
> the pleasure of loving and the illusion of believing myself beloved. It
> is true that I have lost that happy condition, and not without its cost-
> ing me many tears.

In writing these pages, she still fancied she could
hold fast to what she called the "immutability" of her
heart, and that the peaceful sentiment of friendship,
joined to the passion for study, would suffice to keep
her happy. She was then forty years old and, stoic
and geometrician that she was, she might well think
herself in port, when, having gone with Voltaire to
pass part of the years 1747 and 1748 at the little Court
of Lorraine, this, in two words, is what happened.

She there met, in the society of the Marquis de
Bouflers, a man thirty years of age; elegant, agreeable,
witty, although of a somewhat dry and barren mind;
known at that time by an "Epistle to Chloe," a rather
pretty piece in the sensuous style. This was M. de
Saint-Lambert. He played the gallant to her; and she
forgot for him her philosophic reflections, or, rather,
she remembered them. Feeling that passion revived
in her, she took it at its word, and, putting her principles into action, she gave herself up to it. The
results are well known; an incident, half-grotesque,

indecent, and fatal followed, which occupied the minds and tongues of society, and led to the death of Mme. du Châtelet six days after the birth of her child, September 10, 1749.

The impression that this death made on Voltaire was keen, and did honour to his sensibility. His secretary, Longchamps, relates, in great detail, the manner in which he took the whole affair; his first anger and fury at finding himself deceived, then his half-laughable, yet touching resignation. The loss of Mme. du Châtelet drew real tears from his eyes, interrupted now and then by some of those sharp, petulant, sensible words he never could refrain from saying, and which incline us to apply to him, in parody, Homer's saying: "He wept with an outburst of laughter." Three or four days after this death, as he fretted much about a ring Mme. du Châtelet wore, which had his portrait under the setting, Longchamps told him that he had taken the precaution to remove the ring, but the portrait within it was that of M. de Saint-Lambert. "O Heaven!" cried Voltaire, raising and clasping his hands: "such are women! I displaced Richelieu, Saint-Lambert turns me out! that's in the order of things; one nail drives out another: so goes the world!"

Mme. du Châtelet's eyes were scarcely closed, before Voltaire wrote to Mme. du Deffand to announce the death: "It is to the sensibility of your heart that I have recourse in my despair." We remember the satirical portrait; verily, the friend in despair chose a good confidant!

Voltaire's existence was stranded and everything thrown again into doubt and confusion by the death of Mme. du Châtelet. Deprived of the friend who had steadied him, who had held the tiller for him, he neither knew what to do nor where to turn. He was very near doing something desperate. His first idea was to retire to the abbey of Sénones, near Father Calmet, and to plunge into study; his second was to go to England, near to Lord Bolingbroke, and give himself up to philosophy. He took, at first, a wiser course, which was to go to Paris and talk of Mme. du Châtelet with d'Argental and the Duc de Richelieu, and to distract his mind by having his tragedies acted before him in his own house. But the cajoleries of the King of Prussia, which Mme. du Châtelet had counteracted as best she could and as long as she lived, returned to tempt him. He resisted no longer, and he went, at fifty-six years of age, to that last and sad *schooling* of Prussia, whence he returned less agitated, and, apparently, a little wiser.

Frederick the Great was Prince Royal of Prussia, and twenty-four years of age, when he began his correspondence with Voltaire in 1736, four years before he ascended the throne. Voltaire was then living at Cirey, where he received from the young prince, not a letter of compliment but a truly passionate declaration. We may smile to-day at that first letter, awkward as it was, in which Frederick mixes his admiration for Wolff with that he feels for Voltaire, and speaks to the latter in the name of "sweetness," and "the support that you give to all those who are vowed to art and the sciences." But all through the singular style of Frederick's first letters a noble thought makes itself felt. Considering Voltaire from a distance and by his works only, embracing him with that enthusiasm of youth which it is honourable to have felt once in our lives, Frederick proclaims him the sole heir of the great century that has lately ended, "the greatest man of France and a mortal who does honour to language." He admires and salutes him, without as yet perceiving the faults of the man, and solely for the beauties of his mind and the graces of his style. He declares himself his disciple—his disciple not only in his writings but in his actions; for, deceived by distance and the golden mists of youth, he sees in him almost a Lycurgus and a Solon, a legislator and a sage. Let us not smile too broadly. No one ever felt more truly than this young prince what Letters might be in their highest inspiration, what they have in them that is lofty and useful, what their glory possesses that is durable and immortal. "I count it one of the greatest honours of my life to be born the contemporary of a man of such distinguished attainments as yours." This sentiment shines through the whole of this phase of their correspondence. Voltaire is charmed; he flatters also; he thanks, he lauds, he enchants; one cannot truly say that he is scoffing under his breath; and no doubt he did not then laugh too much at certain solecisms and vulgarities of tone that often accompanied this Northern homage. In return, he thinks the young prince "writes verses like Catullus in Cæsar's time"; he plays the flute "like Télémaque — he is Augustus-Frederick-Virgil." "Enough!" says Frederick, who here has the advantage in good sense and good taste: "I am not, I assure you, a candidate for a great man; I am merely a simple individual who is known only to a small part of this continent, and whose name, according to all appearance, will not do more than decorate a genealogical tree and then drop into obscurity and oblivion." Voltaire had the face to tell him, on one occasion, that he wrote better French than Louis XIV; that Louis the XIV did not know how to spell, and other puerile things of that sort ; as if Louis XIV had not been one of the men in his kingdom whose speech was of the best! Here, again, Frederick stops Voltaire, and teaches him a lesson in tact :

" Louis XIV," he said, "was a great prince in a vast number of ways; a solecism, a mistake in spelling could not tarnish in the least the glory of his reputation, established by so many actions that have immortalised him. He could say in every sense : *Cæsar est supra grammaticans* . . . I am great in nothing; nothing but my diligence will ever make me of use to my country; and that is all the glory to which I aspire."

The first meeting of the two men took place **in**

1740, at the château de Meurs on the Meuse, where Voltaire went to pay his respects to the new king in the first months of his reign. It was ten years later (1750) that he made his visit to Berlin, after the death of Mme. du Châtelet.

In Frederick's admiration for Voltaire, there was a mixture of truth and justice and of error and illusion. He felt with delight "the gaiety of that brilliant imagination." He enjoyed that lively, familiar, joyous genius: "It is not given to every one," he told him, "to make the mind laugh." No words could better render the species of attraction, the sparkling, gushing gift so peculiar to Voltaire. Even towards the end, and while wishing him "kinder feelings," he still salutes him as "the finest organ of reason and truth." All that is truly felt and accurately expressed. But when Frederick admired in Voltaire a great poet above all others, when he saw in the *Henriade* the *ne plus ultra* of epics, and puts it above the "Iliad" and the "Æneid," he proves his want of ideality, and shows to what a point he limited his horizons in this direction.

"What pleasures can surpass those of the mind?" he cries—the mind,—that is to say, brilliant reasoning, gay and lively reasoning; that is the whole secret of his passion for Voltaire. This passion (for that is the right word) was reciprocated. Voltaire cannot conceal that he, the great coquette, was captivated by Frederick, and in the witty but contemptible libel, so untrustworthy. which he wrote after his flight from Berlin to avenge himself on the king, he could not refrain from saying, in speaking of Potsdam: "The suppers were very agreeable. I do not know if I am mistaken, but it seems to me there was much wit; the king had it, and brought it out in others." Observe the charm even in the anger. Such was the irresistible seduction they exercised on each other, and which survived even friendship.

It was Frederick's desire to assemble around him the *élite* of the distinguished men of his time, and he seemed for a while to be succeeding. He expected to lead abreast matters of science and the *personnel* of all the great minds with a precision that was almost administrative: "My *savants* arrive in the autumn," he writes, "and I hope to collect in Berlin all that this age has produced that is most famous." These hopes were crowned when, in 1750, he obtained Voltaire. But he paid dear, as we know, for that brief satisfaction, and Voltaire also. The manner in which Frederick writes of him to his sister, the Margravine of Baireuth, and of his other *beaux esprits* is piquant.

Voltaire, in this famous sojourn, quarrelled finally with Frederick because he had begun suit after suit, wrangling first with his *confrères,* the other men of Letters, and introducing civil war into the Academy.

"Voltaire's affair" (a suit against Hirschel) "is not yet finished," writes Frederick to his sister, February 2, 1751. "I think he will shuffle out of it; he will not be less clever, but his character will be more de-

spised than ever. I shall see him when it is all over.
But, in the long run, I would rather live with Maupertuis than with him. Maupertuis's character is sure,
and he has more of the art of conversation than the
poet, who, if you do not take good care, will
dogmatise."

This is the first time that I find Voltaire accused of
dogmatising; and I am not surprised that so few people have made that accusation—very few were in a
position to do so. Voltaire on becoming celebrated
had no equals; every one in his presence lowered his
flag, and listened willingly. Provided he came forward and was himself, no one thought that he talked
too much. Frederick, who liked to contradict in his
turn, and to cross swords without yielding ground,
encountered in Voltaire an interlocutor, both peremp-
tory and intolerant: they were, after all, two *king
minds;* they could have fine interviews, rather than
habitual and equal conversations.

Under the seduction of Voltaire's mind, Frederick
held out as long as he could against the squabbles and
dissensions to which the great man's sojourn in Berlin gave rise. He expresses, however, more than one
thought of sound good sense and practical morals,
which might serve as a lesson to literary men of all
time:

"Here," he writes to his sister, March 13, 1752, "the Devil is
incarnate in my men of Letters; there is no doing anything with
them. These fellows have no intelligence except for society; they

are severe on their own works for fear of being criticised by others, and indulgent to their conduct—which is usually ridiculous, for they believe it will never reach posterity."

" You behold me still terrified (June, 1752), by my adventures with these gentlemen my *beaux esprits;* I have been a good deal splashed, as always happens where you try to separate folks who are fighting."

" It must be a consolation to animals to see that people with minds are often no better than they."

I give only the moralising of Frederick upon his strife with Voltaire. As for his judgments on the man, they are too severe, too harsh for any French pen to copy them willingly. The Margravine of Baireuth, who had seen things from some distance, continued, even at the moment of the great outburst, to be indulgent to the poet. He continued to write to her, and in the height of the storm he took pains to conciliate her. She was won by the charm, the witty, amusing, charming gift that won back Frederick himself later; she did as posterity has done; she laughed, and was disarmed. In that she was very French.

In after years, at a critical and decisive moment after the battle of Kolin, in 1757, she bethought herself of using Voltaire's devotion to her and his desire to repair the wrongs he had done to Frederick. She wrote to him in the month of August of that year. The object was to save Frederick, detach him from the Coalition, or at least to check France by convincing her, in one way or another, that it was not to her interest that the King of Prussia should be destroyed; and that if evil happened to him, she would later repent of it. Voltaire, then living in Switzerland, set to work with

great activity (the details of this belong elsewhere).
Frederick, informed by his sister, sent Voltaire the following lines:

> " For me, threatened by shipwreck,
> I ought, facing the storm,
> To think, live, die, as a king."

In Voltaire's reply he redeemed his past ill-con-
duct by the good sense and the frankness of his
remonstrances:

> " The Catos and Othos, whose death Your Majesty thinks noble,
> had nothing else they could do but fight or die; Otho, in fact, was not
> sure whether he would be allowed to live; he prevented, by a volun-
> tary death, a death he might have been made to suffer. Our mor-
> ality and your situation are far from requiring such an act. In a word,
> your life is needed; you know how dear it is to a numerous family,
> and to all those who have the honour to approach you; you know that
> the affairs of Europe are never long on the same basis, and that it is
> the duty of a man like you to hold himself in readiness for events. I
> dare to say more: believe me, if your courage led you to that heroic ex-
> tremity, it would not be approved; your partisans would condemn it,
> and your enemies would triumph."

In the second part of Voltaire's Correspondence with
the King of Prussia, when they were reconciled after
their quarrel, we find a totally different tone from that
in the first part.   All illusion is over; nothing is left
but that keen delight in intellect which still manifests
itself.   The primitive Frederick, the juvenile enthusiast
has disappeared; he has given place to the philosopher, to the experienced, superior man, who is no
longer tentative in anything.   Also the *king* is felt

oftener. Each tells the other truths, and, what is rare, endures them. Voltaire utters them to the king, and Frederick returns them: "You have done me great wrongs," he writes to Voltaire. "I have forgiven them all, and I even wish to forget them. But if you had not had to do with a *madman in love with your noble genius,* you would not have got off so well." Yet, after these severe words, too strong not to be just, after these words of the *king,* the *madman in love* with the brilliant mind still lets himself be seen when he adds:

"Do you want sweet things? Very good; I will tell you some truths. I esteem in you the finest genius that the ages have borne; I admire your poesy, I love your prose; above all, those little pieces in your literary *Mélanges.* Never has any author before you had a tact so keen, a taste so sure and delicate as you have. You are charming in conversation; you know how to amuse and instruct at the same time. You are the most seductive being that I know, capable of making yourself loved by all the world when you choose. You have such graces of mind, that you can offend and yet at the same time deserve the indulgence of those who know you. In short, you would be perfect if you were not a man."

Who will say now that he who appreciated Voltaire to this degree, and could practise these French ways of insinuating sweetness after bitterness, was not the man of his time who ranked close to Voltaire in wit?

I think I am well within the truth when I say that the attraction of mind between these two men survived even friendship; though it is evident, when we read the last half of Voltaire's Correspondence with Frederick, that friendship itself was not dead within them; that it had revived with a lingering of charm combined with reason, and that it was founded no longer on the extravagant, but on the serious and elevated sides of their nature. Frederick, while he combats the always irascible and choleric instincts of Voltaire, now growing old, supports and favours, as much as he can, his beneficent and humane tendencies. He takes pleasure in praising, in encouraging the defender of humanity, of tolerance, the man who reclaimed and repeopled the waste lands of Ferney, as he himself had peopled the sands of the Brandebourg; in a word, he recognised and embraced in the great practical poet his collaborator in a social work and in civilisation. With a remnant of the old worship, or, if you like, with an idolatry still touching, in all the comparisons he establishes between them he gives the advantage to Voltaire, and this in a tone of feeling that cannot be doubted. Speaking of that future of perfected reason of which he scarcely sees the dawn, although, sceptic as he is, he does not despair of it in the future of humanity, he says: "All depends for a man on the time when he comes into the world. Though I came too late, I do not regret it, for I *have seen Voltaire;* and now, though I see him no more, I read him, and he writes to me."

The journey to Prussia in 1750, and his attempt to establish himself in Berlin, were, as we have seen, a sad campaign for Voltaire, about which enough has been said and written, and from which, like him, we are glad to escape as soon as possible. On his return to France, he was like a man who feels himself over, conscious of bruises on all his limbs. He was very undecided on the choice of a retreat; we find him, successively, at Strasburg (August, 1753), at Colmar, at the abbey of Sénones, at Plombières in the Vosges, and then again at Colmar. He was feeling, at a distance, the pulse of opinion about him in Paris ; meanwhile he searched for some frontier region where he could settle in safety. A year went by in observation and restlessness; he was then in his sixty-first year. He went to Lyons in November, 1754, to confer with his friend the Maréchal-Duc de Richelieu; the cold reception he met with from the archbishop, Cardinal de Tencin, uncle, nevertheless, of his friend d'Argental, made him realise to what an extent he was compromised at the Court of France. It was then that he made the decision to go at once into Switzerland with his niece, Mme. Denis. He settled first at Lausanne and, soon after, at *Les Délices,* outside the gates of Geneva.

These first years in Switzerland are marked by much joy and gaiety. Voltaire felt that he was once more free; he mingled in the life of the region, and made it accept his own life; he acted his comedies and tragedies at home, and found actors at hand, and not at all bad ones, for the principal parts. At the same time he renewed a close correspondence with his friends in Paris, d'Alembert in particular, with whom he began an intercourse of letters that never afterwards ceased. This Correspondence of Voltaire with d'Alembert is essential as giving the key to his life. It should be read by itself, and consecutively, as it appears in the first edition, and not as it is given in the Beuchot edition, where it is fused into the general Correspondence. The life of Voltaire was a comedy: the Correspondence with d'Alembert lets us see behind the scenes and back of the stage; the rest is, more or less, before the footlights.

Voltaire was hardly settled in Switzerland, before he began to send to d'Alembert articles for the *Encyclopédie,* which until then had pursued its way in peace and unmolested. Voltaire now gave d'Alembert excellent literary advice on the method of carrying on such an enterprise; but he was not long in mingling with it counsels of another order, for instance: "During the war of the parliaments with the bishops, sensible people will have a fine chance; you will have freedom to stuff the *Encyclopédie* with truths it would not have dared to utter twenty years ago. When pedants fight, philosophers triumph." The squabbles now began. D'Alembert who wrote the article *Genéve* in the *Encyclopédie,* calling in question the sincere faith in Jesus Christ of the Protestant ministers, roused public opinion in Geneva, and Voltaire, being on the spot, was made to feel it. He wrote, nevertheless, to d'Alembert: "Do not retract, do not seem to yield to these wretches by renouncing the *Encyclopédie.*" For d'Alembert was disgusted, and the enterprise was beginning to meet with serious opposition in Paris. Here Voltaire, while he was leading in Switzerland the life of a great seigneur, apparently occupied only with pleasures of the mind, shows himself, in his letters to d'Alembert, as the ardent organiser of all that concerns and affects the common cause. In every line we find the fervent zealot, the grand-master, or the general-in-chief haranguing his lieutenants, of whom d'Alembert is, in Paris, the leader: "I cannot conceive why those who work for the *Encyclopédie* do not assemble and declare they will renounce everything unless they are sustained. Make yourselves a body, Messieurs; a body is always respected. . . . Rise up, and you will be masters."

I said once that at the time of Montesquieu's death the army of the men of Letters was neither afoot nor enrolled. It was to set it on its feet that Voltaire worked ardently.

Voltaire in his youth had been alone, without partisans, without support; the recollection of his life so often broken up, so agitated, made him feel the importance of making for himself a party, an army, which he would fain organise from a distance, without putting his own person too much under fire; hence he spurred on d'Alembert and his friends. The *Encyclopédie,* which rallied the men of Letters, seemed to him an excellent opportunity. When the existence of that heavy machine is threatened, he talks of nothing but of rushing, all of them, sword in hand, a "square battalion," to defend it. But, meanwhile, he leads a free and joyous life in his country-house on the shores of the lake, and invites to dinner the very ministers whose susceptibility and conscience d'Alembert has wounded. "It is not at all to make fun of them," he writes, "but one must be polite. You can scoff at everything and be gay."

D'Alembert, on the other hand, less petulant and more stable, plays a cool game; holding back Voltaire and keeping his hold upon him; often excited by him, he, in turn, excites Voltaire if he sees him relaxing, and winds him up again; he irritates him through his little passions, and carefully foments his anger; he suggests to him, by name, certain victims. All this Correspondence is *ugly;* it has an odour of schemes and plots, of confederates and secret societies. From whatever point of view we consider it, it does no honour to men who erected falsehood into a principle, and who regarded contempt for their fellows as the first step towards enlightening them: "Enlighten and despise the human race!" Sad trumpet-call, but it was theirs. "Advance, with a sneer, brethren, in the path of Truth!" That was their perpetual chorus.

But Voltaire, who had been caught in a net more than once, thought best to be on his guard. His country-house, *Les Délices,* was too near Geneva; it would not be glorious for him who had been under the claws of a king in Berlin to fall under those of a little republic of *bourgeois* sovereigns: "I have a house in the neighbourhood which cost me more than one hundred thousand francs," he writes in January, 1757, "but they have not yet pulled it down." This proves that the idea of some such danger had come to him. It was then that he began to seek more than one abiding-place, where he could make his home at various times; and he bought Ferney (in October, 1758), which became, in the end, his only and all-sufficient residence.

One of his first cares in his retreat was to bring up, educate, and provide a dowry for the grand-niece of Corneille; he also undertook a commentary on Corneille's works. Whatever judgment may be passed on that work as a whole, he planned it for a good purpose, and began it with great zeal:

"The enterprise is a delicate one," he writes to a friend in Paris; "I must give an opinion on thirty-two plays; I consult the Academy by every post, and I submit all my opinions to it. I hope that, with this precaution, the work will be useful to Frenchmen and to foreigners. One must give oneself all the occupation one can to make life supportable in this world. What would become of us if we wasted our time in saying: ' We have lost Pondicherry '—' the king's notes have gone down sixty per cent,' etc.? . . . You will admit that such talk would be very dull. So I spend my life in planting, building, commenting on Corneille, trying to imitate him at a distance, and all to escape idleness. . . . The farther I advance in life, the more I find work necessary. It becomes, in the long run, the greatest of pleasures, and takes the place of the illusions we have lost."

In all that I have written of Voltaire, I have endeavoured to present him, not completely, but in his most honourable and desirable aspect; without, however, concealing the other side; and allowing the man himself to be seen in his verity.

Voltaire [or rather, Jean-François Arouet, for "Voltaire" was a mere fancy name which he took as a youth on coming to make his way in Paris]—Voltaire in his youth was carried along and favoured by circumstances; he never failed to have the wind astern of him from the day when Ninon bequeathed him "enough to buy books" to the day—the first serious and painful day of his life—when he had his encounter with the Chevalier de Rohan. After that, the long residence at Cirey was a period of varied study and happiness. When he quitted Prussia after his second unfortunate experience, he was past middle age, and the man of all others best endowed and best prepared to put to profit the leisure of the retirement into which he entered; where he multiplied productions of all kinds with a facility and an abundance which in these days might seem less astonishing, but in his day appeared phenomenal. His health even, of which he was always complaining,—that "Voltairean constitution" at all times "sufficiently robust to sustain the most active labours of the mind, and yet too delicate to bear any other sort of excess,"—was to him a precious fund which he managed, under an air of liberality, with a truly prudent economy. He himself, in one of the prettiest letters in the general "Collection," has reduced to its true value the exaggerated reputation for universal intelligence which people took pleasure in giving him:

"I have just read a piece," he writes to M. Daquin, censor and critic (1766), " in which you assure people I am happy. You are not mistaken; I think myself the happiest of men; but I ought not to say so; it is cruel to others.

"You quote M. de Chamberlan, to whom you say that I have written that all men are born with an equal portion of intelligence. God preserve me from ever writing such a falsehood ! I have, since I was twelve years old, felt and thought quite the contrary. I divined then the enormous quantity of things for which I had no talent. I know that my organs are not arranged to go very far in mathematics. I have proved that I have no inclination for music. God has said to every man : ' Thus far shalt thou go ; thou shalt not go farther.' I have some turn in me for learning the European languages ; none at all for the Orientals : *Non omnia possumus omnes.* God gave a voice to the nightingales and the sense of smell to dogs, but there are some dogs that have none. What folly to imagine that every man could be a Newton! Ah! monsieur, you were formerly a friend of mine. do not attribute to me the greatest of all impertinences.

"When you have anything curious in the *Semaine* [a sort of literary review published by M. Daquin], send it to me. Rely upon the esteem, the friendship of an old philosopher, who has the folly, in truth, to think himself a very good farmer, but who has not that of thinking he has all the talents."

When Voltaire is in the right, there is no one like him for giving proof of it lightly and easily. His was one of those keen, quick minds that divine more than they know, which have not the patience to carry a demonstration to its end but often grasp at first sight a great truth, and succeed in expressing it in a manner that delights the learned themselves.

We are not to suppose, however, that Ferney changed Voltaire; he was of those who learn nothing

from experience, and correct themselves very little.
He lived without constraining himself, according to
his whims and inclinations. In him was the irreligious, anti-Christian man, whom the life of Ferney
only strengthened by security, and confirmed in his
audacity. This characteristic appears in his most
ordinary letters; they have all a charming tone, something piquant and brisk, with a graceful air, and then,
in the best pages, we nearly always come upon a touch
of license, or of impiety, that makes itself felt, even
jokingly, at the moment we least expect it. Writing
to M. Bordes of Lyons, on the election of Clement
XIV, he says (July, 1769):

"I don't know what that friar, Ganganelli, will turn out; all I know
is that Cardinal de Bernis nominated him for pope; consequently, he will
certainly not be a Sixtus Fifth. It is a pity, as you say, that they did
not give us some blunderhead. We needed a fool and I am afraid
they have given us a wise man. . . . Abuses are never corrected
till they become outrageous."

Those are detestable sentiments, and give a false
view of the real interests that are most important to
men united in society. Very imprudent and senseless
is he who, in any walk of life, prays for excess of
evil under a pretext of a total and coming reformation;
and complains when at the head of human powers
he sees moderation and wisdom.

This same M. Bordes, to whom Voltaire thus wrote,
was a former friend of Jean-Jacques Rousseau, who
had since become the latter's refuter and adversary.
In writing to him of Rousseau, Voltaire gives way to

his antipathy for that competitor and powerful collaborator, in whom he persisted in seeing only a madman whom he pitilessly insults:

"Ah! monsieur," he writes to M. Bordes, March, 1765, "you see now that Jean-Jacques resembles a philosopher as a monkey resembles a man. . . . People are rejecting his sophistries, and his person is held in horror by all honest men who have sounded his character. . . . What sort of philosopher is a mischief-maker and an informer? How can any one imagine that the Corsicans have written to him? I assure you there is nothing in it. Let us leave the miserable man to his own opprobrium. Philosophers do not count him among their brethren."

There are not enough insulting words in his vocabulary with which to blast Rousseau; he is "a miserable creature whose heart is as ill-made as his mind"; he is "the dog of Diogenes gone mad." In a letter to M. Thomassin de Juilly, another of Rousseau's opponents, he says:

"That miserable monkey of a Diogenes, who thinks he has taken refuge in the old planks of his cask, but who has not even his lantern, never wrote anything with either good sense or good faith. Provided he can sell his quack medicines he is satisfied. You call him Zoïle; he is that in all the talents and all the virtues."

But in all this violence against Rousseau we must not see jealousy. Voltaire was never jealous; he was passionate, unjust, and in the present case he yielded blindly to all his antipathies of taste and temper against a man who never jested, who turned everything, not to laughter, but to bitterness; who wrote with exaggeration [*emphase*], whose very elevation of tone seemed to Voltaire exaggeration, and who declaimed as a republican against the arts, the stage: "Remember how that miserable little Jean-Jacques, the turncoat, wrote to me a year ago: 'You corrupt my Republic in return for the asylum she has given you.'" The explanation of Voltaire's contempt for Rousseau is in those words. He understood nothing of the ardent earnestness of this new apostle, or of his hold upon young souls; he saw only a grotesque being, who was now and then eloquent.

Voltaire was not a democrat, and it is well to call this to the minds of those who, at this distance, and in support of their own systems, wish to give us a Voltaire seasoned with Jean-Jacques. When one likes to study men, and see them as they are, one cannot away with these symbolised statues that threaten to be the idols of the future. Voltaire was against majorities, and he despised them; in the matter of sense, the masses seemed to him naturally stupid; he believed that good sense was to be found among the few only, and it was enough for him if by degrees that little group could be enlarged:

"It seems by the late riot," he writes to M. Bordes (November, 1768), "that your people of Lyons are not philosophers; but provided honourable men are, I am satisfied. . . . France would be a very pretty country to live in were it not for the taxes and the pedants. As for the populace, they will always be silly and barbarous—witness what has happened at Lyons. They are oxen who need a yoke, a goad, and fodder."

Miserable words! Voltaire elsewhere ridicules the rumour that his estate at Ferney was to be erected

into a marquisate: "Marquis Crébillon, Marquis Marmontel, Marquis Voltaire!" he exclaims, "good for
nothing but to be shown at the fair with Nicolet's
monkeys." It is his good taste which scoffs at the
title; but his mind, his nature, was aristocratic, and
on occasion it carried him far; he was brutally feudal.
It has been said that the Revolution, had he lived to
witness it, would have distressed him deeply; one
thing, however, is very certain, the horrors and the
excesses, which mingled from the first with useful reforms, would not have surprised him. In '93, had he
been present, he would surely have said: "There they
are, my Gauls! I recognise them!" No one has so
vividly and frequently exhibited the contrasts that are
noticeable in the character of Frenchmen and Parisians
at the various epochs of our history. Here is one
passage, among a dozen others:

"I have always found it difficult to conceive," he writes to the
father of Benjamin Constant in January, 1776, "how a nation so
agreeable should be at the same time so ferocious; how it can pass so
easily from the Opera to a Saint-Bartholomew, be sometimes composed of monkeys dancing, and sometimes of bears growling; at one
and the same time so intelligent and so imbecile, so brave and so
cowardly."

And again, more gaily (September, 1770):—"I
think nothing can prevent the Pamphlet of La Chalo-
tais from appearing." [The solicitor-general of Brittany, accused of writing anonymous letters to Louis
XV, defended himself in a pamphlet.] "The public

will laugh, argue, and get heated; in a month all will be over; in five weeks forgotten."

It must be a Frenchman as French as Voltaire, saying these things of his nation of those and former days to justify a Frenchman of to-day in repeating them. Let us add, in order to be accurate, that in all his pungent and sagacious expressions of opinion, capricious as they sometimes were, Voltaire forgot, or did not foresee, a gradual softening of manners, an insensible and continual progress, to which he himself contributed. The people of Paris have shown in our day, and even in periods of great excesses, that they are no longer the same as the unformed masses who issued from the old society preceding '89.

On settling at Ferney, Voltaire took the whole of himself, his imagination and his caprices, his principles of agitation and of restlessness, with him. We find him, especially in the first years, begetting all sorts of bickerings, even with his own happiness, flying into a passion about his eternal *Pucelle*—for if he did wrong to make her, she punished him well—creating ideal dangers, fancying that Parliament was about to proscribe him, keeping his trunks packed even in mid-winter, and through months of snow, to be able to spring across the frontier, if need be, at a jump. But after a while, he began to feel more secure, thanks to the protection of the Duc de Choiseul [prime minister of Louis XV]; and then he abandoned himself with incredible ardour to the pleasure of building,

planting, peopling his neighbourhood, establishing in-
dustries and watch factories, introducing joy, health,
and ease of life.   He obtained for his manufactories at
Ferney and Versoix certain exemptions which favoured the birth of his little colonies.   At the fall of
M. de Choiseul he was able, while remaining honestly
faithful to the dismissed minister — the "illustrious
Barmecide" as he called him—to obtain the protection
of Chancellor Maupeou.   Voltaire felt no aversion to
that minister, so unpopular in Paris; distance served
him well, and enabled him to see justly on one point
at least.   He hated the Parliaments, and considered
it a great thing to have got rid of those obsolete
and henceforth restraining bodies, which would be a
perpetual obstacle to all ameliorations and reforms
emanating from the royal power.   He would never
have advised their resuscitation.   But it was not
until the ministry of M. Turgot and the hopes to
which the accession of Louis XVI opened the way,
that Voltaire, philosopher and farmer, manufacturer
and labourer, seemed to take new life.   His letters of
this period show very plainly the old man of eighty
suddenly rejuvenated, exerting himself to write to the
reforming minister and to those who served him,—
Trudaine, De Vaines, Dupont de Nemours, etc.,—and
gaily crying out: "We are in the Golden Age up to
our necks!"

It happened to Voltaire, as it always happens naturally to every great literary renown when joined to a

certain social position, but to him more than to others because of his prodigious activity and the startling proofs he gave of it, that every one, far or near, claimed his good offices; people consulted him, related the wrongs of which they were victims, and solicited the help of his pen and his credit. It was not at Ferney alone that request after request, of all forms and kinds, poured in upon him: sometimes it was Lally-Tollendal, pleading with him to rehabilitate the memory of his father; then it was the directress of a theatre at Lyons whose license had been withdrawn; to-day it was one thing, to-morrow another. Certainly it is a noble idea, which cannot be wholly an illusion, that the more a man is cultivated the better and kinder he must necessarily be; and that in a lofty position, with a reputation made, he cannot fail to be more easily impartial, and thus owes himself to all.

Voltaire seems to me, judging by his letters, to have busied himself actively during the last years of his life with the public welfare of the region about him, and also with the private interests that, from far and near, appealed to him for help; he pleaded continually with ministers and sub-ministers in behalf of his various colonies, for whatever could give security to their existence and add to their comfort. And this, not only for those around him at Ferney, but for others at a distance, who had trusted themselves to him. He is the benevolent and zealous advocate of more than one good cause. What in earlier years may

have seemed feverish excitement became in the end a
noble solicitude for the general interests. This honours his old age; it explains why the world has ended
by attaching to his name a fame more real and more
grandiose than so much waywardness and inconsistency would seem to warrant.

Madame Du Deffand.

Madame Du Deffand.

OF late many of our classics have been reprinted, and some which are not classics at all. The letters of Mme. Du Deffand, I know not why, have not had that honour. The largest collection of those letters was published for the first time in London, in 1810, from the manuscripts found among the papers of Horace Walpole. This edition was reproduced in Paris in 1811, 1812, and 1824, with some corrections, and also certain *suppressions.* Since then, no one has taken the trouble to reprint the text, purging it, and comparing it with the London edition to restore the parts that were altered or suppressed. Yet Mme. Du Deffand well deserved that care; for she is one of our classics in language and in thought, and one of the most excellent of them. It is this characteristic that I should like to make plain to-day.

I have spoken here of Mme. de Sévigné, and quite recently of Mme. Sand. Between these two women, so far apart, so distant, which are the names that really count? that deserve to stand in the first rank of women celebrated for their talent as writers? By the side of Mme. de Sévigné, with less imagination in her style and less genius for detail, but gifted with a poetic and romantic invention full of tenderness, and an incomparable ease and accuracy of expression, we find Mme. de La Fayette. Then we have Mme. de Maintenon, just mind, sound head, agreeable language, which was perfect within a certain defined circle. At the other extremity of the chain we shall find Mme. de Staël. But between Mme. de Maintenon and Mme. de Staël, what a vacuum! We have, to be sure, Mme. de Staal-Delaunay, author of charming Memoirs, a solid and lofty as well as delicate mind, but she did not live long enough, and, through the circumstances of her early position, she never mingled enough in the full centre of society to personify it to our eyes.

The whole eighteenth century would therefore, we may say, be lacking in this direction, and would be represented in literature only by women of unequal merit and of mixed taste, were it not for Mme. Du Deffand. Mme. Du Deffand belongs, in her origin, to the period of Louis XIV, to the excellent form of language that resulted from it. Born in 1697, dying in 1780, she passed through nearly the whole of the eighteenth century, the bold opinions of which her own mind anticipated while she was still a child. But at no moment during her life was she led away by its infatuations of doctrine, by its metaphysical or sentimental jargon. With Voltaire, she is, in prose,

MARQUISE DU DEFFAND
After the painting by Chardin

our purest classic of that epoch, not excepting any one of its great writers.

Born of a noble family of Burgundy, Mlle. de Chamrond received a very irregular and very incomplete education; it was her own mind alone that worked its way. It is related that in a convent of the rue de Charonne, where she was brought up, she early conceived doubts on matters of faith, and spoke of them freely. Her parents sent no less a personage than Massillon to correct her. The great preacher listened, and merely said, as he went away: "She is charming." The abbess insisted on knowing what book she ought to give the child to read. Massillon replied, after a moment's thought: "Give her a five-sous catechism." And they could get nothing further from him. He seemed to despair of her from the first day. Mme. Du Deffand had one peculiarity at least that distinguished her among the free-thinkers of her time, she put no bravado into her opinions; she felt that the philosophy that blazons itself ceases to be philosophy, and she was content to remain in perfect sincerity with herself. When Mlle. Aïssé in dying asked for a confessor, it was Mme. Du Deffand, aided by Mme. de Parabère, who procured him.

Mme. Du Deffand often regretted that she had not had a different education, and cursed the one she had received.

"People often ask themselves," she said, "if they would live their lives again. Oh! I would not be a young girl again on condition of being brought up as I was, to live with the people with whom I lived, and have the same cast of mind and character that I had; I should have just the same misfortunes over again. But I would willingly go back to four years old to have for tutor a Horace . . . ";

and thereupon she traces a plan of education under an enlightened, well-informed man, such as her friend Horace Walpole. The plan she imagined was serious and noble, but the education which she had given herself, or rather that which she owed to nature and experience, made her an exceptional, and far more original person. What she really was would never have been known, nor what her mind was worth for clearness and rectitude of judgment, if she had not derived all she was from herself. At all times, she was one who least asked her neighbour what she ought to think.

They married her, according to that fine custom, to a man unsuited to her except by birth. She judged him at a first glance, took a dislike to him, left him, tried now and again to live with him, found the annoyance too great, and ended by allowing herself frankly all the misconduct that was prejudicial to respect, even in that society of relaxed and easy morality. In the bloom of her beauty under the Regency she inhaled the spirit of it. She was the mistress of the Regent, and of many others. Going from one disappointment to another, she was always trying to repair her last error by some new experience. Later, in her old age, quite at the close of it, we see her doing all she can to fill the voids or diversify the monotony of old acquaintances by gaining new ones; she did the same thing with her lovers during the first half of her life.

After a certain period, however, we find her established on a fairly honourable footing of regular *liaison* with President Hénault, a man of intelligence, but incomparably inferior to herself. She accommodates herself to him finally, as sensible persons do in what is called a marriage of reason. About this time (1740) Mme. Du Deffand has a *salon* which becomes a centre. She is intimate with all that is most illustrious in Letters, and in the great world. Long the friend of Voltaire, she is also that of Montesquieu and of d'Alembert. She knows them and judges them in their persons and in their characters more readily than in their writings; she estimates their mind at its source, without devotion to any of them, with perfect independence. If she reads them her judgment is expressed at once and is never checked by any outside consideration. The keenest and most accurate sayings that have survived about the celebrated men of her day were said by her.

The distinctive trait of her mind was to seize upon the truth, the reality of things and of persons, without illusion of any kind. "Is it not intolerable," she said of the factitious society about her, "never to hear the truth?" And then, as if she had been searching for something beyond it, when she discovers that

truth, that reality, she is not satisfied: disgust and
ennui begin. *Ennui* was her great terror, her dreaded
enemy. With an ardent nature beneath her stiff,
cold air, she wished to repulse that mortal *ennui* at
any cost; it would seem as if she bore within her
some nameless instinct that was ever vainly seeking
its object.

One of the persons of her society whom she most
appreciated was the Duchesse de Choiseul, wife of
the minister of Louis XV, a good and virtuous
woman, well-conducted and withal charming ; who
had no other defect in Mme. Du Deffand's eyes than
that of being too perfect, and to whom she wrote,
one day :

> "You say you do not suffer from *ennui,* dear grandmamma " (the
> name was a jest between them), " and I believe it because you say it.
> 'Your life' you add 'is not occupied but it is full.' Permit me to
> tell you what I think : it is that if it were not occupied it would not
> be full. You have indeed some knowledge of life, but for all that,
> you lack one experience which I hope you will never have : it is the
> deprivation of sentiment with the sorrow of not being able to do
> without it."

Here we touch the profoundly sensitive point in this
nature, thought so cold, and which was not so. It is
through this feeling of impotence and desire that
Mme. Du Deffand makes, in a way, the link between
the eighteenth century and ours. Mme. de Maintenon was also a victim to *ennui,* but with her it was
not the same, it was far more reasonable. If I did not
fear to commit an anachronism of language, I think I

should not commit a moral one by saying that there was in Mme. Du Deffand what was hereafter to be in *Lélia,* but a Lélia without affectation.

She looked about her for that resource that a woman rarely finds in herself and herself only. She sought *another,* or rather she sought no longer. She had vainly hoped to find that other in society where her inexorable eye saw nothing but a collection of absurdities, pretensions, and follies. The men of Letters of her time, when they called themselves Voltaire, Montesquieu, or d'Alembert, amused her fairly well; but in none of them was there enough to satisfy her fully; their atoms and hers never more than half grappled. She had a keen attraction of mind towards the charming Mme. de Staal-Delaunay, whom she lost early. Yet she had one true friend, Formont, one habitual friend, President Hénault, and enough social intimacies to fill to overflowing a less exacting being; but the whole together did little more than slightly amuse her.

During a journey for health which she made in the summer of 1742 to the Baths of Forges, she wrote several letters to President Hénault, receiving a goodly number from him. We have this correspondence, which is curious in tone. Mme. Du Deffand, scarcely arrived at Forges, awaits the president's letters with an eagerness not to be imagined, and from it she deduces proofs of the liking she has for him, lest he should be ignorant of it :

"I see with sorrow that I am as susceptible of *ennui* as of old ; but I comprehend that the life I lead in Paris is more agreeable than I thought, and I should be extremely unhappy if I had to renounce it. Conclude from this that you are as necessary to me as life itself, inasmuch as I prefer to be with you than with all the other persons whom I see ; this is not a blandishment that I am saying to you, it is a geometrical demonstration that I give you."

To these sweet words of so reasonable a kind, the president responds by gallantries in his style, which is not always very delicate. He gives her news of the Court, and of his own suppers : "My supper was excellent, and, what will surprise you, we all amused ourselves. I own that after it, had I known where to find you, I should have gone in search of you; the weather was fine, the moon was beautiful. . . ." We can fancy how Mme. Du Deffand teased him about the moon; she reduced that flash of sentiment to its due value, and while trying to say a few pleasant words, she gives the key to her whole physical and moral nature : *"Ni tempérament, ni roman,"* she tells him plainly : "Indifference physically, and morally no romance."

Add to the above a consuming activity that knew not how to satisfy itself, and you will begin to comprehend her.

Such she was at the age when the last rays of youth expire. About a dozen years later she began to feel that her sight was gradually failing, and to foresee in the near future a dreadful blindness. Pursued by the idea of solitude and eternal *ennui,* she attempted to find a companion in Mlle. de Lespinasse. The story is well known: the young companion, after a few years, quarrelled with her patroness, and carried off a part of the latter's circle of friends, d'Alembert at their head. This defection made a great noise, and divided society into two camps. Every one took sides for or against Mlle. de Lespinasse; in general, youth and learning, and the Encyclopædists *en masse,* were for her. What can be said is, that the union could not last between these two women when each put much of herself into it. They both had too much intellect, minds too exacting, and they belonged to two different generations. Mme. Du Deffand represented the century before Jean-Jacques, before the romantic inspiration; her maxim was: "The tone of romance is to passion what copper is to gold." Mlle. de Lespinasse was one of that second half of the century into which romance entered in full force. The divorce, sooner or later, was sure to come.

Mme. Du Deffand, now blind, had an apartment in the convent of Saint-Joseph, rue Saint-Dominique, the same formerly occupied by the foundress, Mme. de Montespan. She was sixty-eight years old; she lived in the great world as if she were not afflicted with the saddest infirmity, forgetting it as much as she could, and striving to make others forget it by force of skill and charm:—rising late, turning night into day, giving suppers at home, or supping out in company, having for intimates President Hénault,

Pont-de-Veyle, the circle of the Choiseuls (to whom she was related), the Maréchales de Luxembourg and de Mirepoix, with many others whom she cared for more or less—this was her life when, in the autumn of 1765, there arrived in Paris an Englishman, highly distinguished for intellect, Horace Walpole. This was the great event, literary and romantic (that, for once, is the right word), of Mme. Du Deffand's life, the one to which we owe her only letters of real feeling and all that makes us know her best.

This blind old woman fell in love, instantly, with the keen, bold, delicate, and brilliant mind of Horace Walpole, cut out on a pattern she had not seen for fifty years. She perceived in him the qualities proper to a man so distinguished in himself, and also those of the powerful race to which he belonged: she was grateful for them all; and she who had never loved with love, who had had caprices only and no romance, who, in the matter of friendship, could count but three serious ones in her whole life,—Formont and two women, one of whom had deceived her,—she, this moralist of satirical temper, became suddenly tender, emotional as well as amused, full of active, passionate solicitude; she no longer belonged to herself. In short, blind and sixty-eight years of age, she gave her heart, and this time (for the rarity of the thing) she gave it to an Englishman, much distinguished and welcomed by society, a man of fifty, whose mother she could very well have been, whose life was lived

away from her, and whom she greatly embarrassed
by her vivacious tenderness. So true is it that she
was destined, as some one said, to be wise in judgment, and always foolish in conduct.

But as for me, I do not think it folly; for it shows a
noble side in Mme. Du Deffand, which uplifts her, and
proves that while she had economised her sensibility
until then, she was not without it, and was even
capable of passion. In fact, if we pardon Mme. de
Sévigné for having loved her daughter to idolatry,
we must also pardon Mme. Du Deffand for having
felt for Walpole a passion one knows not how to
qualify, which entered through her mind into her
heart, and was fervent, lofty, and pure.

The first time that Horace Walpole saw her in
Paris, he wrote of her to one of his friends (October
6, 1765). After a few details as to his own variations
of humour and impressions since his arrival, he goes
on to say:

"I now begin, in English fashion, to claim the right of doing as I
please. I laugh, I say what comes into my head, and I oblige others
to listen to me. There are two or three houses in which I am wholly
on that footing. . . . I pay no tribute to their great authors of
the day. Every woman here has two or three who never budge from
her salon. . . . Old President Hénault is the pagod in that of
Mme. Du Deffand, a blind old woman, a debauchee of mind, with
whom I supped last night. The president is almost completely deaf
and has more than run his course."

In writing thus he little thought that she whom he
called "a debauchee of mind" was to feel for himself

a true passion of the mind, and that this passion in her would become a passion of the heart, perhaps the only one she had ever experienced, which would last fifteen years, as living on the last day as on the first.

Except for a certain number of letters of Mme. Du Deffand to Horace Walpole, and from Voltaire to her, by far the longest "Correspondence" of hers that we possess is one that passed regularly between three persons: Mme. Du Deffand herself, the Duchesse de Choiseul, and the Abbé Barthélemy. The Duc de Choiseul does not appear in it, except by a few very short notes, but there is mention of him in nearly every letter.

The correspondence, begun in May, 1761, during the great days of M. de Choiseul's ministry, is continuous and lasts without interruption or slackening till August 20, 1780, one month before Mme. Du Deffand's death. It becomes very eager and animated after the fall of the Duc de Choiseul and his exile to Chanteloup. It may even be said that we do not know the life at Chanteloup and that triumphant exile, or form a just and complete idea of it until we have read these letters, which are like a confidential bulletin, in which the enthusiasm of intimate friends and interested persons never weakens for a moment.

The new element in this "Correspondence" is the Duchesse de Choiseul, whom we already knew for her mixture of grace and good sense through the universal testimony of her contemporaries, but never to

the degree in which her natural self is shown in this
series of lively, witty, sensible, serious, even logical
letters, and impassioned, too, whenever the fame and
interests of her husband are in question. The Abbé
Barthélemy, the guest of Chanteloup, the friend who
has given himself once for all ; and whom the spell
has irrevocably bound, also appears to advantage, and
is seen in all the aspects of his character, the most
polished of learned men, amiable and estimable, gay
and moderate, a "good fellow," all things to all men,
a social treasure, having hours, however, when he
regrets, under his breath, the independence of his
former life, and the free delights of study.

The one who gains least is Mme. Du Deffand ; and
yet, all things considered, she does not lose, for, as the
intelligent editor of the "Correspondence" remarks,
she appears such as her well-wishers liked to see her,
"less sensible than affectionate, and more discouraged
than incapable of loving others or herself." She is
full of *ennui;* she judges herself, and more severely
than is needed ; she distrusts others, but, above all,
herself ; she does not think it possible that any one
can truly love her: at the most she admits they endure
her. "I cannot be a burden to you," she repeats incessantly to Mme. de Choiseul, who wants her to
stay at Chanteloup : "I cannot contribute to pleasure
or to amusement ; I should owe it to your goodness,
—I will say the word—to your compassion, to suffer
me near you !" She was only half mistaken : the

Duchesse de Choiseul, in sending, later, this collection of letters to M. Beausset (the future Cardinal), said : "The letters of Mme. Du Deffand have the charm of naturalness, the choicest expressions, and depth of sentiment in *ennui*. Poor woman! I still pity her." *Pity,* that was the feeling she inspired. "Poor woman !" are still the words that come most naturally to our minds after reading her letters ; but we ought instantly to add : "clear and upright judgment, excellent mind, language still more excellent."

Mme. de Choiseul was sketched by Horace Walpole in a few strokes that are indeed those of a painter who was the compatriot of Spencer and of Shakespeare :

"My last new passion, and also, I think, the strongest," he writes during a visit to Paris (January, 1766), "is the Duchesse de Choiseul. Her face is pretty but not very pretty ; her person is a little model. Gay, modest, full of attentions, with the happiest propriety of expression and the greatest vivacity of reason and of judgment, you might take her for the Queen of an Allegory. A lover, if she was the sort of woman to have one, might desire that the allegory should end, but as for us, we say: Let it never end!"

And again, in a subsequent letter :

"The Duchesse de Choiseul is not very pretty, but she has fine eyes ; she is a little wax model, who, for some time, was not allowed to talk, being thought incapable of it, and having both shyness and modesty. The Court has not cured her of modesty; her shyness is redeemed by the most touching tones of voice, and is soon forgotten in the elegant turn and exquisite propriety of her expressions. Oh ! she is indeed the most dainty, the most lovable, the most gracious little being that ever issued from a fairy's egg. So true in her words, in her thoughts ; so considerate, so kindly by nature! Every one loves her, except her husband, who prefers his own sister, the Duchesse de

Grammont, a tall amazon, proud, haughty, who loves and hates according to her caprices, and is detested. Mme. de Choiseul, passionately in love with her husband, has been the martyr of this preference; she has ended by submitting with a good grace ; she has gained some influence over him in consequence, and is thought still to adore him.—But I suspect," adds Walpole, " that she takes too much pains to make it believed."

In this Walpole was mistaken. The attitude of Mme. de Choiseul was in accordance with the truth ; she continued very sincerely, very tenderly, in love with the man of whom she was proud, of whom she said that not only was he " the best of men but the greatest that the century had produced," and of whom she wrote one day, with charming artlessness : "It seems to me that he is beginning to be less ashamed of me ; and it is a great point gained no longer to wound the self-love of those by whom we want to be loved." She had reason to congratulate herself on the exile to Chanteloup, and was, perhaps the only one fully to enjoy its brilliant peace ; she saw in it the means of keeping near her the object of her worship and, if not to reconquer him wholly, at least to possess him, to hold him in her hand, and not to lose sight of him for a single day.

One fundamental pleasantry runs through this "Correspondence," and gives the tone to it. Mme. Du Deffand had had a grandmother, who had married, as her second husband, a Duc de Choiseul; she had had, therefore, a Duchesse de Choiseul as a "grandmamma." Born herself some thirty-five or forty years before the present Duchesse de Choiseul, she amused herself by inverting the rôles and the ages, calling the duke and the duchess "grandpapa" and "grandmamma," while they called her their "granddaughter." That is the alpha and omega of all their letters; it is the pretext for much pretty jesting and childish nonsense when there was nothing better to write about.

Would you see a Duchesse de Choiseul at Versailles, as the wife of a prime minister, in grand toilet and in all her pomp ; courted, surrounded, wearied with homage and civilities, without a moment to herself, and trying to describe to her "granddaughter" at odd moments her hurried morning, her crowded day ?—Mme. Du Deffand had spoken to her in one letter of certain persons from Versailles whom she saw in Paris, and with whom she had promised to have Mme. de Choiseul sup on her next visit to Paris; this is the answer :

"Spare me, my dear child, those Versailles people ; it is now, as you truly say, five months that I have been here. . . . The more people you invite, the more I shall be hindered from seeing you —I am hindered now in the pleasure of writing to you; I am made desperate. I have just torn myself out of bed to have the dressing of my hair—begun yesterday—finished : four heavy hands are on my poor head. And that is not the worst for it—I hear tongs at my ears, and curl-papers—it is too hot ! . . . 'What jewels will Madame put on to-day ?' . . . 'Those go best with such or such a gown.' . . . 'Angélique, bring the headdress '—' Marianne, prepare the panier '—You understand that it is the supreme authority, Tintin, who gives these orders. She has had much trouble in cleaning my watch with an old glove ; she now wants me to see that the inside is still black. But that is not all : a soldier perorates about the expulsion of the Jesuits; two doctors are talking, I believe, about war—or else they are making it on each other ; an archbishop is showing me an architectural decoration ; this one wants to attract my eyes, that other one to occupy my mind, and all to obtain my attention : you alone interest my heart.—They are calling to me from the next room: ' Madame ! it has struck the three-quarters ; the king will be going to Mass '—Quick ! quick ! my cap, my hood, my muff, my fan, my book ! I must not scandalise any one ; quick ! my chair, my porters, and off we go !—I return from Mass ; a woman, a friend of mine, comes in as soon as I do. She is in full-dress ; my very little cabinet is filled up with the *vastitude* of her hoop. She tells me to continue what I am doing: ' I cannot, madame ; I would not be so much my own enemy as to deprive myself of the pleasure of seeing you and listening to you. . . . At last she is gone ! I resume my letter—but here they come to say that the courier to Paris is just starting, has Madame any commands ? ' Oh, yes, yes ! I am just writing to my dear child ; tell him to wait.' Here a little Irish girl comes and solicits me to procure her a favour, which I shall not obtain for her ; a manufacturer from Tours comes to thank me for a benefit I did not procure for him. Some one is presenting to me his brother, whom I do not see ; there is no one, down to Mademoiselle Fels [a famous opera singer] who does not come here to see me.—

"I hear the drums: the chairs in my antechamber are knocked over, the officers of the Swiss guard rush into the courtyard.

"The *maître d'hôtel* comes to ask if I wish dinner to be served; he informs me that the salon is full of people, that Monsieur has come in and demands dinner. Well, well, I must end. There is the exact picture of what I experienced yesterday and to-day in writing to you —and at nearly all times. Judge if I am not weary of people, and whether you ought to give yourself the trouble to procure me more; judge also how I love you to keep on writing to you, and how provoked, out of patience, pulled about, and harassed your poor grandmamma is! Pity her, love her, and you will console her for all."

But this is only the great lady in the days of her ministerial state; I prefer her in her later days of tranquillity and active good sense. It is worth while then to hear this pretty little person, this pretty thing, with her dainty wax face, grow animated, and talk of

public affairs, literature, authors, Rousseau, Voltaire,
the Empress Catherine, putting them all in their true
light; talking, descanting (for she does descant now
and then when she feels at her ease, and it is, perhaps, a
fault); we ought to hear her in such moments become
indignant, rebellious, breathing forth fire and flame;
she has no hesitation then, nor any shyness; she says
all she thinks, all she has in her heart; her reflections
overflow like a restrained passion. She is a marvel to
Mme. Du Deffand and the "great abbé," and as for
us, she amazes us. She has maxims, principles, which
contrast with her period, with her youth, with her
childlike air:

"Let us above all," she says, "distrust those who oppose themselves with such rancour against what they call the prejudices adopted
in society. If they would examine societies, they would see that
laws can foresee and be enacted against actual things only; they may
be the terror of criminals and the curb on crimes, but prejudices are
the only curb on morals. Now governments are founded equally on
morals and on laws; destroy either the one or the other, and you
overthrow the edifice. . . .

"The employment of the mind to the injury of public order is one
of the greatest wickednesses, because, by its nature, it is the most un-
punishable, or the most unpunished; yet it is the most dangerous,
because the coil it produces is extended and promulgated by the very
penalty inflicted on the guilty, and for centuries after. That species
of crime is a seed sown; it is the tares of the Gospel.

"A true citizen will serve his country best by his mind and by his
talents, but he will not write on the social contract in a way to make
us doubt the legitimacy of Governments, and to load us with chains
the weight of which we have never yet felt. I have always mis-
trusted that Rousseau, with his singular systems, his extraordinary
accoutrements, and his pulpit of eloquence perched on the roofs of
houses; he has always seemed to me the charlatan of virtue."

Mme. Du Deffand was shocked by a passage in an article by Fréron, in which he spoke "insolently" of Horace Walpole in relation to Walpole's mystifying letter to Jean-Jacques. She complained to her "grand-papa," then prime minister, in order that he might castigate Fréron; at which Horace Walpole, when he heard of it was much annoyed: "We love so much the liberty of the press," he wrote, "that I would rather be maltreated by it than see it suppressed." All that Fréron had done, moreover, was to report a book translated from the English; there was no other blame that could be laid on him; "In strict justice," said M. de Choiseul, "it is the censor who did wrong and not Fréron; however, they shall both be corrected." Mme. de Choiseul had been set to work on this affair, but she soon felt that she had better be involved as little as possible in such squabbles, in which plenty of others took pleasure:

"Let us not thrust ourselves into literary quarrels, my dear child," she writes; "if we did so at first, it was only to pull your friend out, and not to mingle in it ourselves; such quarrels are good for nothing but to depreciate talent and bring to light absurdities. But—between ourselves be it said—it ought to be rather pleasant for us to see the tyrants of our opinions destroying each other by the same arguments they use to subjugate our minds. That is the surest way to enable us to escape their dominion while profiting by their lights."

Mme. Du Deffand was really of the same opinion. Since the defection of Mlle. de Lespinasse, who had withdrawn from her, carrying with her certain of the leaders of the Encyclopædists, she was much opposed to whatever resembled partisan interests either in philosophy or in literature. But as Voltaire, with malicious pleasure, tried to provoke Walpole and bring him, by pique or by prodding, to a discussion on the merits of Racine and Shakespeare, and as, moreover, he seemed in the humour to wrangle with the two ladies on the subject of La Bletterie, whom they protected and he disliked, Mme. de Choiseul wrote again to her old friend:

"I think that we should do well to let him alone; as for me, I do not want to enter upon a literary dispute; I do not feel myself in a condition to make head against Voltaire. Besides, the animadversion of men of Letters seems to me more dangerous than the plague. I like Letters, I honour those who make them a profession, but I desire their society only in their books; I find them good to see in their portraits only.—I hear the granddaughter saying: 'Grandmamma is right; she seems to have all my experience.' Admit, dear child, that none of them, except our very dear and good abbè, is without venom; he is, because he keeps his superiority for himself, his fine mind for us, and his kind spirit for everybody. But he fears men of Letters as much as we do."

Thus Mme. de Choiseul and Mme. Du Deffand united their sentiments of prudence and propriety in this matter, making no exception among literary men, except for their wise and gentle Anacharsis.

The younger of the two was full of good, practical advice, and she gave it without making it unsavoury; she relieved it by a vivacious turn of expression, that justifies the eulogy of Horace Walpole:

"Chanteloup, May 17, 1767. You tell me of your sadness with the greatest gaiety, and of your *ennui* in the most amusing fashion. Do you also make courage for yourself, dear child? That is the best thing to make when we have not any. Between *making* and *having* there is a long way; yet it is only by dint of making that we ever acquire any. Oh! how much I have made in my life! *Make courage* is not, I know, a French expression; but I must speak my own language before that of my nation; we often owe the irregularity of our expressions to that of our thoughts—we have to render them such as they are. . . . From all this, I gather that you are ill and full of *ennui;* this grieves me. You are sad because you are ill and ennuyéd, and you are ill because you are sad and ennuyéd. Sup less, open your windows, drive out in a carriage, appreciate people and things. So doing, you will love less, but you will hate less; you will not have great enjoyments, neither will you meet with great disappointments; and you will no longer be sad, ill, and weary with *ennui*. Write to me always in your sad moments; it will be a distraction. Do not fear to make me share your *ennui;* I shall share your feelings only; and mine will be infinitely tender for you."

I may be mistaken, but this letter seems to me in a tone wholly modern, more modern than that of Mme. Du Deffand. It is essentially new and distinguished. Such a letter might have been written from 1800 to 1820 by a Mme. de Beaumont, or a Duchesse de Duras, by one of those women of heart and thought who were no longer of the eighteenth century.

The dismissal came: the Duc de Choiseul was exiled to Chanteloup; we know with what honour. Seeing such evidence of public esteem and favour, the heart of the duchess is filled with feelings of pride, satisfaction, and conjugal delight; she overflows, her measure is full, she is proud; she extols the happy exile—happy at least for her,—she would not reduce it in any way; the exercise of power seems to her less enviable, less sweet. And when fears are expressed that these popular manifestations might irritate the duke's enemies, and perhaps provoke more severity, she replies:

" What more do you expect them to do to us? the king never strikes twice. . . . Terror has attacked our friends to such a point that some of them fear the public interest will be embittered against us. Let it be embittered! in the meantime, if further harm is attempted against us, it will be the public interest that holds it back; they dare not; there would be general revolt. Let that interest go on; it is too flattering to us to deprive us of it. Let it be perpetuated, if possible. It secures the fame of my husband; it rewards him for twelve years of toil and anxiety; he has bought it with his services; it might cost even a higher price and yet we should not feel that we had paid too highly for the immense happiness, and of a new kind, which we have caused France to enjoy. M. de Choiseul feels this; as for me, I own my head is turned by it. . . ."

Thus we see her heroically elating herself for her lord and master; all his interests are hers; she embraces them without reserve, without calculation; she exaggerates his fame; she sees him pure and spotless; if any one holds back, if they do not grant all, or if they seem to compromise with the inimical powers, she is provoked to anger, she is like a lion—above all, and before all, she is a woman, honestly coquettish, tender, assiduous, showing herself in love, as on the first day, with the man who, until then, had certainly not made too much of her, and to whom, more than ever, she now consecrates herself:

" Chanteloup, January, 1771. . . . You wish me to tell you all I feel, all I do, all I experience! I have no longer those feelings of suffocation, the journey has absolutely cured them. I did not take cold. Our rooms are beginning to get warm, thanks to paper stuffing the chinks of all the windows, and sheepskins round all the doors. Our chimneys, too, begin to smoke rather less. . . . We have pretty good food; we pass our nights tranquilly, and our mornings in adorning ourselves in pearls and diamonds like princesses of romance. I have never had my hair so well dressed or thought so much of my adornment as I do now. I want to be young again, and, if possible, pretty! I shall try at any rate to make the grandpapa think I am both, and as he will have few objects of comparison, I shall manage it more easily."

Mme. de Grammont, nevertheless, was there, and shared habitually the same exile. But here, from the first day, yielding to a generous emotion, the rivalry was disarmed, and without altogether ignoring its cause they worked in concert to soften the exile of the fortunate mortal for whom, the very day before, they were at arms. The treaty of peace which Mme. de Choiseul signed with her sister-in-law, at a first interview, in presence of her husband, the conditions she laid down, the limits she clearly established around her in her own house, as a devoted wife and the accomplished mistress of a household, all show the action of a very firm, very delicate person, perfectly gentle and without temper, but who chooses to be reckoned with, a woman capable of more than one sacrifice that does not concern dignity. This agreement, we must add, was very well observed on both sides; tact, good taste, and knowledge of the world prevented difficulties in the beginning, and in the long run Mme. de Grammont ended by winning something not only of the esteem but even of the affection of her whom she had so long distressed. If we were still sensitive to these subtleties of the old society, I should say that we were witnessing, veritably, the triumph of its manners.

We can gather from these letters a description in fullest detail, of an ideal ministerial exile in the eighteenth century. Chanteloup, seen through the eyes of Mme. de Choiseul, or through those of the good abbé, was an Eden. But the agreeable incidents that occurred to enliven it and to diversify the scene disappear for us before grave reflections. What illusion in this intoxication! in this long ovation over a fall, in which fashion played at popularity; in this hope, secretly nourished and ever present, of a future recall, and a triumphant return to the head of affairs! What illusion in that fame which they believed to be eternal, in that building, costing forty thousand *écus,* erected at the extremity of the artificial lake, a true pagoda, on the marble walls of which were carved the names of all who visited Chanteloup during those four years, with this inscription made by the Abbé Barthélemy:

" Étienne-François, Duc de Choiseul,
Deeply touched by the testimonies of friendship,
Kindness and attention
With which he was honoured during his exile
By a vast number of persons who hastened
To come to him in this place,
Has caused this building to be erected
To eternalise his gratitude."

How small that ministerial obelisk, inaugurated ten years before the French Revolution, at a few steps from the volcano that was about to engulf the monarchy,

how small, seen from afar, it looks, and how it misses
its effect in the perspective!—unless, indeed, we regard it simply as a domestic chapel, dedicated by a
loving and enthusiastic woman to her worship of her
husband.

Let me add here that Mme. de Choiseul, on the
death of her husband in 1785, retired to the Convent
of the Récolettes, to enable her to pay the enormous
debts that he left and thus do honour to his memory.
During the last years of her life she lived in the rue
Saint-Dominique, in a house afterwards occupied by
Maréchal Soult. One day, during the Directorate, or
the Consulate (for she did not die till 1801), M. Pas-
quier, going to see her, found her much agitated. He
asked her the cause, fearing it was some bad news:

" No, not that," she answered. " But just now they told me that
a man from Chanteloup was there, and wished to see me. I told them
to bring him in. I saw a tall man, neatly dressed, who asked me if I
recognised him: ' Do you not remember, Madame la duchesse, little
Pierre who picked up stones on the road, and to whom you were so
good because, when you passed, you saw he put his heart into his
work? Well, I am little Pierre. You asked me one day what I
needed to set me up in business; and you bought me a donkey and a
cart. That brought me luck. I worked, I made my way. I am
now a contractor for roads. Do you know I am one of the first men
in my region. I am rich. But, Madame la duchesse, all that belongs
to you; they tell me you are not well off. I have come to return to
you what is yours.' "

The emotion of Mme. de Choiseul in relating the
little story was too much for her; tears choked
her voice.

The Abbé Barthélemy, as I said before, gains by the publication of these letters, of which a goodly number are from him. It is true that his descriptions seem in these days rather long and tiresome, his grand chronicles of Chanteloup dull and long-winded, his jokes stiff and starched: it needs a magic of the pen, which he lacks, to make us find pleasure in the monotony of those, to him, happy days. Let me say, to be just, that it was not for us that he wrote, but for the persons of his coterie, who found all he said very good, very kind, and very amusing. But, when we enter into the spirit of this correspondence with the two distinguished women whose union he cemented and sustained, we cannot fail to estimate at his true value this essential friend, this equable and safe character, compliant without baseness, agreeable and serviceable without flattery. A true sentiment, conceived early, and nourished by him for thirty years, chained him to the feet of his noble friend, Mme. de Choiseul. I know not whether, like Walpole, he began by taking her for a Queen of Allegory; but he was certainly patient, for he seems never to have wished that the golden mists should part, or the allegory vanish.

One day, however, when Mme. Du Deffand, with the curiosity of a bored woman, questions him rather closely as to his private sentiments, as to how he stands with Mme. de Grammont, and how he governs himself between her and Mme. de Choiseul, he goes, in his reply, rather beyond the meaning and bearing of her letter, and adds, after a few explanations:

" . . . This is all that I can say to you on the subject. I am greatly touched by the curiosity you express to me about it; it can come only from the interest you feel in me, and that interest will be satisfied with my reply; for, if you put aside the favourable prepossessions you have for me, you will see that I am very fortunate in being so well treated. In the main, I am not agreeable; thus I am not fitted to live in society; circumstances, which I did not seek, tore me from my study, where I had long lived, known to a few friends, infinitely happy because I had a passion for work, and because a rather flattering success in my own line promised me greater still. Chance brought me to know the grandpapa and the grandmamma; the feelings that I vowed to them led me astray from my career. You know to what a point I am penetrated with their goodness to me; but you do not know that in sacrificing to them my time, my obscurity, my peaceful life, and, above all, the reputation I might have won in my profession, I made them the greatest sacrifices of which I was capable: sometimes they come into my mind and then I suffer cruelly. But as, on the other hand, the cause is a noble one, I put aside such ideas as best I can, and let myself be carried along by destiny. I beg you to burn this letter. I have been led to open my heart to you by the marks of friendship and kindness with which your letter is filled. Do not attempt to comfort me; assuredly I am not to be pitied. I know so well the value of what I possess that I would give my life not to lose it. In God's name, let nothing transpire of all this; neither in your letters nor in your conversations with the grandmamma; she would be grieved if she suspected that I still regretted some things. Do not be grieved for me yourself; for these regrets of mine are not of long continuance, and I feel daily that they grow less keen. It is not so with the sentiments that attach me to you."

If the Abbé Barthélemy received much from his noble friends, he brought them much of his own in return; he sacrificed to them more than he let them see; he was aware of it, yet he kept it secret within himself: all that honours him.

Mme. Du Deffand, as we feel in the midst of our impatience, and even of our smiles, at her perpetual lamentations, had, in general, one merit — she was *true*. She shows herself to us as she was, not seeking to embellish herself; she does herself justice, or blame, but does not flatter herself. Always doubting and distrusting that she is loved, she has the desire to be. At her advanced age, she still kept burning, as in her earliest years, the *thirst for happiness,* and she knows no means of quenching it. When we consider her in her relations with Horace Walpole and with the Choiseuls, we see her on her best side, the side to which she clings in her endeavour to love. There are moments when she flatters herself that at last she is loved, and then she cries out: "I enjoy a happiness I have always desired, but have come near to thinking a pure chimera: *I am loved*—by you and by my Horace. . . ." But these moments are rare and soon pass; they give place to long periods of hardness and sterility. At such times she wants to know what others think of her at bottom; whether they love her truly, and in what manner: "You *know* that you love me," she says to Mme. de Choiseul, "but you *do not feel* it."

She seems convinced of the truth of that terrible and cruel maxim, which others besides her have professed to believe and for which Christianity alone can supply the corrective or the remedy, namely: "To know a human being truly to the depths of his nature,

and to love him, is an impossibility." Nothing said
or done reassured her, nothing changed that belief.
In vain did Mme. de Choiseul try to instil into her
mind her own excellent precepts of practical wisdom:
"In the matter of happiness, we ought not to question the 'why' and the 'wherefore'; the best way
and the safest is to take it as it comes. It is only
evil in which we should search for causes and for the
means of pulling out the thorn that wounds us."
Nothing availed. They invited her to Chanteloup;
they assured her of the pleasure she would give, of
their happiness in having her; she dares not believe
it; she lacks *faith* in friendship as in everything else.
The abbé preached to her, and there is a very pretty
letter of his, written from Chanteloup, on the 2nd of
February, 1771; it begins abruptly in these words:

" The other day, one of our Franciscan Friars from Amboise preached
on the cardinal virtues, and here is an extract from his sermon:
" ' Without faith, hope, and charity there is no salvation in this world,
nor in the other. Let us begin with the two latter, which we know
best, because they are nearest to us.   Everybody knows the force of
hope and of love; but what can those virtues do without faith, without the confidence which is their foundation ?
" ' My dear Brethren, examples will convince you better than
reasons. If a little girl, far from her parents, wrote to them: " I hope
to go and see you; that hope makes me happy, because I love you as
much as any one can love; but I fear I shall not seem to you lovable ";
her parents would answer her: " Why do you doubt that we should
love you, inasmuch as you would not have us doubt that you love
us ? " Are you ignorant that charity, according to Saint Paul, covers
a multitude of sins ? Are you ignorant that Saint Augustine said:
Love, and all shall be forgiven you ? Are you ignorant that persons
do really displease when they are always fearing to displease ? Distrust

poisons and destroys feelings; it is not a work of nature. Look at
children; see with what frankness they love. If they do wrong,
they are whipped; but at your first caresses they will fling themselves
into your arms. Do you know why, dear Brethren? Because they
trust; they do not calculate. Reason invented calculation, hence suspicions, fears, false interpretations. Instinct knows neither principles,
nor consequences, nor errors; it is by instinct that we truly love and
are loved. Trust to that, my very dear Brethren; that will guide you
better where feelings are concerned than all the great arguments of
philosophers, the deceitful experience of the world, or the dangerous
sophistries of your own reason '. . . .

" The good Friar said more, but I came away, because he began to
tire me, and my instinct tells me not to bear *ennui* :—but I thought I
saw in his discourse a few truths applicable to the granddaughter."

It was thus they treated the sick old child, who had
so abused and misused in youth the faculty of loving
that she no longer had the force or the faith of love in
her last days : but it was at least something, better
than nothing, to have kept the desire and its torture.
She said of herself, comparing that self with Mme.
de Sévigné, and humbling herself in the comparison
(this time it is to Horace Walpole that she writes) :

" You find, you say, my letters very short. You do not like me
to speak to you of myself; I weary you when I communicate my
thoughts, my reflections ; you are right ; they are always very sad.
If I tell you about this or that person, what interest could you take in
them? Unfortunately, I am not like Mme. de Sévigné in anything ; I
am not moved by things that are nothing to me. Everything interested her, and warmed her imagination ; mine is iced. I am sometimes animated, but only for a moment ; that moment gone, all that
brightened me is so effaced that even the memory of it is lost."

It is not for us to take pleasure in adding our commentary to hers and crushing her with the presence
of Mme. de Sévigné :—Yes, Mme. de Sévigné had

indeed received from a fairy at her birth *Imagination,*
that magic gift, that golden horn of plenty ; but, more
than that, she had known how to control her life and
her feelings.

Curious without interest, eager for the new without
hope of better, tired of all things without ceasing to
be agitated, Mme. Du Deffand wrote one day to
Mme. de Choiseul : " What think you of the new
minister (M. de Saint-Germain) ? I remember how
often I heard the late Mme. de Staal say : ' I am
charmed to make new acquaintances ; I always hope
they will be worth more than the old ones ; I am at
least certain they cannot be worse.' " To which Mme.
de Choiseul replied, as if poison had been presented
to her : " Your quotation from Mme. de Staal is a
horror to me. I am far from thinking as she did ;
it seems to me that I am not dissatisfied with any of
my acquaintances, and I am enchanted with my
friends."

Those words issued from a healthy soul. Mme. de
Choiseul has indeed the honours of this correspondence. Her name should be added to the list of
women who have thought well and written well.
She is one conquest the more won by literature from
the old French society.

I have lately studied very closely the relation between Mme. Du Deffand and Horace Walpole, and I
think that, in general, justice has not been done to
either of them. In Walpole people have seen only

the fear he felt of incurring the ridicule of a most satirical society through this proclaimed passion of a blind old woman ; and as for Mme. Du Deffand, we judge her too much as did Grimm, Marmontel, the whole Encyclopædic clique, through whom the tradition about her has come down to us. We judge her too much as if we were on the side of her enemy, Mlle. de Lespinasse, or on that of Mme. Geoffrin. The true, deep, and serious judgment on Mme. Du Deffand, in this matter, ought to be formed from the "Letters of Horace Walpole"; for Walpole, in spite of his harshness, more apparent than real, appreciated his old friend at her true value, and admired her extremely. He returned many times to Paris expressly to see her. In a letter addressed to the poet Gray, written in January, 1766, three months after the one I have previously quoted, he says, in describing delightfully the two rival figures of Mme. Geoffrin and Mme. Du Deffand :

" Her great enemy, Mme. Du Deffand, was for a time the mistress of the Regent ; she is now very old and blind ; but she retains all her vivacity, wit, memory, judgment, and charm. She goes to the Opera, to the theatre, to suppers, and to Versailles ; she gives two suppers a-week, has all the new books read to her, writes songs and epigrams that are truly admirable, and remembers all that has been done in that line for eighty years. She corresponds with Voltaire, dictates delightful letters to him, contradicts him, is not bigoted for him, nor for any one, and laughs at Clergy and philosophers alike. In discussion, to which she inclines readily, she is full of warmth, yet she is very seldom in the wrong. Her judgment on every subject is as correct as possible ; but on all points of conduct she is as much mistaken as any one can be ; for she is all love and all aversion, ardent to enthusi-

asm for her friends, always anxious that they should love her and concern themselves with her ; a violent enemy, but frank."

In this first portrait, to which Walpole added, later,
many a touch of his brush, we can see a Mme. Du
Deffand far more living and animated than she has
usually been painted.

Walpole quitted Paris April 17, 1766, after a stay of
seven months, and Mme. Deffand wrote to him on the
19th. She had received a letter from him the evening
before, written especially to urge her to secrecy and
prudence. Why such prudence? it may be asked.
Because there was then a secret chamber where letters
were unsealed, and a too tender, too ardent letter from
an old woman of seventy might go to the king, to
the Court, amuse the courtiers, and make this rather
singular intercourse the topic of satirical couplets,
such as Mme. Du Deffand herself knew so well how to
write. Walpole would not willingly subject himself
to that. Mme. Du Deffand was better inured to it.
" You say that people are laughing at us," she writes,
" but here they laugh at everything, and do not think
of it the next instant." This fear on the part of Walpole returns perpetually; he restrains his old friend as
much as he can; he rallies her for being " romantic,"
" sentimental " ; he piques her by taxing her with
metaphysics, which she abhors above everything.
She replies with anger, with submission, with sentiment. She persists in returning constantly to the
topic he forbids, to that constant thought which is

for him alone. If he is ill, if he does not write often
enough, she threatens him, gaily, with the most violent measures:

"Take notice," she says, "that it is not letters that I exact; simply
bulletins; if you refuse me this kindness, I shall instantly say to Viart
(her secretary): ' Start! take your boots, and go, at one flight, to London; proclaim in all the streets that you come from me, that you have
orders to live near Horace Walpole, who is my guardian, that I am his
ward, that I have for him an unbridled passion, and that I shall, perhaps, arrive myself directly, and settle at Strawberry Hill; in short,
there is no scandal I am not willing to cause.

"Ah! my guardian, quick! get a bottle of salts; are you fainting?
This, however, is what will happen if I do not hear from you twice a
week."

Here, of course, she is jesting, but at other times she
is sad, bitter, and casts a despairing glance on life:

"*Ah, mon Dieu!* you are right enough! what an abominable, detestable thing is friendship! where did it come from? to what does it
lead? on what is it founded? what good can we expect or hope to
get from it?   What you have said to me is true; then why are we on
this earth? above all, why should we live to grow old?   . . .
Last evening I wondered much at a numerous company who came to
see me; men and women seemed to me machines with springs that
made them go and come, talk and laugh, without thinking, without
reflecting, without feeling; each played his or her rôle from habit:
Mme. la Duchesse d'Aiguillon laughed convulsively; Mme. de Forcal-
quier disdained everybody; Mme. de La Vallière jabbered about everything. The men played no better parts; and I, myself, was sunk in the
blackest reflections; I thought how I had spent my life in illusions;
how I had dug for myself all the abysses into which I had fallen; how
all my judgments had been false and rash, and always too hasty; how,
in short, I had never truly known any one; that I had never, moreover, been known by any one, and that, possibly, I did not know myself. We desire a support, we let ourselves be charmed by the hope
that we have found one; it is a dream; a dream which circumstances
soon dispel, and on which they have the effect of an awakening."

We have the two tones. The last tone, that is to say, the serious and penetrating one, the one that goes to the bottom of everything, is not rare in the letters of Mme. Du Deffand to Walpole. He, good Englishman that he is, in spite of his flashes of French wit, makes her read Shakespeare; which she instantly enjoys, crying out, as if on the discovery of a new world: "Oh! I admire your Shakespeare. I read 'Othello' yesterday, and I have just read 'Henry VI.' I cannot express to you the effect those plays have had upon me; they have resuscitated me." She, too, in her way, sees into the depths like Shakespeare; in her 64th Letter I find what I call her Hamlet monologue. I invite the inquirer to read the passage that begins with these words: "Tell me why, detesting life, I fear death." . . . and ends thus: "I own that a dream would be better." An English critic, at the time when these Letters were published in London, remarked, very justly, that Mme. Du Deffand seemed to combine in the character of her mind something of the qualities of the two nations: the charm and liveliness of the one, with the boldness and vigorous judgment of the other.

What she liked first of all in Walpole was his freedom of thought and of judgment. She loved truth above all else, and that people should be truly themselves. The taste of her time disgusted her: "What people call eloquence to-day has become to me so odious that I would prefer the language of the markets;

by dint of searching for wit they smother it." Her
literary judgments, which must have seemed excess-
ively severe at the time, are nearly all confirmed
to-day. "That Saint-Lambert," she said, "has a
cold, tasteless, false mind; he thinks he abounds in
ideas, but he is sterility itself." What she said of
Saint-Lambert, she says, with variations, of many
others. How she *selects* in Voltaire! how she distinguishes in him the good from the second-rate; that
which came from the living spring from mere idle
repetitions [*rabâchage*]. She does the same with Jean-
Jacques: "Not knowing what to read, I have gone
back to Rousseau's *Héloïse;* there are very good parts
in it, but they are drowned in an ocean of eloquent
verbiage." On Racine, on Corneille, she passes sound
and correct judgments. There is only one work that
she would like to have written; one only, because it
seems to her to have attained, in all respects, to perfection; and that is *Athalie*. It was said of Mme. Du
Deffand that in the matter of reading "she denied herself nothing but the necessary." The saying is witty
but shallow. Undoubtedly, she did not have a solid
foundation of regular, systematic reading. As she was
not told in advance what she ought to admire, she had
only her own clear opinion, her honest and luminous
instinct, and they usually guided her aright.

" You English," she writes to Walpole, " you subject yourselves to
no rule, no method; you let genius grow, without constraining it to
take this or that form; you would have all the intellect you have, if
no one had had any before you. Oh! *we* are not like that; we have

books; some on the art of thinking; others on the art of speaking, writing, comparing, judging, etc."

But if here she seems to flatter Walpole and to espouse the taste of his nation, she does not always compliment him, and she knows at need how to oppose him. She stands firm for Montaigne, whom Walpole did not like; she is amazed at that, and gives him her reasons in many places:

"I am very sure that you could accustom yourself to Montaigne; one finds in him all that one has ever thought; and no style is more energetic. He teaches nothing, because he decides nothing; it is the very opposite of dogmatism. He is vain—Hey! all men are, are they not? and those who seem modest, are not they doubly vain? The *I* and the *me* are on every line; but how should we ever have any knowledge except through the *I* and the *me*? No, no, my tutor, he is the only good philosopher and the only good metaphysician there ever has been."

In another charming passage, in comparing Montaigne with Walpole at his manor of Strawberry Hill, she exclaims: "No, no, Horace resembles Michel more than he thinks he does!" What she likes especially in Montaigne is that he had a friend and believed in friendship. Thus this woman, sceptical as to everything, came, in extreme old age, to believe in something; and for that much must be forgiven her.

Mme. de Sévigné was then extremely in vogue in society; people were reading her Letters, then recently published; and the unpublished ones relating to Fouquet's trial were lent about. Horace Walpole doted on her and called her "Our Lady of Livry." Oh! how many times did Mme. Du Deffand, to please him, envy the style of "that saint of Livry." "But beware of imitating her," writes Walpole; "your style is yours, as hers is hers." Mme. de Sévigné, be it said, is admirably judged by Mme. Du Deffand, and so is her cousin, Bussy Rabutin. Mme. de Maintenon, also, is clearly apprehended: "I persist in thinking that that woman was not false; but she was cold, austere, unfeeling, without passion. . . ." This whole portrait of Mme. de Maintenon should be read; it remains the best likeness of all that have been made of her. One might be tempted to apply a part of it in its conclusions to Mme. Du Deffand herself if she had not, in loving Walpole with this unlooked-for rejuvenescence, given the lie to her former reputation for insensibility.

Walpole was a collector, an amateur, antiquary, bibliophile, having all sorts of tastes, and perhaps a few manias. Mme. Du Deffand envied him because he never felt *ennui* in solitude; but, with her severe taste, she could not comprehend how any one could like, pell-mell, so many things; read, for instance, Shakespeare and Voltaire's *Guerre de Genève,* admire Mme. de Sévigné and find pleasure in the novels of Crébillon *fils.* She tells him so. In the matter of memoirs and of history she congratulates herself that their tastes are alike. I must be allowed to quote one more passage, because Mme. Du Deffand has been accused of not liking Plutarch, and I am certain that, if she did not like him, she must have thought she discovered in him something too much of a rhetorician;

"I like real lives also," she writes: "I can read only facts written by those to whom they happened, or by those who have witnessed them; and furthermore, I want them related without phrases, without additions, without reflections; I wish the author not to be so concerned to say things well; I want the tone of conversation, vivacity, warmth, and above all, facility, simplicity. Where is that to be found? In a few books we know by heart, and which, assuredly, are not imitated in the present day."

This indicates the side that I call classic, in the highest meaning of the word, in Mme. Du Deffand; that by which she is above and outside of her epoch. I shall not dwell here on the portraits which she drew of the personages of her social world. She excelled in such portraits; fixing into them, ineffaceably, absurdities and follies in a picturesque manner. In the different ways of human beings, she saw only varieties of the universal folly. From the depths of her armchair, blind as she was, she saw all; she uses continually the word "see"; she forgets she has no eyes, and others forget it as they listen to her. She judged even the acting of actors and actresses; and it was she who stamped with a single sentence the characteristic of Mlle. Rancourt, visible on her first appearance: "She is a demoniac without heat."

I have said that Horace Walpole came from England several times to see her. It is curious to gather the impressions of that clever and clear-sighted friend: he raises himself in our estimation and makes us absolve him for his occasional harshness and coldness toward her, by the manner in which he speaks of her to others. He does not shrink from calling her his "dear old friend." At each journey he thinks she grows younger — a miracle in which he certainly counts for much:

"At seventy-three years of age," he writes (September 7, 1769), " she has the same fire as at twenty-three. She makes couplets and songs, and remembers all those that have been made. Having lived from the most agreeable to the most reasoning epoch, she unites what is best in the two periods, without their defects : all that the first had that was charming without its conceit, all that the second has that is reasonable without its arrogance. I have heard her discuss with all sorts of people all sorts of subjects, and I have never found her mistaken. She can put down the learned, lift up disciples, and find the right word for all. As lively in her impressions as Mme. de Sévigné " —what praise from the lips of Walpole !—" she has none of her prejudices, but a more universal taste. With the frailest of bodies, her vital energy carries her along in a rush of life that would kill me, if I had to stay here. If we return at one in the morning from a supper in the country, she proposes to me a drive around the boulevards, or a visit to the fair, because, she says, ' it is too early to go to bed.' I had great difficulty, last night, in persuading her, though she was quite ill, not to stand about till two or three o'clock to watch for the comet ; she had, with that intention, ordered an astronomer to bring his telescope to President Hénault's apartment, under the idea that it would amuse me."

Poor President Hénault, as we see, was not dead : but, for some years, he was little better, and was now a mere wreck. Mme. Du Deffand, on the contrary, to the end of her life in 1780, in her 84th year, remained the same, lively, indefatigable, of "herculean feebleness," as Walpole said. She could not sleep; and felt, more than ever, the need of spending her nights in society: "Whether it injures my health or not," she said, "or whether it suits the régime of the people with whom I like to live, I shall not go to bed a minute before I must." Like old Wenceslas, she would not sleep till the last moment: "What I take from my nights I add to my days."

In one of the journeys he made to Paris (August, 1775), Walpole, before his boots are off, sees Mme. Du Deffand arriving at his hotel. She is present at his toilet, in which, as she remarks, there is no impropriety, because she cannot see. Walpole goes to sup with her, does not leave her till half-past two that night, and before his eyes are open in the morning receives a letter from her: "In fact," he says, "her soul is immortal and forces her body to keep it company."

There are two traditions about Mme. Du Deffand: the purely French tradition, which has come down to us through those she judged so severely, through the men of Letters and the Encyclopædists; and the direct, truer, more private tradition, for which we must go to Walpole as its source. In the latter we find, with surprise, an ardent woman, impassioned, capable of devotion, and even kind. *"Ah! mon Dieu!"* she cries, "what a great and estimable virtue is kindness! Every day I make a resolution to be kind; I know not if I make any progress." Place that saying, for contrast, beside those terrible words she said after the manner of La Rochefoucauld: "There is not a single person to whom we could confide our troubles without giving him a malignant joy, or without debasing ourselves in his eyes." Well, those two traditions, the one that makes her unfeeling, and the one that shows her impassioned, must be combined to give a complete idea of her.

But the real key to this heart is in her feeling for Walpole. She regrets in one place that Walpole was not her son, which was quite possible as regards their ages. In fact, we can see in this sudden passion of a sterile old age a sort of maternal tenderness which had never found rest, and which was suddenly aroused, without being aware of its true name. To define the secret instinct and offend no one, let us call it a tenderness of adoption. She loved Walpole as the tenderest of mothers would have loved a son long lost and suddenly restored to her. Many of these singular and erratic passions, in which sensibility misleads itself, are often only a revenge of nature, punishing us for not doing simple things in their right season.

I shall say nothing of Madame Du Deffand's letters from the historical point of view, and the curious light they cast on the last years of Louis XV and the first years of Louis XVI. Nor shall I speak of the tone of her society, which continued quite faithfully, after her, in the circle of the Beauvaus, and even into the salon of the Princesse de Poix under the Empire. I shall only refer to the last letter, so self-restrained, and so touching, which she dictated for Walpole. Her faithful secretary, Viart, could not read it aloud to his mistress after writing it, without bursting into tears; then it was that she said to him, in her naïve astonishment, these infinitely sad words: "So you *do* love me?" The sore of her whole life is there — unbelief and desire.

She had requested that her little dog, Tonton, be sent to Horace Walpole, that he might take care of it. The faithful Viart, in the letter in which he gives Walpole the details of her illness and death, adds, in closing: "I will keep Tonton until M. Thomas Walpole goes to England; I take the greatest care of him. He is very gentle; he bites no one; he was cross only near his mistress." In a letter from Walpole, dated May 4, 1781, I find these words: "The little dog of my poor, dear Mme. Du Deffand has come. She made me promise to take care of him the last time I saw her; this I shall do religiously; I will make the poor animal as happy as possible." I, myself, would not do like Buffon, and forget the dog of the blind.

Lord Chesterfield.

Lord Chesterfield.

AT all epochs there have been treatises intended to form the "Man of Honour," the "Well-bred Man," the "Courtier," where there were Courts, and the "Perfect Knight." In these various treatises on good-breeding and polite manners, if we open them in successive ages, we shall discover, at first sight, parts that are as much out of date as the fashions and the coats of our fathers. Evidently patterns have changed. But looking a little closer, we shall find, if the treatise has been written by a man of sense who knows mankind, that there is still much by which to profit in the study of those models that have been set up before the eyes of preceding generations.

The Letters that Lord Chesterfield addressed to his son, which are a whole school of good-breeding and knowledge of the world, have the particularly interesting merit that their writer never thought of setting up a model; he merely wished to train an excellent pupil in his private life. These were confidential letters which were suddenly brought to light, revealing all the secrets and betraying the ingenious artifices of paternal solicitude. If, in reading them to-day, we are struck by the excessive importance given to incidental and passing particulars, to details of dress, for instance, we are no less struck by the lasting side, that which belongs to the sum of human observation in all ages; and this last part is much more considerable than we might think from a first superficial glance. In seeking to train his son to all that became an honourable man in social life, Lord Chesterfield did not write a treatise "On Duties" like Cicero; he left letters which, by their mixture of right judgment and levity, by certain frivolous airs insensibly mingled with serious graces, hold, fairly well, a middle place between the "Memoirs of the Chevalier de Grammont" and *Télémaque*.

Before enlarging upon the Letters we need to know a little about Lord Chesterfield, one of the most brilliant minds in England in his day, and also one of those most closely allied with France. Philip Dormer Stanhope, Earl of Chesterfield, was born in London, September 22, 1694, the same year that Voltaire was born. Sprung from an illustrious race, he knew the value of his birth and desired to sustain its honour; but he found it difficult not to laugh at genealogical pretensions carried to extremes. To guard himself from them once for all, he placed among the portraits of his ancestors two old figures of a man and a woman; on the frame of one was written Adam Stanhope, on that of the other, Eve Stanhope. Thus, while holding firmly to his real honours, he cut short all chimerical fancies.

LORD CHESTERFIELD
From a portrait by Ramsay

His father took no interest in his education, and he was given over to the care of his grandmother, Lady Halifax. He was early conscious of a desire to excel and be first in everything; a desire he would have liked, later, to excite in the breast of his son, and which, for good and for evil, is the principle of all great things. As he himself, in his first youth, had no guidance, he made mistakes more than once in the objects of his emulation, and conceived a false notion of honour. He confesses that at one period of his inexperience he fell into excess in wine and into other excesses to which he was not naturally inclined, but his vanity was gratified in being called a man of pleasure. So with gambling, which he then considered a necessary ingredient in the composition of a young man of fashion. He therefore plunged into it without any passion at first, but soon could not withdraw from its fascination; and compromised his fortune in that way for years. "Take warning by my example," he says to his son, "choose your pleasures yourself, and let none of them master you."

This desire to excel and to distinguish himself did not always mislead him; he often applied it wisely; his first studies were admirable. Placed at Cambridge University, he took all the courses that were taught there; he studied civil law, philosophy, and mathematics under the learned and blind Saunderson. He read Greek fluently, and gave account in French of his progress to his old teacher, a French refugee pastor,

M. Jouneau. Lord Chesterfield had learned the French language in childhood from a Norman nurse who took care of him. When he came to Paris for the last time, in 1741, M. de Fontenelle, having remarked in his pronunciation something of the Norman accent, asked him if he had not originally learned the language from a person of that province; which was in fact the case.

After two years at the university, he made the tour of the continent, according to a custom of the young noblemen of his country. He visited Holland, Italy, and France. Writing from Paris, December 7, 1714, to this same M. Jouneau, he says :

"I will not tell you my sentiments about Frenchmen, because I am often taken for one of them, and more than one Frenchman has paid me the greatest compliment they think they can make to any one, which is : ' Monsieur, you are exactly like us.' I will only tell you that I am insolent, I talk much, very loud, and in the tone of a master ; that I sing and dance as I walk along ; and finally that I am furiously extravagant in powder, feathers, and white gloves, etc."

He will do justice, later, to our serious qualities, but here we see the mocking spirit, satirical and slightly insolent, which makes its point at our expense.

In his Letters to his son, he pictures himself, on the occasion of his first entrance into polite society, as still covered with the rust of Cambridge, shamefaced, silent, and finally taking his courage in both hands to say to a lady : "Do you not think it is very hot to-day, madam ?" Lord Chesterfield tells that to his son not to discourage him, but to show him from what beginnings he himself had advanced. He

does the honours of his own person to embolden
the lad, and the better to draw him closer to himself.
I do not allow myself to take him at his word in
this anecdote.   If he were ever for one moment
embarrassed in society, that moment must have been
short indeed !

Queen Anne had just died; Chesterfield rejoiced in
the succession of the House of Hanover, of which he
was to be one of the declared champions.   He had a
seat in the House of Commons, and made his first appearance there on a good footing.   Yet it is said that
an apparently frivolous circumstance held him in
check and paralysed, in some degree, his eloquence.
One of the members of the House, who was not distinguished for any other superior talent, had that of
imitating to perfection the speakers to whom he replied.   Chesterfield feared ridicule (a foible of his),
and he was silent upon certain occasions oftener than
he wished to be, lest he should afford opportunity for
the mimicry of his colleague.   He soon after inherited
the peerage on the death of his father and passed into
the House of Lords, the surroundings of which may
have been better suited to the grace, refinement, and
urbanity of his eloquence.   But he never compared
the two scenes as regarded the importance of their debates, or the political influence to be acquired in them :

"It is unheard of," he said later of Pitt, at the moment when that
great orator consented to enter the Upper House under the title of
Earl of Chatham : "it is unheard of that a man in the plenitude of

his power, at the very moment when his ambition had just obtained the most complete triumph, should quit the House which had procured him that power, and which alone could secure it to him, to retire into that hospital for incurables, the House of Lords "

It is not for me to estimate here the political career of Lord Chesterfield. If I dared to hazard a judgment upon it as a whole, I should say that his ambition was never wholly satisfied, and that the brilliant distinction with which his public life was filled covered, in the depths below, many disappointed aspirations and wasted hopes. Twice, in the two decisive circumstances of his political life, he was stranded. Young, and in the first fire of his ambition, he early staked his whole career on the side of the presumptive heir to the crown, who became George II. He was of those who, on the accession of that prince in 1727, had a right to count upon favour and a place in power. But, able as he was, in seeking to turn to the side of the rising sun he did not do so with perfect judgment. He had long courted the mistress of the prince, believing in her coming influence, but he neglected the legitimate wife the future queen, who proved in the end to have the only real power. Queen Caroline never forgave him. This was the first check to the political fortunes of Lord Chesterfield, who was then thirty-three years old and in the full tide of his hopes. He was too hasty and he chose the wrong path. Robert Walpole, less active and apparently less clever, took his measures more carefully, and calculated better.

Thus thrown with some scandal into the Opposition, and especially after 1731, when he was forced to resign his offices at Court, Lord Chesterfield worked with all his strength for ten years to overthrow the Walpole ministry, which did not fall till 1742. Even then, he did not attain to power; he was still left outside of the new combinations. When, two years later, in 1744, he entered the administration, first as ambassador to The Hague, then as Viceroy to Ireland, next as Secretary of State and member of the Cabinet (1746–1748) his actual power was more specious than real. In a word, Lord Chesterfield, at all times an eminent public man in his country, whether as one of the leaders of the Opposition, or as an able diplomatist, was never a directing minister, nor even a very influential minister.

In public affairs, he certainly had the distant *coup d'œil,* and that outlook upon the future which comes from breadth of mind; but he possessed these qualities far more than he did the persevering patience and the practical firmness in daily work which are so necessary to men in government. It would be true to say of him, as of La Rochefoucauld, that public life served to make an accomplished moralist of an incomplete man of action.

In 1744, at the age of only fifty, his political ambition seemed to be partly worn out; his health was enough affected to make him think with satisfaction of retirement. Besides which, he had a secret ideal and a real ambition, the object of which is now known to us. He had had, before his marriage and about the year 1732, a son by a French lady (Mme. du Bouchet), whom he had met in Holland. To that son he attached himself with extreme tenderness; he wrote to him in all sincerity: "From the first day of your life, the dearest object of my own has been to render you as perfect as the weakness of human nature will allow." To the education of this son all his aspirations, all his predilections and worldly hopes had turned; whether Viceroy in Ireland, or Secretary of State in London, he found time to write him long, detailed letters, directing his every action, for the purpose of perfecting him in the serious and polite arts of life.

The Chesterfield whom we prefer to study is, therefore, the man of intellect and experience, who has passed through public office and tried all rôles of political life only to know their every mechanism and to give us the last word upon them; the man who, in his youth, was the friend of Pope and of Bolingbroke, the introducer into England of Montesquieu and Voltaire, the correspondent of Fontenelle and Mme. de Tencin; he whom the Academy of Inscriptions elected to its membership, who united the mental qualities of the two nations, and who, in a witty Essay, but more particularly in his Letters to his son, shows himself to us as a moralist, as agreeable as he is finished, and as one of the masters of life. It is the La Rochefoucauld of England whom we are now studying.

Montesquieu, after the publication of the *Esprit des Lois,* wrote to the Abbé de Guasco, who was then in England: "Tell Lord Chesterfield that nothing has gratified me so much as his approbation; and that as he is reading me for the third time, he will be well able to tell me what to improve and to rectify in my work; nothing could be more instructive than his observations and his criticism." It was Chesterfield who, speaking one day to Montesquieu of the proneness of Frenchmen to revolution and of their impatience with slow reforms, summed up our whole history in the pithy sentence: "You Frenchmen know how to make barricades, but you will never know how to raise barriers!"

Lord Chesterfield certainly enjoyed Voltaire; he said, apropos of the *Siècle de Louis XIV:* "Lord Bolingbroke taught me how we ought to read history, Voltaire teaches me how it ought to be written." But at the same time, with that practical sense that never deserts men of intellect on the other side of the Channel, he perceived Voltaire's imprudences, and disapproved of them. When old, and wholly retired from society, he wrote to a French lady:

"Your good authors are my principal resource; Voltaire, above all, charms me, except for his impiety, with which he cannot keep himself from larding all he writes. He would do better to suppress it wisely: for after all is said, no one ought to disturb the established order. Let every man think as he will, or rather, as he can, but not communicate his ideas when they are of a nature to trouble the peace of society."

What he said then, in 1768, Chesterfield had already said twenty-five years earlier in writing to Crébillon *fils*—singular correspondent, and singular confidant in the matter of morals!   He was speaking of Voltaire, with reference to his tragedy of *Mahomet* and the daring things he had put into it:

" What I cannot pardon, for it is unpardonable, is the trouble he gives himself to propagate a doctrine as pernicious to civil society as it is contrary to the common religion of all countries.   I doubt very much whether it is permissible for a man to write against the worship and belief of his nation, even though he be sincerely convinced that it is full of errors, on account of the confusion and disorder he will surely cause; but I am very certain that it is not at all permissible to attack the foundations of morality and break the bonds, already too weak, that hold men to their duty.

In writing thus Chesterfield was not mistaken as to Voltaire's great inconsistency.   That inconsistency, in two words, was this: Voltaire, who considered all men as fools or as children, who had not laughter enough with which to ridicule them, nevertheless placed loaded weapons in their hands without troubling himself as to the use they might make of them.

Lord Chesterfield himself, in the eyes of the puritans of his country, has been accused, as I ought to state, of making a breach of morality by the Letters he addressed to his son.   The severe Johnson, who in other respects was not impartial in regard to Chesterfield and thought he had grounds of complaint against him, said, when the Letters were first published, that they " taught the morals of a wanton and the manners of a dancing-

master." That judgment is superlatively unjust; if
Chesterfield, in some particular case, insists on graces
of manner, and on being agreeable at any price, it is
because he has already dwelt on the solid parts of education, so that his pupil is not so much in danger of
sinning on the side that renders a man "respectable"
as on that which renders him agreeable. Though more
than one passage in these Letters may seem very
strange coming from a father to a son, taken as a whole
they are inspired by a true spirit of tenderness and
wisdom. If Horace had had a son, I fancy he would
not have written to him otherwise.

The Letters begin with the *a b c* of education and instruction. Chesterfield teaches, and sums up in French
for his son, the first elements of mythology and history.
I do not regret that these first letters have been published: excellent advice is slipped into them. The
little Stanhope was only eight years old, when his
father drew up for him a manual of rhetoric suited to
his understanding, by which he tried to instil into him
good language, and distinction in the manner of expressing himself. He especially recommends to him
attention in all he does, and he gives full value to that
word. It is *attention* only, he tells him, that impresses
objects on the memory: "There is not in all the world
a surer sign of a small and paltry mind than inattention. All that is worth the trouble of doing, deserves
and requires to be well done, and nothing can be well
done without attention." This precept he repeats

incessantly, and he varies its application as his pupil grows older and is more in a condition to understand it to its full extent. In pleasure or in study, he wishes that each thing done should be done well, done fully, and at its right time, without hindrance or distraction. "When you read Horace," he says, "pay attention to the accuracy of his thought, to the elegance of his diction, to the beauty of his poesy, and do not be thinking of the *De Homine et Cive* of Puffendorf; and when you read Puffendorf do not think of Mme. de Saint-Germain." But such free and firm disposal of thought by the action of the will is in the power of very great or very good minds only.

M. Royer-Collard was wont to say that "what specially marked our age was *respect* in the moral order, and *attention* in the intellectual order." Lord Chesterfield, with his less serious air, would have been capable of that saying. He was not long in realising what was lacking in the son he was trying to form, and who was, indeed, the occupation and object of his life:

"In scrutinising your personality to its depths," he writes, "I have not, thank God, discovered as yet any viciousness of heart, any weakness of the brain; but I have discovered laziness, inattention, and indifference; defects which are only pardonable in aged persons who, in the decline of life when health and vigour lessen, have a kind of right to that sort of tranquillity. But a young man should be ambitious to shine and to excel."

Now, it is precisely this sacred fire, this spark that makes the heroes, the Alexanders, the Cæsars,—*to be first in all that they undertake,*—it was this motto of

great hearts and of eminent minds of all classes that
nature had neglected to put into the worthy but thoroughly commonplace soul of young Stanhope. "You
seem to lack," his father says to him, "that *vivida
vis animi* which stirs, which instigates most young
men to please, to shine, to outdo others."—"When I
was your age," he says again, "I should have been
ashamed that another could learn his lesson better than
I, or could beat me at any game; and I should have
had no peace till I recovered the advantage."

The whole of this little Course of Education by
letters has a sort of continued dramatic interest. We
follow the effort of a keen, distinguished, energetic
nature, such as that of Lord Chesterfield, in its struggle with an honest but indolent nature, a soft, lethargic
dough, of which the father desires to make, at any
cost, an accomplished masterpiece, agreeable, original;
succeeding, finally, in making nothing better than an
estimable copy. What sustains this struggle, — in
which so much art is expended and the eternal counsel recurs, always the same at the bottom, under
all its metamorphoses, — what sincerely touches the
reader, is the true, paternal affection which inspires
the delicate and excellent master, patient this once,
however eager, prodigal of resources and skill, never
discouraged, inexhaustibly sowing on that barren soil
the elegances and graces of life. Not that this son,
the object of so much culture and zeal, was unworthy
of his father in any way. It has been said that no

one was ever more stupid, more sulky than he; and a harsh saying of Dr. Johnson is quoted in proof of it. But such opinions are caricatures that go beyond the truth. It appears, from more accurate testimony, that Mr. Stanhope, without being a model of grace, had, in reality, the air of a well-bred, polished, agreeable man. But do we not feel that the discouraging point is just there? It might, perhaps, have been better to fail totally than to have made, with so much care and trouble, an insignificant and ordinary man of society, one of those of whom it is said, for all judgment, that there is nothing to say. There was surely enough to discourage and make the work seem pitiful to any but a father.

Lord Chesterfield thought, at first, of France, as the best place to refine his son and give him the pliancy and ease that he never afterwards acquired. In his private letters to a lady in Paris, Mme. de Monconseil, we see that he thought of sending him there in early youth:

" I have a boy," he writes to this friend, " who is now thirteen years old. I will confess to you that he is not legitimate, but his mother is a person well born, who showed me kindnesses that I did not deserve. As for the boy, perhaps it is prepossession, but I think him lovable; he has a pretty face, much vivacity and, I believe, intelligence for his age. He speaks French perfectly, he knows much of Latin and Greek, and he has history, ancient and modern, at his fingers' ends. He is at present in school; but as no one dreams here of training the manners and morals of young men, who are nearly all boobys, awkward and impolite, in short, such as you see them when they come to Paris at twenty or twenty-one years of age, I do not wish my boy to stay here long enough to get those bad tendencies.

That is why I intend, as soon as he is fourteen, to send him to Paris.
. . . As I love this child extremely, and pique myself that I can
make something good of him, because I think the stuff is there, my
idea is to unite in his person what I have, so far, never found in any
one individual, namely: what there is of good in the two nations."

He enters into the details of his plan and the means
he expects to employ: an English teacher for the
mornings, a French tutor for the afternoons, aided,
above all, by the gay world and good society. The
war that broke out between France and England post-
poned this project of a Parisian education, and the
young man did not make his first appearance in French
society until 1751, when nineteen years of age and
after completing the grand tour of Switzerland, Germany, and Italy. All had been arranged by the most
attentive of fathers for his success and his welcome
on this new stage. The youth is lodged at the Acad-
émie, with M. de la Guérinière; in the mornings he is
to do his exercises; the afternoons he must devote to
society: "Pleasure is now to be the last branch of
your education," writes the indulgent father; "it will
soften and polish your manners; it will induce you to
seek and then to acquire the graces." On this latter
point Chesterfield is exacting and gives no quarter.
The *graces;* it is to them that he returns perpetually,
for without them all efforts are vain: "If they do
not come to you, seize them!" he cries. As if to
know how to seize them were not already having
them!

Three ladies, friends of his father, are specially

charged to watch over and guide the young man at his start; they are his *governesses* for society: Mme. de Monconseil, Lady Hervey, and Mme. Du Bocage. But these introducers seemed essential for his start only; after that, the young man must go of himself, and choose some more charming and intimate guide. On the delicate subject of women, Lord Chesterfield breaks the ice: " I shall not speak to you on this topic as a theologian, a moralist, or a father " ; he says, " I put aside my age to consider yours only. I wish to speak to you as one man of pleasure would do to another if he has good taste and intelligence." And he explains his meaning; stimulating the young man as much as he can towards "honourable arrangements" and refined pleasures in order to turn him from easy and coarse habits. He has for principle that " an honourable arrangement becomes a man." All his morality, in this respect, may be summed up in Voltaire's line: " Nought is evil in good company." it is at such points that Johnson's grave modesty veils itself; ours only smiles.

The serious and the frivolous mingle incessantly in these letters. Marcel, the dancing - master, is much recommended; Montesquieu no less. The Abbé de Guasco, a sort of hanger-on to Montesquieu, is a useful personage as an introducer here and there:

" Between ourselves," writes Chesterfield, " he has more knowledge than talent; but a clever man knows how to get some good out of every one, and every man is good for something. As for

President Montesquieu, he is, in every respect, a precious acquaintance. He has genius, with the most extensive reading in the world.
Draw from that source as much as you can."

Among authors, those that Chesterfield recommends, especially at this epoch, are La Rochefoucauld and La Bruyère: "If you read in the morning
a few of La Rochefoucauld's maxims, consider them,
examine them well; compare them with the originals
you will meet in the evening. Read La Bruyère in
the morning, and judge at night if his portraits are
good likenesses." But these excellent guides are not
themselves to have other utility than that of a geo-
graphical map. Without personal observation and
experience they would be useless, and even lead to
error, as a map would do if we relied upon its
complete knowledge of towns and provinces. Better
read one man than ten books: "The world is a
country that no one has ever known through descriptions; each of us must travel over it in person to get
initiated."

Here follow a few precepts and comments that are
worthy of a master of human morals:

"The most essential knowledge of all, I mean knowledge of the
world, is never acquired without great attention; I know a goodly
number of aged persons who, after living much in society, are still
mere children in knowledge of the world. . . .

"Human nature is the same the world over; but its workings are
so varied by education and by habit, that we ought to see it under all
its customs before we can say that we know it intimately. . . .

"Nearly all men are born with all the passions to a certain degree;
but there is scarcely any man who does not have a ruling passion, to

which the others are subordinate. Discover in each individual that ruling passion, pry into the folds of his heart; and observe the diverse effects of the same passion in different natures. And when you have found the ruling passion of a man, remember never to trust him wherever that passion has an interest. . ."

"If you wish to win the good graces and affection of certain persons, men or women, try to discover their most salient merit, if they have one, and their ruling weakness, for every one has that ; then, do justice to the one, and a little more than justice to the other. . . .

"Women, in general, have but one object—their beauty ; in regard to it there can hardly be flattery too gross for them to swallow. . . .

"The flattery that will most truly touch women who are really beautiful, as well as those who are decidedly ugly, is that which applies to their minds. . . ."

As regards women, though he seems at times very contemptuous, he makes reparation to them at other times; and, above all, whatever he may think himself, he never allows his son to say much evil of them:

"You seem to think that from Eve to the present day they have done much harm ; as for the aforesaid lady, I give her up to you; but since her day, history will show you that men have done far more evil in the world than women; but, to tell you the truth, I advise you to trust to neither more than is absolutely necessary. What I also advise you is never to attack whole bodies of persons, whatever they may be. Individuals pardon sometimes ; but bodies and societies never pardon."

In general, Chesterfield recommends to his son circumspection and a sort of prudent neutrality, even as regards both the rascals and the fools who swarm in the world: "Excepting their friendship, there is nothing more dangerous than their enmity." This is not the morality of Cato and Zeno; it is that of Alcibiades, Aristippus, and Atticus.

On religion he says, in reply to certain cutting remarks made by his son: "The reason of every man is, and ought to be, his guide; I should have as much right to exact that all men should be of my height and my temperament, as to insist that they should reason precisely as I do."

In all things it is his opinion that we ought to know and love the good and the best, but not to make ourselves the champions thereof against all and every one. We ought to know, even in literature, how to tolerate the weakness of others: "Let them tranquilly enjoy their errors of taste as well as of religion." Oh! how far we are from such wisdom in our bitter trade of criticism as we now make it!

He does not, however, counsel falsehood: he is explicit on that point. His precept is: Never say all, but never lie. "I have always observed," he repeats frequently, "that the greatest fools are the greatest liars. For myself, I judge of a man's veracity by the strength of his mind."

The serious, as we see, blends readily in Chesterfield with the agreeable. He is constantly demanding of the mind both firmness and flexibility, gentleness in manner with energy beneath it. Lord Chesterfield truly felt the seriousness of France and of all which the eighteenth century brought with it that was fruitful and redoubtable. According to him: "Duclos, in his *Réflexions,* is right in saying that a germ of reason is beginning to develop in France; and I confidently predict," adds Chesterfield, "that before the end of this century, the business of king and priest will be more than half gone." The French Revolution was thus predicted by him in 1750.

He cautioned his son from the outset against the idea that the French are purely frivolous: "The cold inhabitants of the North consider the French a frivolous people, who whistle and sing and dance all the time: this idea is a long way from the truth, though many *dandies* may seem to justify it. But those very dandies, matured by age and by experience, are often metamorphosed into very capable men." The ideal, according to him, would be to unite the good qualities of both nations; but he seems in this mixture to incline more to the side of France: "I have said several times, and I really think it, that a Frenchman who adds to a foundation of virtue, erudition, and good sense the manners and politeness of his country attains to the perfection of human nature."

He united fairly well in himself the merits of the two nations, with an additional trait that belongs to his race. He had imagination in his intellect. Hamilton had this distinctive quality, and carried it into his French intellect. Bacon, the great moralist, is almost a poet in expression. The same cannot be said of Lord Chesterfield, and yet he had more imagination in his wit and in his intellect than we find in Saint-Évremond and in our brilliant moralists in general. In this respect he is like his friend Montesquieu.

Although, in these Letters to his son, we are obliged, without being rigorous, to note certain points of a somewhat corrupt morality, we must also point out, by way of compensation, the very serious and altogether admirable passages in which he speaks of Cardinal de Retz, of Mazarin, of Bolingbroke, of Marlborough, and of many others. It is a rich book. We cannot read a page without retaining in our minds some valuable observation.

Lord Chesterfield destined this son, so dear to him, to diplomacy; at first he found some difficulty in carrying out his plans because of the young man's illegitimacy. To put an end to such objections, he made him enter Parliament, as the surest means of overcoming the scruples of the Court. Mr. Stanhope in his maiden speech, had a moment's hesitation, and was forced to have recourse to his notes. He never again renewed the attempt to speak in public. It seems that he succeeded better in diplomacy; but always in secondary rôles that required only solid worth. He filled the post of envoy extraordinary to the Court of Dresden. But his health, at all times delicate, gave way in youth, and his father had the grief of seeing him die before him at the early age of thirty-six (1768).

At this period, Lord Chesterfield was living a sequestered life on account of his infirmities, of which the most distressing to him was total deafness. Montesquieu, when his sight was failing, had formerly said to him: "I know how to be blind." But Chesterfield admitted that he could not say as much, for he knew not how to be deaf. He wrote oftener to his friends, even to those in France: "Intercourse by letters," he wrote, "is the conversation of the deaf and their sole link to society." He found his greatest consolation in his pretty country-house at Blackheath, to which he had given, in French fashion, the name of Babiole [the Bauble]. There he busied himself in gardening and in cultivating pineapples and melons; he said he "vegetated in company with them":

> "I have vegetated this whole year," he wrote to a lady in Paris (1763), "without pleasures and without troubles: my age and my deafness forbid the first; my philosophy, or perhaps my temperament (they are often mistaken for each other), guarantees me from the latter. I always derive the best I can from the tranquil amusements of gardening, walks, and reading; meantime, I await death without desiring it or dreading it."

He undertook no long works, for which he felt himself too weary, but he sometimes sent agreeable Essays to a periodical called "The World." These Essays confirm his reputation for refinement and urbanity. But nothing approaches the work which, to him, was no work at all; namely: these Letters, which he never expected that any one would read, but which are to-day the fund of his literary wealth.

His old age, beginning rather precociously, dragged slowly along. His wit played in a hundred ways on that sad theme; speaking of himself and one of his friends, Lord Tyrawley, who was equally old and in-

firm: "Tyrawley and I," he said, "have been dead
these two years, but we don't wish it known." Voltaire, who while claiming to be always at death's
door, still remained young, wrote to him (October 21,
1771) this pretty letter, signed "The Old Sick Man of
Ferney":

". . . Enjoy your honourable and fortunate old age, after
passing through the trials of life. Enjoy your mind, and preserve the
health of your body. Of the five senses that we all share, you have
but one that has weakened ; Lord Huntingdon assures me that you
have a good stomach, which is worth more than a pair of ears. Perhaps it might be for me to decide which is the saddest, to be deaf, or
blind, or unable to digest, as I can judge of these three conditions
from thorough knowledge ; but it is long since I gave up deciding
about trifles, and longer still about important things. I confine myself to believing that if you have sun in the beautiful house you have
built for yourself, you must have tolerable moments ; that is all we
can expect at our years. Cicero wrote a fine treatise on old age, but
he did not prove his work by his life; his last years were very unhappy. You have lived longer and more happily than he. You
have had nothing to do with perpetual dictators, or with triumvirs.
Your lot has been, and is still, one of the most desirable in this great
lottery where the lucky tickets are rare, and where the grand prize of
continual happiness was never won by anybody. Your philosophy
has never been upset by chimeras which have sometimes muddled
very good brains. You have never been, in any way, a charlatan, or
the dupe of charlatans ; and I count that as an uncommon merit
which contributes to the shadow of felicity which we enjoy in this
short life."

Lord Chesterfield died on the 24th of March, 1773.
In thus indicating his charming course of worldly
education, it has not seemed to me out of place to
take lessons in good breeding and polite manners,
even in a democracy; and to take them from a man

whose name is so closely connected with those of Voltaire and Montesquieu; a man who, more than any other of his compatriots, showed remarkable predilections for our nation; who more than was reasonable, perhaps, delighted in our agreeable qualities; who also appreciated our graver qualities, and of whom one might say, for all eulogy, that his mind was French, if he had not possessed in the warmth and vivacity of his wit that gift of imagination which is the sign-manual of his race.

Franklin.

Benjamin Franklin.

THERE are certain foreign names which, in some respects, belong to France, or, at least, touch her very closely. The eighteenth century had several which, at certain moments, have been welcomed and almost adopted by us; they would form quite a list from Bolingbroke to Franklin. In naming those two men, I have named two great inoculators in the moral or philosophical order; but Bolingbroke, in exile, and coming at the beginning of the century, affected a few persons only, whereas Franklin, coming later, and at an epoch of general fermentation, operated on a great number. The history of ideas and of public opinion in the years that preceded the French Revolution would be incomplete if we did not pause to study Franklin. I shall try to do so by the help of certain published works upon him, but, above all, by studying his own words.

Franklin wrote his "Memoirs," which, unfortunately, he never finished. The first part, addressed to his son, was written during his stay in England, in 1771; in it he gives a detailed and intimate history of himself until his twenty-fifth year. The great public

affairs in which he was soon more and more deeply
engaged leaving him no leisure, he did not resume
his narrative until urged by friends to do so during his
sojourn in Paris in 1784. This second part of the
" Memoirs," which shows him busy with affairs of
public interest and with the political management of
Pennsylvania, comes down to the period of his first
mission to England in 1757, when, at the age of fifty-
one, he is commissioned by his compatriots to go and
plead their interests against the descendants of William
Penn, who were abusing their rights. From that
period we have nothing more than fragments of narrative and his " Correspondence," which, it is true, is
very complete, and leaves little to be desired. (Nevertheless, the judicious, shrewd, and amiable guide does
not lead us by the hand to the end, and that is a distinct loss. The two parts of the " Memoirs " that we
do possess are fully sufficient, however, to show us
the man himself, and they make the most original and
most profitable reading to be found in this familiar
and wholly modern style of book.

Franklin was a man rightly named, and he well
justified his name ; for that word "Franklin" signified
primitively a free man, a freeholder, enjoying on a
little property of his own a rural and natural life. His
family were natives of Northamptonshire in England,
where for more than three hundred years, they had
possessed a small holding, to the products of which
were added the profits of a forge. These blacksmith

BENJAMIN FRANKLIN
From a portrait by Duplessis

farmers were Protestants of the old stamp, faithful to
the Anglican dogma, even under the persecuting reign
of Queen Mary. Towards the close of the reign of
Charles II, an uncle of Franklin and his father adopted
the doctrines of certain non-conformist preachers.
The father emigrated young, in 1682, carrying wife
and children to America, where he settled at Boston
in New England. Benjamin Franklin was born in
Boston, January 17, 1706, the last son of a numerous
family: two sisters were born after him, making, in
all, sixteen children by two mothers. His father, who
had been a dyer in England, started in Boston a manufactory of soap and candles. He thought at first of
devoting Benjamin to the service of the Church, as the
tenth, or tithe, of his sons; but, his small means not
permitting it, he put him into his own business, and
employed him in cutting wicks and filling moulds
with tallow. Young Franklin had a decided taste for
the sea; he would there have found a career well
suited to the exercise of his natural qualities of boldness, prudence, and constant observation. His father
opposed it. This father, a simple artisan, was, according to his son, a man of strong sense and solid mind,
a good judge in all matters of private or general interest that demanded caution. His advice counted for
much, and the people of his region were not slow,
when need was, to consult him. He died at eighty-
nine years of age; and his wife, Benjamin's mother,
died at eighty-five; the boy, therefore, in his humble

sphere, came of a strong and healthy race; he was its emancipated scion, and he brought it to perfection in himself.

This emancipation of his intellect seems to have suffered neither obstruction nor delay. From childhood he had a passionate love for reading; his father's library, we can well believe, was ill-supplied; it consisted chiefly of books on religious polemics. He read them; but above all, he read " Plutarch's Lives," which, by a lucky chance, was among them. He bought a few books of travels; a little later, a dilapidated volume of Addison's "Spectator" fell into his hands and served him to form a style. Half from recollection, half by invention, he himself tried to write on some of the same subjects; then, comparing what he had written with the original, he corrected his faults, and he fancied sometimes that on points of detail he was not always worsted.

When he read this ragged volume of the "Spectator" he was no longer working in his father's shop. The latter, seeing his repugnance to the business of making candles, and having tried to turn him to some mechanical trade properly so called (upholsterer, turner, etc.), finally apprenticed him to another of his sons, a printer. Benjamin was then twelve years old, and he remained an apprentice till he was twenty-one. His great anxiety was to procure books and to husband the time to read them, all the while doing his work faithfully. Having read, when he was about sixteen, a book which recommended an exclusively vegetable diet, he resolved to try it, as being more philosophical as well as more economical. When his comrades left the printing-office to get their meals, he quickly ate his, which he had frugally prepared himself, and the time he thus gained he spent in reading, studying arithmetic and the first elements of geometry, but above all, in reading Locke on the "Human Understanding," and the "Art of Thinking" by the gentlemen of Port-Royal.

Never did a more vigorous and healthy mind train itself with less cost, and react upon itself with greater freedom and fewer scholastic prejudices. Let us consider what Boston, or any other city in North America, was at that date. There were provinces in which Quakers made nearly one-third of the population; the various Presbyterian or dissenting sects were the majority. From the first consideration that he gave those sects, all, more or less, emanating from Calvin, Franklin was unable to accept their anti-natural and crushing dogmas. He was a freethinker and a deist; and at first he was so with that fresh ardour and need of proselyting which is so natural to youth. He liked arguments on such subjects, which sharpened his dialectic subtlety, but, little by little, he corrected himself of that tendency. Having obtained a copy of the "Memorable Sayings" of Socrates, by Xenophon, he took pleasure in striving to reproduce its method; he owned afterwards that he sometimes abused it. He amused himself by leading the person he talked with into making concessions of which the latter did not foresee the consequences, and then he triumphed in the inextricable muddle into which he had led him. One of the master-printers (Keimer), for whom he afterwards worked in Philadelphia, had been caught so often, that finally he refused to answer Franklin's simplest questions without first asking him, " What are you aiming to infer ? " This rather Scotian and sophistical method, which Socrates himself does not seem to me to have escaped wholly, was one of the perversities of Franklin's youth ; he cured himself gradually, limiting the expression of his thought to the dubitable form, and avoiding a dogmatic appearance. He had reflected much on the manner of persuading men through their own interests, and he recognised that for that end we must not seem too sure of our own opinion; men will agree better and consent more readily to receive from us what they think they partly find in themselves.

Montesquieu, in the *Lettres Persanes,* speaks of a person with a positive and dictatorial tone—such as we still know in these days: "I found myself lately," writes Rica to Usbek, " in company with a man very content with himself. In one quarter of an hour he had decided three questions of morals, four historical problems, and five points of physics. I never before met so universal a *decisionist."* Franklin was quite the contrary of that man. He ended by suppressing in his vocabulary the words *certainly, undoubtedly:*

"I adopted in their place," he says, "'I conceive,' 'I presume,' 'I imagine,' that such a thing is thus or thus; or else I say: 'It seems to me at present.' When a person puts forward something that I believe to be an error, I refuse myself the pleasure of contradicting him promptly, and instantly demonstrating the absurdity of his proposition; in replying, I begin by observing that in certain cases or circumstances, his opinion might be just, but that, in the present case, it *seemed to me* that there might be some difference, etc. I soon found the advantage of this change of tone. The conversations I had were more agreeable; the modest manner in which I put forth my opinions procured them a readier reception and less contradiction; I had less mortification myself when I found out I was wrong; and I was more able to make others see that they were wrong and bring them to agree with me when I was right. This method, which I did not adopt without doing some violence to my natural inclination, became to me in the long run easy, and so habitual that perhaps no one, for the last fifty years, has heard a dogmatic expression escape my lips."

He attributes to this precaution—after his known character for integrity—the influence he obtained with his compatriots in his various proposals for the public good. He tells us his secret; the artifice is simple and innocent, it comes originally from Socrates; let us beware of confounding it, in any case, with the deception of Ulysses.

Franklin's brother began, about the year 1720, or 1721, to print a newspaper; it was the second that appeared in America. Benjamin, who saw its making, who heard the talk of those who contributed by their pens, and who himself worked at printing it, had a desire to write a few articles, but feeling sure they would be rejected with contempt on account of his youth, if the writer were known, he sent them anonymously, disguising his writing. The articles succeeded, he rejoiced inwardly, and kept the secret until he finished all that he then had to say. His brother was soon after arrested and imprisoned by order of the President of the General Assembly of the province for having inserted an opposition political article; and was released only under prohibition of continuing to print his newspaper. He evaded the prohibition by issuing the paper under the name of his brother, young Benjamin, to whom he returned, as a mere form, his bond of apprenticeship with the release therefrom. It was settled, however, by a new agreement intended to to be kept secret, that Benjamin should continue to serve as apprentice to the end of the term originally agreed upon. Here we find the confession of a fault by Franklin, or what he calls, in his language as a printer, "one of the first errata of my life." Ill-treated by his brother, who was violent and sometimes came to blows, he resolved, after one of these quarrels, to quit him, and he did so on the warranty of the certificate of release from apprenticeship, knowing well that his brother would not dare to produce the secret agreement.

The confessions that Franklin makes of his wrongdoings (and we find three or four in these years of his youth) have a character of sincerity and simplicity which leaves no doubt as to the nature of the man who makes them. When Rousseau, in his "Confessions," makes such avowals, he is very near to boasting of them at the moment he confesses them. Franklin, who, in any case, has only slight wrong-doings with which to reproach himself, is less severe upon his actions and does not boast of them at all. He says, in a charming manner, at the beginning of his "Memoirs," that he would have "no objection to live the same career over again, from beginning to end, claiming only the privilege that all authors have, to correct in the second edition the faults of the first."

On leaving his brother's printing-office, he could not find work in Boston and started for New York, thence for Philadelphia, which became his city of adoption. He arrived in a pitiable plight, in workmen's clothes, soaked with rain, having rowed the boat during the crossing. He had little money left in his pocket, yet he wished to pay his passage to the boatman. They refused at first to take it, saying he had paid his way by rowing; but he insisted on giving them his shilling in coppers. "Men," he remarked, "are sometimes more generous when they have little than when they have much; perhaps to prevent people from suspecting how little they have." He made his entry into the city carrying three loaves of bread which he had just bought, one under each arm and eating the third. He passed thus before the house of his future wife, Miss Read, who was at her door, and thought his appearance extraordinary. He was now seventeen years of age, and alone in a strange city to make his way in the world.

He found employment with one of the two printers of the city, and soon saw that both knew little of their business. He was noticed by the governor, Sir William Keith. In those new countries there was less distance between the classes than there was in the old countries. The governor, who seemed to take a fancy to him, made him, secretly, fine promises and great offers to induce him to set up for himself. After a year's stay, Franklin paid a visit to Boston to obtain his father's permission to go into business for himself. He was well dressed, he had money in his pocket, which he jingled when he went to see his old comrades in the printing-office of his brother, who never forgave him. His father, who did not think him sufficiently mature, and who distrusted a certain tendency he fancied he saw in him to satire and pamphlet-writing, turned a deaf ear to a letter from Governor Keith, but did not forbid his son to return to Philadelphia. Franklin returned, and, while remaining a journeyman-printer, continued to train himself by study to literary composition; he made friends of certain young men of the city who liked reading, as he did, he knew Miss Read, and paid a little court to her; then, tempted again by the promises of the governor, who talked to him incessantly of setting up in business for himself, he resolved to go to England and buy the outfit for a small printing-office.

He embarked on this first voyage to England at the close of the year 1724, being then nineteen years of age. He found, on arriving, that the pretended letters of introduction given him by Governor Keith were lures or decoys; in short, he had been hoaxed. He found work in the great printing-office of Palmer, then with Watts, perfected himself in his trade, moralised to his comrades, tried to teach them a better hygiene, a more healthy regimen, and preached to them by example. He met a few men of Letters. When "composing," as printer, a book on "Natural Religion," by Wollaston, the idea came to him of writing a short metaphysical "Dissertation" to refute some points in the book. This little work, of which a few copies were printed, brought him into relations with certain freethinking men. In short, during this stay of eighteen months in London he launched himself in more ways than one; he learned from several schools; but especially did he mature quickly in practical knowledge of men and of life.

On leaving Philadelphia he had exchanged promises with Miss Read, whom he expected to marry. One of the errors, the errata of his life, was that soon after his arrival in London he wrote a single letter to this very worthy young girl, telling her that it was improbable he should return to Philadelphia as soon as they had expected. From this indifference it resulted that the young lady, urged by her mother, married another man, was very unhappy, and Franklin did

not marry her till some years later when, her first
marriage being dissolved, she had recovered her
liberty.

Here a reflection begins to dawn upon us. An ideal
is lacking in this healthy, upright, able, frugal, laborious nature of Franklin—the fine flower of enthusiasm,
tenderness, sacrifice,—all that is the dream, and also
the charm and the honour of poetic natures. In what
I have to say of him I shall not assume to depreciate or
belittle him in any way; I simply seek to define him.
Let us take him in the matter of love. Young, he
feels no irresistible, all-constraining sentiment; he sees
Miss Read, she suits him; he conceives both respect
and affection for her; but all is subordinate to what is
possible and reasonable. Arrived in England, having
exchanged promises with her, he begins to doubt
whether they can be fulfilled; he tells her so honestly,
without otherwise showing much grief. " The fact
is," he says, by way of excuse, " the expenses I have
had to incur make it impossible for me to pay my passage." Later, when he returns to Philadelphia, with
good prospects, and sees Miss Read, sad, melancholy,
a widow, or nearly so, he returns to her; but not
until he has himself missed another marriage, and because he thinks the state of celibacy full of vices and
inconveniences. ''Marriage, after all," he says, '' is
the natural state of man. An unmarried man is not a
complete human being: he resembles one-half of a
pair of scissors without its other half, and conse-

quently, is not even half as useful as if the two were put together."

He tries to correct his first mistake and succeeds. Married at twenty-four years of age, he finds in his wife for many years a tender and faithful companion, who aids him much in the work of his shop. That is his ideal: do not ask more of him. When he is old and in Paris, he spends a day at Auteuil, talking nonsense with Mme. Helvétius; telling her he wished to marry her and that she was very foolish to resolve to be faithful to her late husband, the philosopher. The next morning he writes a very pretty letter to her, in which he pretends that he has been transported in a dream to the Elysian Fields; where he finds Helvétius in person, who has married again, and is much astonished to hear that his former wife on earth persists in being faithful to his memory. While he talks very pleasantly with Franklin, in comes the new Mme. Helvétius, bringing coffee which she has prepared with her own hands:

"Instantly," writes the lively old man, "I recognised her as Madame Franklin, my former American wife. I claimed her; but she said, coldly: 'I was your good wife for forty-nine years and four months, almost half a century; be satisfied with that. I have formed here a new connection which will last through eternity.'— Displeased with this refusal of my Eurydice, I at once resolved to quit those thankless shades and return to this good world to see the sun and you. Here I am; let us avenge ourselves."

All that is gay, a pretty, piquant, social jest, but the lack of sentiment reveals itself.

Also, there is a flower, a bloom, of religion, of honour, of chivalry, which we must not ask of Franklin. He is not obliged to comprehend chivalry, and he gives himself no trouble to do so. When the founding of the Society of the Cincinnati is in question, he opposes it with good reasons, but he makes no reservation in favour of chivalry, considered historically and in the past. He forgets Lord Falkland, that perfect result of delicate and gallant chivalry grafted upon ancient loyalty. He applies to the examination of chivalry a method of moral arithmetic which he is fond of employing, and starting from the principle that "a son derives only half from the family of his father, the other half from that of his mother," he proves by figures that in nine generations (supposing a pure, intact genealogy) there remains in the person who inherits the title of "Knight" only the five-hundred-dozenth part of the original knight or noble. He brings everything down to arithmetic and strict reality, assigning no part to human imagination.

So with religion. He returns to it, after his early freethinking, in a sincere and touching manner. I know no deist who shows a more living sense of faith than Franklin; he seems to believe, on all occasions, in a Providence actually present and perceptible. But there again, what was it that most contributed to bring him back to religion? It was seeing that, during the time when he was decidedly a sceptic, he failed in fidelity to a trust, and that two or three other sceptics of his acquaintance allowed themselves to do him certain wrongs involving money and integrity. "I began to suspect," he says, "that these doctrines, though they may be true, are not very profitable." Thus he returns to religion through utility. The useful is always, and preferably, his measure.

Franklin is by nature above all the anxieties of a Childe-Harold, all the susceptibilities of a Chateaubriand. We, of the hasty and vivacious French race, would like him to have had a little of ourselves in him. The devotion of a Chevalier d'Assas, the passion of a Chevalier Des Grieux, the folly of Parisina or Ariel, all that is in our thoughts, and we feel that the wings to soar are lacking, at any rate in youth, when a man cannot pass at will from one of these worlds to the other. Nevertheless, let us see Franklin just as he was in his moral beauty, and in his true stature. That judicious, firm, shrewd, comprehending, honest man will be unshaken, immovable, when injustice assails him and his compatriots. He will also do all in his power, for years, with the mother-country, to enlighten opinion, and prevent extreme measures; until the last instant he will strive to bring about a reconciliation founded on equity. One day when a man of great influence in England, Lord Howe, gave him hopes (on the very eve of the rupture), a tear of joy rolled down his cheek; but when injustice hardened itself and an obstinate pride plugged its ears, then the purest and most invincible of passions swept him

along, and he who thought that "all peace is good
and all war evil" was for war then, for the holy war
of a legitimate and patriotic defence.

In the ordinary current of his life Franklin is ever
the most gracious, smiling, and persuasive of utili-
tarians.   "I approve, for my part, that people should
amuse themselves now and then with poesy," he says,
"as much as is needed to perfect their style; but not
beyond that."   Yet he himself, without being aware
of it, has a form of imagination and a way of saying
things that make him not only the philosopher, but
sometimes the poet of common sense.   In a little Diary
of travel, written at the age of twenty (1726) during
his return from London to Philadelphia, speaking of I
know not what atrocious description that was given
him of a former Governor of the Isle of Wight, he says:

"What surprised me was that the old fellow of a porter spoke to
me of the governor with a perfect notion of his character. In a word,
I believe it to be impossible that a man, had he the craft of a devil, can
live and die a wretch and yet conceal it so well that he could take with
him to the grave the reputation of an honourable man. It will always
happen that, by one accident or another, he is unmasked. Truth and
sincerity have a certain natural and distinctive lustre which can never
be counterfeited; they are like fire and flame, no one can paint them."

Pointing out a method of economy that would en-
sure having money at all times in our pocket—a
method that consists (independently of the fundamental counsel of work and honesty) in "spending
always a penny less than the net profit," he adds:

"In that way thy flat pocket will begin to swell and will no longer cry out that its belly is empty. Thou wilt not be insulted by thy creditors or harassed by want, gnawed by hunger, or numbed by nakedness. The whole horizon will shine brighter to thine eyes, and pleasure will gush from the innermost recesses of thy heart "

If ever the doctrine of economy came into the world with contentment and mirth and a sort of familiar poesy of expression, we must look for it in Franklin. An inward warmth of feeling animates his prudence; a ray of sun lights up and cheers his honesty.

Franklin returned to Philadelphia from his first journey to England in 1726; and, after a few attempts, he established himself as a printer at twenty-one years of age, first with a partner, but soon alone. He makes a sort of moral inventory of himself at this decisive moment of his life. He enumerates his principles, from which he never afterwards departed. "I was convinced that *truth, sincerity,* and *integrity* in the relations between men are of the first importance for the happiness of life, and I formed the written resolution, which is always placed in my Diary-book, to practise them as long as I live." To this real and fundamental probity, Franklin took pains to add the legitimate social profit that accrued from it. But, while observing the constant little cares that he gave and the minute pains he took to make himself more and more virtuous within, and more and more considered without we must never separate in him the appearance from the reality. He was, if you will, the shrewdest and most prudent of honest men, but also the least hypocritical.

" In order to insure," he says, " my credit and my reputation as a merchant, I took care to be laborious and economical not only in reality, but also to avoid all appearance to the contrary.   I clothed myself simply; I was never seen in any of the resorts of idle company.   I joined no fishing or hunting parties; it is true that a book sometimes debauched me from my work; but that was rarely, and at home, without causing scandal.   To show that I was not above my trade, I sometimes took to the printing-office, through the streets on a wheelbarrow, the paper I had bought in the shops.

Franklin's wheelbarrow has sometimes been cited in contrast with his future destiny; but, as we see, it was a legitimate little device on his part, rather than a necessity of his position.

About this time, Franklin formed a club of the educated young men whom he knew, to discuss and improve themselves in culture of mind and in the search after truth.   After writing some articles in the "Journal" already established in Philadelphia, he was not long in having a newspaper of his own, the "Gazette," which he printed; thus obtaining the principal means of influence and of civilisation in the city and in the province.

In order to judge Franklin as a literary man, an economist, and inventor of several useful inventions, we must picture clearly to ourselves this young man of his time and place, in the midst of compatriots who were rough, unequally educated, and little trained in the arts of life.   Franklin appears among them as an indefatigable educator and civiliser.   In the first articles that he wrote weekly for the "Gazette," he endeavoured to polish manners and customs, to cor-

rect bad and uncivil habits, coarse jesting, visits too
long and intrusive, and persistent popular prejudices
inconsistent with good practices. We must not
ask of these Essays a general purpose that they have
not. Later, in diplomatic relations, Lord Shelburne
when negotiating with Franklin observed that his
principal characteristic in dealing with public affairs
was, "not to embarrass himself by trying to bring
about events, but only to profit well by those that
happened," adding that he had "the science of ex-
pectant medicine." In the first part of Franklin's life,
although he seems full of inventions and a great pro-
moter of all matters of public utility, he is so only to
the degree that is immediately applicable; he never
goes beyond that limit; he is practical in all things.

"It is an amazing thing," remarks a writer of the
Franklin school, "that one of the passions that men
have less of and which it is most difficult to develop
in them, is the passion for their own comfort and
convenience." Franklin did all he could to inoculate
his compatriots with that passion, and make them
take an interest in the useful arts and thus ameliorate
their lives. He contributed not only to found, by sub-
scription, the first public library, the first Academic
Society (which became the University of Pennsylvania), and the first hospital, but he showed men
how to warm their homes by economical stoves, how
to pave their streets, how to sweep them by day,
and how to light them by night with lamps of con-

venient shape. What he did not invent himself, he
perfected; and the idea, passing through him, became
simplified, yet more ingenious. When entering into
such minute details, he feels the need of excusing himself; but at the same time he thinks that nothing is to
be despised that is serviceable every day to everybody. "Human happiness is less the result of great
prizes of good fortune, which rarely come, than of
the many little enjoyments that reproduce themselves
daily."

During these years of his youth and of the first half
of his life, not a single project of public interest in
Pennsylvania came up that his hand was not in it.
His fellow-citizens knew this well, and when some
new enterprise was proposed to them for subscrip-
tion their first words were: "Have you consulted
Franklin? what does he think of it?" And he, before proposing anything directly, was careful to prepare the public mind by writing something about it
in his "Gazette." He avoided signing his name, however, in order to spare the self-love of others. No
one has ever used a newspaper better or more salu-
tarily than he. We may say that he was wily for the
public good. Counsellor, teacher, benefactor of his
city, such, in short, was his rôle before the collision
of the colonies with the mother-country.

He takes pains to inform us that this application to
the general good was carried on without injury to his
private interests; in no wise does he think that in

order to perform public duties well we should be content to do our own badly. He attained, by l'aborious ways, to an honest fortune and to an independence that placed him in a position to follow his tastes for study and for the sciences.

During his whole life, Franklin made a steady and progressive advance, which was guided by an unvarying plan. When about twenty-four years of age, he conceived the bold and difficult project of attaining to *moral perfection,* and to do so he set to work like a skilful physician who, by means of very simple and right measures which he combines, obtains quite often great results. He explains to us in detail his almost commercial method: his memorandum book of thirteen virtues (temperance, silence, order, resolution, economy, etc.), and the little synoptical list, on which he specified his faults every day of the week, occupying each week with a single virtue especially; then passing to another, so as to make the course complete in thirteen weeks; making four courses of virtue a year:

"Just," he says, "as a man who has a garden to weed does not undertake to pull up all the weeds at once (which would exceed his capacity and strength), but he works on one patch first, and having finished that he goes to the next—in the same way do I hope for the encouraging pleasure of seeing on my pages the progress made in a virtue, in proportion as I free those pages from their bad points, until at last, after a certain number of turns I shall have the happiness of seeing my note-book clean and clear."

It is difficult for us not to smile in seeing this Art of Virtue thus set up for his individual use, and to hear

him tell us, moreover, that at this same epoch in his
life, he had conceived the plan of forming, among
the men of all nations, a "party united for virtue."
There, indeed, Franklin shows that he had his hidden
corner of dreams and of excessive moral ambition,
from which the most practical of men are not always
exempt. He was much struck with the immense
changes in the world that a single man of reasonable
capacity can bring about when he applies himself
with continuity and fixity to his object, when "he
makes it his business." In his hours of speculative
musing he very willingly let his thoughts run, sometimes in the moral order, sometimes in the natural
science order, to conjectures and hypotheses that were
very bold and very far-reaching. But for him who
mastered his passions and governed himself by prudence, such vagaries of speculation, such escapes into
space, had no dangers; he returned, in the practice of
daily life, to experience and to the possible; in which
his disciples, as we shall see, did not always follow
him.

Nothing, therefore, came to mar or thwart his early
and well-considered plans for the amelioration of the
moral and social state of his compatriots. Among his
means of action, we must place the Almanacs that
he published from 1732, under the name of Richard
Saunders, otherwise called Poor Richard. Franklin
had by nature the popular gift of thinking in proverbs and of speaking in parables. I will here recall

only a few of the best-known proverbs that he coined and put in circulation:

> "Idleness is like rust, it consumes faster than use wears out. The Key that is used is always bright."
>
> "Little as you may love life, do not waste time; it is the stuff life is made of."
>
> "A labourer on his legs is taller than a gentleman on his knees."
>
> "If you are labourers you will never die of hunger: hunger may look in at the door of the man who works, but it cannot enter."
>
> "The second vice is lying; the first is to run in debt. Lies mount astride of debt and ride it."
>
> "Lent is very short for those who have to pay at Easter."
>
> "Pride is a beggar that cries as loud as want, and is much more insolent."
>
> "Poverty often deprives a man of all spirit and all virtue; it is difficult for an empty sack to stand up straight."

More than one of these proverbs, both in meaning and in turn of phrase, recall Hesiod and La Fontaine; but especially Hesiod, speaking in prose and in modern fashion, among a rude and practical race which had never been visited by the Muses.

As for the fables and tales, they were an habitual form of speech or writing with Franklin; everything supplied him with matter or pretext. In his old age, he scarcely spoke consecutively unless he were telling a tale. Some of these tales when written down may seem rather childish; others are very pleasing; but most of them lose much in not coming from his half-smiling lips.

He began to enter public affairs, properly so-called, in 1736, when thirty years of age, as secretary of the General Assembly. It was for him a very important position in itself, and also for the printing matter that it procured for him. The first year he was elected without opposition; but the second year an influential member spoke against him, and declared that he should oppose and thwart him in future. Franklin imagined a means of winning him over without solicitation or baseness, namely, to make this member do him a little service:

" Having heard," he says, "that he had in his library a very rare and curious book, I wrote him a line in which I expressed my great desire to look over the volume, and asked if he would do me the favour to lend it to me for a few days. He sent it to me immediately, and I returned it at the end of the week, with another note, warmly expressing my gratitude for the favour. The next time we met in the Assembly he spoke to me (which he had never done before), with much civility; and after that he always showed an eagerness to serve me on all occasions, so that we became great friends and our friendship lasted till his death. This is only another proof of the truth of an old maxim that I once learned, which says: ' He who has once done you a service will be more inclined to do you another, than the man whom you have yourself benefited.' "

It was by such degrees of moral sagacity, of judicious conduct, of rectitude and skill, love for the public weal and for good understanding in all things, that Franklin prepared himself, little by little, and without knowing it, for the important rôle that events were reserving for him. But, worthy and respected as he was among his own people, it would have been difficult to divine in him, at this date, the man of whom Pitt was one day, in defending him from insult, to say so magnificently in the House of Lords, that he was a man "who did honour not only to the English nation, but to human nature.'

Franklin's "Memoirs" are full of interest for all those who have had a toilsome early life, and have experienced the difficulties of existence and the lack of generosity in men, but who are, nevertheless, not embittered, not posing as misanthropes, nor as virtue unrecognised; not spoiled either, nor fallen into the corruption and intrigues of self-interest; men who have preserved themselves equally from the evil of Jean-Jacques and from the vice of Figaro, who, wise, prudent, discreet, starting from hard and honest gains, putting cautiously, but boldly if need be, one foot before the other, have become, in various degrees, useful, honourable, and even important members of the great human Company—to all such, and to all whom the same circumstances await, these "Memoirs" are a source of observation that will always be applicable, and of truth that will always be felt.

I am not writing the life of Franklin; it is written by himself, and where he stops we must look for its continuation in the excellent work of Jared Sparks, which ought to be translated into French. My desire is to show the philosopher and the American statesman in his early conditions, with an existence already so full before his arrival and his favour in France, and before he embraced Voltaire. It is thus only that we shall feel how different were those two men and the two races which they represent.

Franklin was nearly seventy-one years of age when he came to France at the close of 1776. He was fifty-one when his compatriots in Philadelphia chose him, in 1757, to be their agent in England. This second time that he went there he appeared as the most distinguished man of his province, already known in Europe for his experiments in electricity, dating ten years back. The mission with which he was charged, and which is not to be confounded with his later political mission in 1764, was wholly special and provincial. William Penn, the coloniser and legislator of Pennsylvania, in the Charters and fundamental agreements which he had obtained from the Crown, or had himself granted to the immigrant population, had carefully stipulated for his own private interests and those of his family, together with the civil and religious liberties of the colonists. His sons, owners of large territorial possessions, who were invested with the extraordinary right of appointing the governors of the province, assumed that their estates were exempted from taxation. The Assembly of Pennsylvania opposed so flagrant an inequality, and Franklin was commissioned by that body to go to England and plead the cause of the public rights against the sons of William Penn, by making an appeal to the officers of the Crown. The interest of Pennsylvania, at that time, was that the Crown should intervene more directly than it did in colonial administration, and that it should free the province from the species of petty feudality that entailed these profits on one family.

During the last years of his stay in Philadelphia, Franklin had become more and more respected in the province. Elected a member of the Assembly, of which he had long been secretary, charged, moreover, with the organisation and management of the Posts, he had rendered great services to the English army in the war with Canada (1754). Interposing between the Assembly, not warlike because it was chiefly composed of Quakers, and the English general, he had procured carts and provisions, made contracts with markets, in short, had constituted himself purveyor for the army, without other motive than that of saving the province from military exactions, and doing his duty as a faithful subject. The disasters that followed had not surprised him; knowing the presumptuous character or the incapacity of the leaders first employed in the expedition, he had predicted the result.

After his arrival in England, he was consulted on this war with Canada, and on the means of better conducting it. He did not see Mr. Pitt, the prime minister, who was then a personage of great importance and seldom accessible, but he communicated with his secretaries, and did not cease to press upon them the necessity and the urgency of taking Canada from France; pointing out at the same time the ways and means of succeeding. He even wrote a pamphlet on the subject. To take and keep Canada was to him as favourite a thought as the destruction of Carthage was to Cato; he urged it not only as a colonist, but as an Englishman of Old England, ardently working for the future grandeur of the empire. At this period of his life Franklin knew no difference between his two countries; he had a consciousness of the growing and illimitable destinies of the young America; he saw it, from the St. Lawrence to the Mississippi, peopled within a century by British subjects; but, if Canada remained French, this development of the British Empire in America would be constantly held in check, and the Indian tribes would find a powerful auxiliary, always ready to gather them into confederation, and hurl them on the colonies.

In seeing the ardour that Franklin puts into this question, which he considers national, we understand how, fifteen years later, when the rupture came between the colonies and the mother-country, he had a moment of keen anguish, when, without being shaken in his determination, he shed tears; for he had, in his most virile years, himself contributed to consolidate England's grandeur; and he could say, in his last letter to Lord Howe (July, 1776):

" Long did I endeavour, with sincere and indefatigable zeal, to preserve from all accident the glory of that beautiful and noble porcelain vase, the British Empire; for I knew that, once broken, the pieces could never keep even a part of the strength and value they had when they formed a single whole, and that a perfect reunion could hardly be hoped for in coming years."

That word "hardly" [à peine], which seems to have a slight gleam of hope, was in reality, at that date, merely a politeness.

But, in 1759, Franklin was still only an Englishman from the other side of the Atlantic, to whom the mother-country did honour by a distinguished welcome. In the intervals of leisure left him by the incidents and prolonged delays of his mission, he cultivated the sciences and learned men. He visited Scotland in the summer of 1759, and there became intimate with men of the first order, with whom that country was then well provided, forming an intellectual group of a distinct character, composed of the historians Robertson, David Hume, Ferguson, etc.:

"In short, I must say," wrote Franklin on his return from this journey to Edinburgh, " that the six weeks I have just passed are, I think, those of the fullest and the *most dense* happiness I have ever had at any time in my life. The agreeable and instructive society that I found there has left so sweet an impression on my memory, that if strong ties did not draw me elsewhere, I think that Scotland would be the country I should choose in which to spend the rest of my days."

David Hume, writing to thank Franklin for sending him, at his request, instructions as to the making of lightning-rods, ends his letter thus:

"I am very sorry that you think of soon quitting our hemisphere. America has sent us many good things, gold, silver, sugar, tobacco, indigo, etc.; but you are the first philosopher and the first really great man of Letters whom we owe to her. It is our fault that we do not keep you; which proves that we are not in agreement with Solomon, that ' wisdom is far above gold '; for we take good care never to send back an ounce of the metal when we have once laid our fingers on it."

Franklin wittily replies to this letter, in the style of an economist:

" Your compliment of *gold* and *wisdom* is very kind to me, but a little unjust to your country. The different value of each thing in different parts of the world is in proportion, as you know, to the demand for it. They tell us that in Solomon's time gold and silver were in such abundance that they had no more value in his land than the stones in the street. You have here to-day precisely such an abundance of wisdom. You should not therefore blame your countrymen if they do not desire more than they have; and, if I have a little, it is only just that I should take it where, by reason of rarity, it will probably find a better market."

We can readily understand Franklin's liking for the Lettered world of Edinburgh; he had in him a philosophy both penetrating and circumspect, subtle and practical, and an industrious as well as lofty observation. As author of moral Essays, and also as experimenter and man of science, as a clear and simple expositor of his methods and his results, it certainly seems as if Scotland were his intellectual country. He wrote something on " Old Scotch Melodies" and the delightful impression they made upon the soul. He tried, in a very acute analysis, much as a Dugald Stewart might have done later, to explain why those old melodies are so charming. His remarks on this subject bear the stamp of that ingenious simplicity of thought which is the sign of a truly philosophical mind. Nevertheless, in the matter of music, as in all else, it is evident that what Franklin likes is simplicity; he wants music conformed to the

sense of the words and the feeling expressed, and this
with as little effort as possible. But, there is a kingdom of Sounds, as there is one of Colour and of Light;
and this magnificent kingdom in which the Handels
and the Pergolèses rise and soar, as in the other we
see the Titians and the Rubenses float and play, Franklin was not formed to enter; he who invented and
perfected the harmonica remained in the principles
of elementary music. In nothing did he like luxury;
and in the fine arts˙ luxury is richness and talent
itself.

In like manner, in religion, and in the worship of
public adoration which the peoples render to Divinity,
there is, if I may dare to say so, a kingdom of Prayer
and of Hymns. There, again, Franklin tried to apply
his method. Taking the Book of Common Prayer,
used by Protestants, he endeavoured to make it, according to his ideas, more reasonable, more moral; and for
that purpose he cut out, and corrected certain parts;
he laid hands on the Psalms, he abridged David. He
who in certain respects seemed so truly to feel, and
even imitate in a way, the parables of the Gospel, he
does not feel nor understand fully either Job or David.
Their obscurities impede him; their words that issue
partly from the clouds bewilder him; he requires that
all be comprehensible; he levels, as best he can, Mount
Sinai. And yet, the moment we accept, as he had the
wisdom to do, public worship and adoration, are there
not in˙the soul of man emotions, in human destiny

mysteries and depths which call for and justify the thunders of the Divine word ? However that may be, he could not, and did not, admire sublime disorder, and he did his best to prevent the lightnings of Moses from descending upon us, precisely as he had warded off the other lightning with his rods. Job, David, Bossuet, old Handel, and Milton go far beyond Franklin, and yet, leader and zealous introducer of the rival and practical race, if you let him alone he will gently compel them to reckon with him.

Here would be the place, were I fitted for it, to speak of him as a man of science, and to mark his position and, so to speak, his level among great men. An excellent English critic (Jeffrey) dropped a word on that point in the only direction in which writers like myself can approach it. Franklin was not a geometrician, he was solely a physicist, a natural philosopher; his works in that line have a character of simplicity, of delicate and searching analysis, of easy and decisive experiments, of clear reasoning within the mental compass of every one, with luminous, gradual, and convincing demonstration. He goes as far as he can with the instrument of common language, and without employing calculations and formulas. Science with him is inventive, and he makes it familiar. "A singular felicity of induction," said Sir Humphry Davy, "guides all his researches, and by very small means he establishes great truths." He did not restrain himself in conjectures and hypotheses whenever natural ones presented themselves to his mind; and he allowed himself to make very bold ones to explain some of the great phenomena of nature; but he did so without attaching other importance to them than that which could properly be granted to speculative conjectures and theories.

The turn of his mind, however, always brought him back to the practical, and to the use that could be made of science for the safety and comfort of life. Thus it was that his general discoveries in electricity led to the invention of the lightning rod. He never, at any time, crossed the Atlantic without devoting himself to experiments on the temperature of sea-water, or on the swiftness of vessels; experiments destined to be of use long after him to future navigators. He liked above all, and searched for, applications of science for domestic use. While guaranteeing buildings from lightning, he invented for the interior of houses convenient, economical chimneys that did not smoke. The scientific and learned man in Franklin always remembered the handicraftsman, the workman, and the industry. Man has been defined in general in many ways, of which some are regal and magnificent; but as for him, he limited his definition to that of "an animal who makes tools."

He had faith in experimental science and in its discoveries; he often regretted, towards the end of his life, that he was not born a century later, that he might have enjoyed all that would then have been discovered.

" The rapid progress that *true* science makes in our day," he wrote to Priestley, February 8, 1780,

" gives me sometimes a regret that I was born so early. It is impossible to imagine the degree to which the power of man over matter may be carried in a thousand years. Possibly men will have learned how to disengage from great bodies their weight, and give them an absolute lightness which will facilitate transportation. Agriculture may diminish its toil and double its product. All diseases may, by sure means, be prevented or cured, without excepting even that of old age, and our life might prolong itself at will to greater length than before the Deluge."

Franklin, in speaking thus, may have smiled a little, but it is very certain that he believed some of these things at heart. When he does dream he has vast horizons, and just such dazzling perspectives; it is the style of illusion of many men of science. One part at least of his predictions is now on the road to being realised.[1] At the same time, he has the good sense to regret that moral science is not in a parallel path towards perfection, and that it makes but little progress among men.

After a stay of five years in England, having obtained, if not all the points of his demand, at least the recognition of the essential principles for which he had

---

[1] Written in 1852, seventy-three years after Franklin wrote to Priestley. What would Sainte-Beuve (not to speak of Franklin) say now, fifty-three years later, to deep-sea cables, wireless telegraphy, electricity lighting our houses, driving our carriages, cooking our dinners ! The spirit of Franklin's predictions is more than fulfilled, but his own works are not obsolete. The " Franklin stove "—a portable open fireplace, made of iron, in which logs of wood are burned, as on a hearth,—are still much used in country regions.—TR.

come to plead in the name of his countrymen, Franklin embarked, at the end of August, 1762, for America. At the moment of setting foot on the vessel he wrote to Lord Kames, a Scotch friend of his:

" I cannot leave this happy isle and the friends I have made here, without extreme regret, though I go to a country and to a people that I love. I depart from the old world to the new, and I fancy that I feel somewhat as a man does in passing from this world to the next: grief at departure, dread of the passage, hope in the future."

Franklin returns often to this idea of death, and always in a gentle, almost smiling manner. He considered it as a crossing, to be sailed in obscurity and doubt as to its length; or else as the sleep of a night, as natural and necessary to the human constitution as the other sleep. "We shall rise fresher in the morning."

Reaching America, welcomed by his countrymen, and caught again into the current of public affairs, Franklin often gives a glance of remembrance to those years in England, so well employed, and where friendship and science had been so much to him. He feels at once, on arriving among his own people in Philadelphia, the difference of the two societies and the two cultures. He writes to Miss Mary Stevenson, his charming and serious pupil, in whose family he had lodged while in London:

" Of all the enviable things that England possesses, that which I envy most is its society. How that little island which, if compared with America, is like a stepping-stone laid across a brook, scarcely higher above the water than is needed to keep the shoe dry, how, I say, does that little island manage to collect, almost in every neighbourhood, more sensible, intelligent, and elegant minds than we can gather through hundreds of leagues of our best forests ? "

He ends, however, by expressing a hope that the arts, ever tending westward, would some day cross the great ocean, and, after they have first provided for the necessities of life, would begin to think of its embellishment.

Franklin, elected member of the Assembly of Pennsylvania, and director-general of Posts, passed more than two years in taking a most active part in local affairs. In the Assembly he was leader of the Opposition; that is to say, he continued to speak for the interests of the population against the privileges of the proprietors, the sons of Penn, represented by the governor. He was appointed, in the end, President of the Assembly. At the same time he paid attention to his administration of the Posts, and formed a military association to control some serious disturbances that took place. The dwellers on the frontiers, often exposed to the attacks of Indians, and grown fanatical in their desire for vengeance, made attacks themselves, unexpectedly, and exterminated whole tribes of inoffensive and friendly Indians. Such summary executions, when the idea of them arises in America, (and it does arise sometimes) meet but little hindrance, because of the lack of an armed force. Franklin contributed at that time, with all his ability and all his energy, to make up for the powerlessness of the governor. He felt that the weak side of democracy and of the form of government that sprang from it lay there; he says it, again and again, to the end of his life and after America has given herself her definitive Constitution (1789): "We have guarded ourselves against an evil to which old States are very subject, namely, the excess of power in governments; but our present danger seems to be the lack of obedience in the governed."

Finally, in the midst of the political contests, already very keen, which Franklin had to sustain in the Assembly and in the elections of Philadelphia, came the news of the famous Stamp Act (1764). In drawing up that bill, the English minister made it very plain that he claimed for the British Parliament the right of taxing the colonies at will, and of imposing duties upon them without their consent. In this conjuncture Franklin was again chosen by his countrymen to be their agent and organ to the Court of London and the British ministry. He left Philadelphia, surrounded by a cavalcade of honour composed of three hundred of his fellow-citizens, who accompanied him to the harbour, where, leaving behind him many devoted friends, and also a goodly number of political enemies, he embarked once more for England (November, 1764). He did not foresee that he was to stay there ten years; which, with his preceding sojourn, made in the end a residence of not less than fifteen years.

Here the scene enlarges, and the subject takes a far

wider range. In Franklin's preceding mission the matter concerned little more than a family suit between the colony and the sons of the coloniser. In the new mission the envoy of Pennsylvania was soon to become the agent and *chargé d'affaires* of the other principal colonies, and to express in their name the prayers and complaints of a nation, very humble at first and very filial, but which already feels its strength, and is determined not to give up its rights. America, at this date, was like a robust adolescent, who is slow in saying to himself, and even in comprehending that he desires to be completely independent: instinct, long repressed, whispers it to him, and at last the day comes when, rising in the morning, he suddenly feels himself a man.

During the ten years residence of Franklin in England, the question passed through many phases, many successive variations, before the final explosion; but we can say, nevertheless, that it never went backward. There was no moment when England was sincerely inclined to yield, or the colonies to give way. The merit of Franklin in this long and ever-memorable struggle was that he never went beyond the spirit of his countrymen but, at that great distance, was able to divine it, and serve it in the exact measure that was suitable. His perspicacity must have early enlightened him as to the inevitable future; but, none the less, he continued his course to the end, and, with unshaken patience, kept his footing.

and drew from the slightest circumstances whatever might conduce to peace and open the way to a settlement. In all that concerns him individually, three principal facts stand forth, and show him publicly before the world with his qualities of strength, prudence, and lofty firmness.

The first of these circumstances was his interrogation before the House of Commons in February, 1766. The new ministry of the Marquis of Rockingham seemed more mildly disposed towards America and ready to give her satisfaction by repealing the Stamp Act. Franklin was summoned before the House to answer any and all questions that might be put to him, either on this particular point or on the American question in general, by the present or former ministers, or by any other member of Parliament. His attitude, his self-possession, the promptitude and propriety of his answers, his profound knowledge of the subject and of the political consequences it involved, his intrepidity in maintaining the rights of his countrymen, his expressions full of point and character, all contributed to make this examination one of the most significant of historical acts and a great prognostic verified by events:—" If the Stamp Act be rescinded," he was asked at the close, " would that induce the Assemblies of the Provinces to recognise the right of Parliament to tax them, and to annul their resolutions?" "No," he replied, " never!"—" Is there no means of compelling them to annul those resolu-

tions ? "—"None that I know of. They will never
do so, unless constrained by force of arms."—"Is
there no power on earth that can bring them to annul
them ?"—"No power, however great it be, can bring
those men to change their opinions." With regard
to the determination taken by the colonies not to
receive any article of English manufacture until the
revocation of the taxes, he was asked: "In what
were the Americans accustomed, up this time, to
take pride ?"—"In making use of the fashions and
the articles of English manufacture."—"And in what
do they now put that pride ?"—"In wearing, and
wearing-out, their old clothes, until they themselves
know how to make new ones."

The second famous circumstance in which he stood
upon the scene was very different in character.
Franklin, closely as he approached, in his literary and
scientific form of mind, his friends of the school of
Edinburgh, had something in him by which he differed from them notably. He had passionate convictions to such a degree that the cold and sceptical
David Hume thought he discovered in him a spirit of
faction, almost bordering on fanaticism. That means
simply that Franklin had a political religion which he
believed in ardently. In the interests of his cause, and
by an action that had more of the citizen than of the
gentleman in it, he thought it his duty to send to
friends in Boston confidential letters, which had been
placed in his hands with some mystery; letters which

proved that the violent measures adopted by England
were advised by certain men in America, especially
by the Governor of Massachusetts, Hutchinson, and by
the Lieutenant-governor, Oliver. The effect of these
letters, which were circulated through the country,
produced before the Assembly at Boston, and recognised to be in the handwriting of the Governor and
of the Lieutenant-governor, was prodigious, and led to
a Petition to the King, transmitted through Franklin,
in defence of which he was summoned on a fixed day
(January 29, 1774) before the Privy Council.

It was there that his enemies awaited him; for by
this time he had many; passions on both sides were
at their height. A crowd of privy councillors, who
seldom attended, were invited as if to a fête; there
were not less than thirty-six present, besides a vast
audience. After a speech made by Franklin's lawyer
in support of the Petition, a speech that was scarcely
heard because the lawyer happened to be hoarse on
that day, the solictor-general, Wedderburn, afterwards Earl of Londsborough, rose to speak. Putting
aside the matter of the Petition, he turned upon Franklin, who was in no way in question: for nearly an
hour he insulted him in regard to the letters, declaring
him to be an incendiary setting fire and flame between
the two countries. He mingled ridicule and sarcasm
in a way to make all the members of the Council roar
with laughter. Franklin sat unmoved, received the
broadside without betraying the slightest emotion,

and retired silently. The next day he was dismissed from the office of director of the Posts in Pennsylvania, hints having been given to him more than once to send in his resignation; to which he replied that it was with him "a principle never to ask, never to refuse, and never to resign an office." In this case, he preferred to lay upon his adversaries the responsibility of the act by which they struck him.

This scene before the Privy Council left a deep impression upon Franklin's soul. He took pleasure in noting that one year, to a day, from that outrage, on the 29th of January, 1775, he received a visit at his house in London from Mr. Pitt, then Lord Chatham, who had made a motion in the House of Lords on affairs in America: "The visit of so great a man, and for an object so important," he says, "flattered my vanity not a little; and this honour gave me all the more pleasure because it occurred one year, to a day, after the other minister had taken such pains to insult me before the Privy Council." On the day of the affair before the Council Franklin was dressed in a complete suit of Manchester velvet. It is related that when presented at the Court of France, four years later, during the first solemn functions of his fortunate and honoured negotiation, he put on designedly the same ceremonial suit, to avenge it and cleanse it, in some degree, from the insults of Mr. Wedderburn. The truth of this statement, which has passed into a sort of legend, has been questioned. I am inclined

to think it true, and to suppose the suit to be the one
mentioned by Mme. Du Deffand in a letter of March,
1778: "Mr. Franklin was presented to the king; he
was accompanied by some twenty insurgents, three or
four of whom wore uniforms. Franklin wore a grey-
ish velvet suit, white stockings, his hair long, spectacles on his nose, and a white hat under his arm."
It was after one of his decisive interviews with the
French ministry, or after this first presentation at
Court, that Franklin wrote: "That suit is henceforth
precious to me; for I wore it when so grossly insulted
by Wedderburn, and now, in the same suit, I have
taken my complete revenge."

The third circumstance in which, as I have said,
Franklin made a brilliant appearance upon the scene
during his mission to London, was the day on which
Lord Chatham made and upheld his motion in the
House of Lords, February 1, 1775. Franklin was
present at the debate as spectator. A fresh and unexpected insult was levelled at him by one of the speakers, Lord Sandwich, who denied that the proposition
could come from an English peer, and

"then," says Franklin, "turning to me who was leaning on the bar,
he added that he believed he had before his eyes the person who had
drawn it up, one of the most cruel and malevolent enemies the country had ever had. This outburst fixed the eyes of a great number of
the lords upon me ; but, as I had no reason to take it to myself, I kept
my countenance as motionless as if my face were made of wood."

When it became Lord Chatham's turn to reply, he
expressed himself about Franklin in the words I have

already quoted, and so magnificently that the latter had difficulty, as he owns, in keeping the same indifferent air and wooden face with which he had just confronted insult.

After this stay of ten years in London, and when the inevitable rupture took place, Franklin returned to America (March, 1775). Henceforth, the "beautiful porcelain vase," as he called it, was broken, and he mourned it. But the man of Old England no longer existed in him. Hostilities began, blood flowed, he lost the last spark of his affection for the country of his fathers; in his acts, in his thoughts we now see only the man and the citizen of the new continent, of that young, emancipated, vast empire, of whose people he is among the first to sign its declaration of independence, and to foretell its grandeur, without one wish to look back or to recede. The position of the United States is critical, but the energetic good sense of Franklin tells him that the hour has come for prudence itself to be rash.

Franklin at this date is seventy years of age. After more than one year passed in active labours and in the most fatiguing missions, having been sent when the winter was scarcely over to rouse Canada, if possible, to insurrrection, he is chosen to go to the Court of France to negotiate with and strive to rally it to the support of the American cause. He sailed, October, 1776, on a sloop of war (not neglecting to make on the voyage, according to his usual custom, observations on marine temperatures), and disembarked upon the coast of Brittany in the Bay of Quibéron, whence he made his way by land to Nantes, arriving in Paris at the end of December. Here it is that, for us, the story of the patriarch of Passy begins; but we could not rightly understand him if we had not seen him as a young man, and then as a mature man, in the completeness of his character and in some of its principal traits.

When he arrived in Paris at the end of December, 1776, his coming, which was destined to become a sojourn of eight and a half years, was instantly made the topic of all conversation. It was not his first visit to France: he had already spent some weeks in Paris in 1767, and again in 1769. Of his first journey he gave an account in a lively letter to his young friend, Mary Stevenson, in which he remarks chiefly upon external matters, the roads, the politeness of the people, the manner of dressing the hair, the rouge worn by women, the mixture of sumptuousness and poverty in the buildings. He had been to Versailles, he tells her; he was presented to the king; he had seen him eat his dinner; Louis XV had spoken to him:

" Enough said about all that," he writes, jestingly, stopping himself as if about to say more ; " for I would not have you think that I was so pleased with this king and queen as to lessen the consideration I have for ours. No Frenchman can surpass me in the idea that my king and queen are the best in the world, and the most amiable."

" Travelling," he says in the same letter, " is a means of prolonging life. It is scarcely a fortnight since we quitted London, but the variety of scenes we have passed through makes that time seem equal to six months spent in one place. I myself have been subjected to greater changes in my person than I should have made in six years at home. I was not in Paris six days before my tailor and hairdresser had transformed me into a French gentleman. Only think what a figure I make with a little bag of hair behind and my ears uncovered ! They tell me I have grown twenty years younger and that I have quite an air of gallantry. . . ."

This Franklin of 1767, thus curled, powdered, and dressed like a Frenchman, differed totally from the purely American Franklin who reappeared in 1776, to ask for the support of the Court of France, in a wholly republican suit and a sable-fur cap, which he kept on his head. It was thus that he first appeared in the salons of the gay world, at Mme. Du Deffand's, beside Mmes. de Luxembourg and de Boufflers. " Picture to yourself," he writes to a friend, "a man as gay as ever, as strong, as vigorous, merely a few years older; very simply dressed, wearing thin grey hair quite flat and coming out below my one *coiffure*—a handsome fur cap, which covers my forehead down almost to my spectacles." However, he did, soon after, suppress the fur cap and continued to the last bareheaded, his hair very spare on the crown, but falling on both sides of his head and neck almost to the shoulders; in short, exactly such as his portraits have fixed indelibly in our memories.

Franklin had long understood French; he set himself to study it in 1733, and could read all books in our language very easily; but he spoke it with difficulty, and this had been an obstacle to his knowing more of French society during his stay in Paris in 1767 and 1769. Mme. Geoffrin, to whom he had a letter from David Hume, had not been able to initiate him, though his arrival was much noticed by scientific men. We find in the "Secret Memoirs," said to be written by Bachaumont, under date of September, 1767: "M. Franklin, that natural scientist, so remarkable for the experiments in electricity which he has made in America, and brought to the most surprising point of perfection, is in Paris. All the scientific men are eager to see and to confer with him."

During the first period of his stay, beginning in 1776, Franklin was compelled to conquer this difficulty of conversation and, in spite of his advanced age, he succeeded by his perseverance. Nevertheless, a few blunders on his part are recorded. Being present one day at a session of the Academy, and understanding the French language but slightly when declaimed, he determined, in order to do the civil thing, to applaud whenever he saw Mme. de Boufflers give signs of approbation; but it so happened that, without knowing it, he applauded, louder than any one, the parts that praised himself.

Franklin's feelings towards France varied during his long career, and even during the period of his last sojourn; it is only just to take account of these differing periods, lest we should think him a scoffer, and ungrateful. A British patriot by origin, and an American of Old England, he began by not liking France, considering her an enemy, as much as he could so consider a nation composed of his fellow-beings. He distrusted France, and during his stay in London, when M. Durand, the French minister plenipotentiary, showed him esteem and tried to draw from him information on the affairs of America, he held himself aloof: "I imagine," he wrote (August, 1767) "that that intriguing nation would not be sorry to meddle in our affairs, and to blow the fire between Great Britain and her colonies; but I hope that we shall furnish her with no such opportunity."

The opportunity had now come, the way was open ten years later, and it was Franklin himself who came to solicit our nation and its king to take part in the struggle and to profit by it. In the early days of his sojourn he is sensitive to annoyances, to absurdities; he finds himself the object not only of admiration but of sudden infatuation, and at first he does not like it. He is besieged by solicitations, by entreaties of all sorts. A generous fever had taken possession of our nation; men were fighting in America, and every soldier wanted to rush there. It was all the rage to go and draw your sword for the "insurgents," as it was, later, to rush to California for gold. No one would believe that Franklin had not come to solicit, first of all, military assistance and engage officers.

"These demands," he wrote, "are my perpetual torment. . . . Scarcely a day passes that I have not a number of such visits of solicitation, to say nothing of letters. They look up all my friends and weary them to weary me. The head functionaries of all ranks in all departments, ladies great and small, not counting professional place-hunters, importune me from morning until night. The noise of each carriage entering my courtyard suffices to alarm me. I fear to accept an invitation to dinner, so nearly sure I am to meet some officer or some friend of an officer who, after a glass or two of champagne has put me into good humor, begins his attack. Happily, in my sleep I do not dream of these disagreeable things, otherwise I should come to dread what are now my sole hours of repose. . . . And all those who are recommended to me are ' experienced officers—brave as their swords—full of courage, talents and zeal ' for our cause; in a word, real Cæsars, each of whom would be an inestimable acquisition for America. . . ."

In these first days Franklin, no doubt, did not rightly estimate the impulse that swept the nation along, and was presently to impel the Government itself to a course by which America was so greatly to profit. Little by little, however, he becomes acclimated; his little banter lessens, the slight irony ceases, and after a year or two spent in France, he is wholly conquered by the general spirit of the nation:

" I am charmed," he writes to Mr. J. Quincy (April, 1779), " with what you say of the French politeness and civil manners shown by the officers and crews of the fleet. The French, in this respect, greatly surpass the English. I find them the most agreeable nation in the world to live among. The Spaniards are thought to be cruel, the English haughty, the Scotch insolent, the Dutch stingy, etc.; but I think that the French have no national vice attributed to them. They have certain frivolities, but those hurt no one except themselves. To dress the hair so that no man can put a hat on his head and therefore carries that hat under his arm, and to fill the nose with snuff, may be called absurdities, but they are not vices; they are merely the results of the tyranny of fashion. In short, nothing is lacking in the character of a Frenchman of all that goes to make a charming and honourable man. He has only a few trifles the more, which we could well do without."

When he quitted France, in July, 1785, Franklin was wholly one of us; he repaid us the hospitality he had received and for the popularity by which he was surrounded, from the first to the last day, by feelings of affection and reciprocal esteem. We may say of him that he was the most French of Americans.

I insist upon this point because to detach such or such a passage from his letters, without distinguishing the times at which they were written, might lead us to infer quite the contrary. In politics, I cannot follow the progress of his negotiations in the complicated circumstances through which he led them; such an analysis would require a long chapter. I shall insist only on this one important point: Franklin was in no way ungrateful towards France. From the moment that the treaty of alliance was concluded, he had but one answer to all the overtures made to him to listen to proposals from England: "We cannot negotiate without France." America had been a submissive daughter until the day when she emancipated herself from England, but in vain did the latter secretly recall her and endeavour to tempt her in underhand ways; America was now a faithful spouse. Such was the principle that Franklin professed on all occasions, public or private; and it drew upon him in America the reputation of being too French. But he believed, contrary to his distinguished colleagues (such as Mr. Adams), that Americans could not express too openly their feelings of gratitude to France, and to her young and virtuous king. He who is not given to the mis-use of words, nor to exaggeration, goes so far on this point as to say:

"If this article" (on continuing the war conjointly with France, and not making a separate peace) "did not exist in the treaty, an honourable American would cut off his right hand rather than sign an agreement with England which was contrary to the spirit of such an article."

At a certain moment negotiations were opened with England with the knowledge and consent of France; France, on her side, opened parallel ones. Each of the two allies thought it wisest to seek to make their treaties of peace separately; promising to inform each other before their final conclusion. Here alone we have the right to notice that the American commis-sioners, to the number of five or six, among them Franklin, rushed their treaty through the last con-ferences, and did not communicate to the French minister, M. de Vergennes, the preliminary articles de-cided upon, though not yet ratified. M. de Vergennes complained to them of this infraction of their former agreement, and even of the instructions they had re-ceived from Congress, and Franklin admitted that there had been a want of courtesy. The fact was that a rather singular distrust felt by the English negotiators, the cause of which it would take too long to explain here, had crept of late into the minds of the American commissioners, and had made them disregard politeness. Nothing, however, in the articles agreed upon was of a nature prejudicial to France: all was well, except the formality which had been omitted. Franklin, more French in mind and inclination than his colleagues, and suspected of being so, thought it best not to separate from them on this occasion; and he was charged with the duty of repairing the ill-effect of this irregularity with M. de Vergennes and Louis XVI. In this he seems to have succeeded almost completely, and, what he was least concerned about, his position at the Court of France and the affectionate consideration he enjoyed from all, were in no way impaired.

I hasten now to speak of his philosophical and social character which specially interests us to-day. Franklin had influence upon us; he had more than he sought to have. No one ever understood the difference between young and old nations, between a virtuous and a corrupt people better than he. He repeated, many and many a time: " None but a virtuous people are capable of liberty, all others are in need of a master: revolutions cannot take place without danger when the peoples have not sufficient virtue." He said it of England; could he have failed to think it of France ? When, towards the close of his life, he heard of the first events of July, '89, he felt as much distrust and doubt of them as hope; the first murders, certain "circumstances" by which the French Revolution was accompanied from the beginning, seemed to him " grievous, afflicting":—" I fear," he says, " that the voice of philosophy will have difficulty in making itself heard through the tumult."—"Purify, but not destroy" was one of his maxims, and he plainly saw from the beginning it would not be followed in France.

Nevertheless, there is no doubt that during his residence in Paris, he did, in his privacy at Passy, influence many of the eminent men who took part soon after in the great Revolutionary movement; and that he contributed to give them more confidence and boldness in their purposes:—"Franklin," says Mallet du Pan, "said more than once to his pupils in Paris that whoso would transport into the body politic the principles of primitive Christianity would change the whole face of society." He is one of those who have advanced with utmost conviction the doctrine of secularising Christianity, and thus obtaining, if possible, good and useful results upon earth. But to take Christianity and drag it so vehemently in that direction is to alter and curtail that which hitherto has been its essence, namely, abnegation, the spirit of sacrifice, and patience founded on immortal expectations. However that may be, the idea of *work and peace,* which, in spite of the checks that it receives from time to time, seems destined to rule more and more all modern societies, owes much to Franklin.

He visited Voltaire during the last journey that the latter made to Paris (February, 1778), where he died. The two patriarchs embraced, and Franklin requested Voltaire to give his blessing to his grandson. It is probable that he knew but little of Voltaire in all his works, and took him merely for the apostle and propagator of tolerance. But such a scene, with the sacramental words pronounced by Voltaire, "God and Liberty!" resounded far and near, and spoke vividly to the imaginations of men.

I like to believe that Franklin, could he have followed his own inclinations solely, and chosen from among us the person of his preference and his ideal, would rather have embraced M. de Malesherbes, "that great man," as he calls him, who came to see him at Passy, and who, renouncing public life and amusing himself with great plantations, was anxious to obtain through him the trees of North America, not yet introduced into France.

Established at Passy in a beautiful house with a garden, enjoying a charming neighbourhood, Franklin usually, at least during the first years and before his health failed, dined out six days of the seven, reserving Sundays for the Americans. whom he entertained at home. His more especial friends were, among other well-known personages: Turgot, the *good* Duc de La Rochefoucauld, Lavoisier, the society that surrounded Mme. Helvétius at Auteuil, the Abbé Morellet, Cabanis, etc. He went always once a year to Moulin-Goli, to stay with M. Watelet; and he paid a certain visit to Mme. d'Houdetot at Sannois, the sentimental memory of which has been preserved. But these excursions were rare; for, independently of his functions as minister and negotiator, he filled the offices of "merchant, banker, admiralty judge, and consul." His countrymen found it more economical to use him, without a secretary, in these employments; which condemned him to a very sedentary life during the day. He compensated himself for this drudgery at night, in a friendly and familiar society for which he was so well fitted. He preferred, as a general thing, to listen rather than speak; and certain women of society could be named who, having gone to some salon out of curiosity to meet him, complained of his silence. He had his times and seasons. These intervals were followed by charming awakenings. When he talked, he liked to go to the end of what he had to say, without interruption. The play of wit, the tales and fables of which he was prodigal at such times, have been in part preserved and depict him to us with his own peculiar stamp. He had a kindly irony. One of his most charming correspondents in England, Miss Georgiana Shipley, to whom he had sent his "Dialogue with Gout" and other nothings that he amused himself in writing and then in printing himself, reminded him of the delightful and serious hours she had formerly passed in his society, in which she had "acquired such taste for playful and reflective conversation" [*pour la conversation badinante et réfléchie*]. Those words, which she put in French, give a good idea of Franklin in his ordinary life.

Franklin's Correspondence during these years is most

agreeable and pleasant reading; the perfect equilibrium, the justness, the absence of all evil passions, all
anger, the good use he learns to make of even his enemies, an affectionate feeling that mingles with his exact
appreciation of things and which banishes their dryness, a lofty sentiment wherever such is needed, a certain smiling air shed over all, make these letters a real
treasury of morality and wisdom.   Brought into comparison with Voltaire's Correspondence, that of Franklin
gives birth to many thoughts; all is healthy, honourable, and as if vitalised by a constant and lively serenity; he called ill-humour "uncleanliness of soul."

More than once he rises to heights; the consciousness of the reality and ardour of his human affection
suggests to him a species of poetry:

"I must soon quit this scene," he wrote to General Washington
(March, 1780), "but you may live long enough to see our country pro-
sper, as it cannot fail to do, in a rapid and astounding manner, when
once the war is over—like a field of young Indian corn, that too prolonged fine weather and too much sun have withered and discoloured,
and which, in that weak condition, being buffeted by storms of rain
and hail and lightning seemed threatened with entire destruction, yet,
when the tempest had passed, it recovers its fresh verdure, lifts its head
with new vigour, and rejoices the eyes, not of its possessor only, but
of all who pass that way."

Is not that a comparison which, by the sweetness of
its inspiration and the breadth of its imagery, recalls
the Homeric comparisons of the Odyssey ?   Franklin,
when old, read the poets very little; one of them,
however, by his nature, his simple grace, the recti-

tude of his sentiment, found the way to his heart: this was William Cooper, the humble poet of moral life and reality. The noblest eulogy that could be made of that poet—of whom we have not the counterpart in our literature—was written by Franklin in a few lines.

While Franklin was thus corresponding with friends in America and in England and with his absent daughter, regretting the joys of his family hearth, but anticipating for his country great prospects for the future, he was popular in France : he was, in fact, the fashion. His portrait in medallions, in busts, and engravings was seen everywhere; it was worn in rings and bracelets, on canes and snuff-boxes. Beneath the engraved portraits were the famous lines addressed to him by Turgot:

> "Eripuit cœlo fulmen, sceptrumque tyrannis."
> ("From heaven he took the lightning, and the sceptre from tyrants.")

Franklin blushed at these lines, and he blushed sincerely; he would greatly have preferred that what he considered "extravagant" praise of him should be suppressed, for it did, in fact, exaggerate his rôle. But he had to do with a monarchical nation which likes above all things that some one person shall be held to do everything, and which needs to personify its admiration in a single name and a single glory.[1]   In

[1] Strange that Sainte-Beuve should give this reason ; it would seem, rather, that in the tumult of French souls conscious that some change

sending this portrait to his friends in America, he called attention, by way of excuse, to the marked characteristic of the French nation of carrying eulogy to extremes, so that ordinary, simple praise becomes almost censure, while excessive praise, in turn, ends by being without significance. To a M. Nogaret, an indefatigable rhymester now totally forgotten, who asked his advice on a translation into French of Turgot's line, Franklin replied with much frankness:

PARIS, 8 March, 1781.

" MONSIEUR:

" I have received the letter you did me the honour to write to me on the 2nd of this month, in which, after overwhelming me with a deluge of compliments which I can never hope to deserve, you ask my advice on your translation of a Latin line that has been applied to me.   If I were, what I really am not, sufficiently conversant with your excellent language to be a competent judge of its poesy, the idea that I am the subject of it would prevent me from expressing any opinion. I content myself with saying that it attributes far too much to me, particularly in the part relating to tyrants.   The Revolution has been the work of a great number of brave and capable men, and it is fully honour enough for me if I am granted a small part in it."

All that he says on this subject in his letters (and he recurs to it at various times) is of pure good sense, in a tone more dignified than scornful, and without false modesty.   Franklin is one of those men who, while honouring humanity and liking to look upward toward heaven, has no aspiration to be taken for an angel.

must come to their nation and yearning for it, they clung with a species of infatuation to the man who personified to them a successful revolution on the highest plane—where, alas for the world! they did not follow.—TR.

Extracts from his "Private Journal" are often quoted in relation to schemes, more or less fantastic and chimerical, that were communicated to him as a common meeting-point, by inventors of projects, machines, systems, or constitutions. All the fools and all the dreamers seem to have set one another on to make this sensible man, coming from afar, their confidant and judge. Among those who submitted to him their ideas or their works, there came one day a certain unknown natural philosopher who was no other than Marat. On another occasion, an author, whose name is not given, but who is thought to have been Thomas Paine, sent him the manuscript of an irreligious work: suppose, if you prefer to do so, that this author, about whom there is uncertainty, was a Frenchman, a philosopher, a pupil of the school of Holbach, or even of that of Auteuil—Volney, for instance, submitting to Franklin the manuscript of his *Ruines*. Franklin replies by a letter, which I shall give entire, because it expresses better than anything I could say the true relation in which he stands with the philosophers of the eighteenth century, and the point at which he separates from them:

"I have read your manuscript with some attention. By the argument it contains against a special Providence,—though you grant a general Providence,—you sap the foundations of all religion: because, without the belief in a Providence who knows, watches, and guides, and can favour some in particular, there is no motive for worshipping a Divinity, for fearing to displease him, or imploring his protection. I shall not enter into any discussion of your principles, although you seem to desire it. I shall merely, for the moment, give you my opinion, which is that, although your arguments are subtle and may prevail with certain readers, you will never succeed in changing the general sentiments of humanity on this subject; and if you print that work the consequences will be much odium heaped upon yourself, great injury to you and no benefit to others. He who spits against the wind spits in his own face. But, supposing you succeed, do you imagine that any good will result ? You may, yourself, find it easy to live a virtuous life, without the help given by religion, you who have a clear perception of the advantages of virtue and the disadvantages of vice, and who possess sufficient strength of resolution to make you capable of resisting all common temptations. But consider how numerous is that portion of humanity which is composed of weak and ignorant men and women, of the inexperienced and thoughtless youth of both sexes, who have need of the motives of religion to turn them from vice, to encourage them to virtue and retain them in the practice of it until it becomes *habitual*—which is the great guarantee of safety. Perhaps you yourself owe to it originally—i mean to your religious education—the habits of virtue of which you now justly boast.

" You could easily display your excellent talents for reasoning on a less hazardous subject, and by so doing obtain a rank among our most distinguished authors: for, among us, it is not necessary, as it is among the Hottentots, that a young man in order to be admitted into the company of men should give proofs of his virility by beating his mother. I advise you, therefore, not to try to unchain the tiger, but to burn this writing before it is read by any one else. In that way, you will spare yourself much mortification from the enemies you will create, and also, perhaps, much regret and repentence. If men are wicked with religion what would they be without it ? This letter, as I think, is a proof of my friendship; I will therefore add no other protestation, but sign myself simply: wholly yours."

Among the philosophers of renown in the eighteenth century, I see none but Montesquieu who would have thought thus; but Franklin expresses it in a manner more affectionate, more emotional, more paternal, than Montesquieu would have done.

If all those who conversed with Franklin at Passy

had truly understood his precepts and his measures, they would have thought twice before undertaking in the Old World a universal recasting. At the same time, I must add (even if some contradiction be found in it) that it was difficult for those who listened to him not to take fire, not to be tempted to reform society radically; for he was himself, in his general way of thinking and presenting matters, a great, too great a simplifier. This practical man had nothing in him that discouraged a Utopia; on the contrary, he rather invited it by the novelties and facilities of the outlook he opened towards the future. He gave, in talking, a desire to apply his ideas, but he did not give in equal measure to those who listened to him (the Condorcets and the Chamforts, for instance,) his temperament, his discretion in details, and his prudence.

A witty critic has very well defined him as the "godfather of a future society"; but I do not know how that same critic could have found means to join the name of M. de Talleyrand with that of Franklin: those two names must swear at seeing themselves thus associated! Franklin, in the midst of his shrewdness and ability, is always upright and sincere. Lord Shelburne had sent his son, Lord Fitzmaurice, to see him; after the young man's second visit, Franklin writes in his Journal (July 27, 1784):

"Lord Fitzmaurice came to see me. His father having asked me to give him such advice as I thought might be useful to him, I took occasion to tell him the old story of Demosthenes replying to the man

who asked him what was the first essential in oratory ? ' Action.'
—And the second ? ' Action.'—And the third ? ' Action.' I told
him that had usually been interpreted as meaning the action of an orator, his gestures in speaking; but that I thought there was another form
of action more important for an orator who wanted to persuade people
to follow his advice, and that was a consistency and a deportment in
the conduct of life which should impress on others an idea of his integrity as well as of his talents; and I added that that opinion once
established, all difficulties, delays, oppositions, which ordinarily have
their cause in doubts and suspicions, would be forestalled; and that
such a man, though he might be a very second-rate orator, would
nearly always obtain the advantage over the most brilliant orator who
had not the reputation of sincerity. . . ."

This was all the more appropriate to the young man
because his father, Lord Shelburne, gifted with many
talents, had the reputation of being the very opposite
of sincere. In all things, Franklin wanted first the
essential, the base, the foundation, convinced that
that foundation would be made manifest and that
the solid respect due to it must bear fruit.

After a stay of eight years in France he returned to
America, being then seventy-nine years of age. Suffering from calculus, he could not bear the motion of a
carriage; a litter of Queen Marie Antoinette, drawn
by Spanish mules, took him from Passy to the port of
Havre, where he embarked. He lived five years
longer, in Philadelphia, and died on the 17th of April,
1790, at eighty-four years of age. His return to his
country, the honours he there received, the slight vexations (for such there are in every life) that he bore
without showing them, his domestic happiness in his
garden, under the shade of his mulberry trees, beside

his daughter, with his six grandchildren playing at his knee, his thoughts more and more religious as years advanced upon him—all these things make the most beautiful and perfect end and crown of old age that the mind can imagine. His Correspondence in these years does not cease to be interesting and lively; it is fed to the last by the same sentiments. Among various passages I have selected the following as well expressing that mixture of serenity and gentle irony, of human experience and hope, which formed his habitual character. It is from a letter addressed to his old friend, Mary Stevenson, now become Mrs. Hewson:

"I have found," he writes from Philadelphia, May 6, 1786, "my family in good health, in good condition as to fortune, and respected by their fellow-citizens. The companions of my youth are in truth, nearly all gone ; but I find an agreeable society among their children and grand-children. I have enough public affairs on hand to keep me from *ennui,* and with them private amusements, such as conversation, books, my garden, and cribbage. Reflecting that our market is as abundantly supplied as the best of private vegetable gardens, I am in process of transforming mine, in the middle of which stands the house, into lawns and gravel walks, with trees and flowering shrubs. Sometimes we play at cards in the long winter evenings, but just as one plays at chess, not for money, but for the honour or pleasure of battling with one another. This will not seem a novelty to you, for you will remember how we played together in this way during that winter at Passy. It is true that I have, now and then, little twinges of remorse in reflecting that I lose time so idly; but another reflection comes to comfort me and murmurs in my ear: ' Thou knowest that the soul is immortal: why then art thou niggardly in this matter of a trifle of time ? hast thou not a whole eternity before thee ? ' So, being easily convinced and, like many other reasonable beings, satisfied with a small reason when it is in favour of my desire, I shuffle the cards and begin a new game."

Letting his thoughts dwell on the hopes and fears, the many and diverse chances of happiness or misfortune which brighten or temper family joys, he says, elsewhere, quoting the words of a religious poet, Dr. Watts :

" He who brings up a numerous family, so long as he is there, living, to look after it, offers himself, it is true, as a ' target for grief ' ; but also he has greater opportunity for pleasure. When we launch upon the Ocean our little flotilla, bound and freighted for different ports, we hope for each vessel a lucky voyage; but contrary winds, hidden sand-banks, tempests, and enemies have a share in the disposition of events ; and although there may result a mixture of mistakes and disappointments, nevertheless, considering the risks on which we can have no insurance, we ought to esteem ourselves happy if some of our ventures return to port."

His ideas of death had never varied for many years, and his hope became more vivid, more keenly felt, as he approached his end. He considered death a second birth: " This life is an embryonic state, a preparation for life. A man is not wholly born until he has passed through death." The peaceful end of his old friends who had lived righteous lives seemed to him a foretaste of the happiness of another life. The recent discourses of Herschel appeared, he thought, to call us to a future and sublime voyage of celestial discovery through the spheres.

By taking him away at that date and thus sparing him two or three more years upon earth, Providence saved him from the horror of seeing those he had best known and loved during his stay in France put to a violent death—the *good* Duc de La Rochefoucauld, Lavoisier, his neighbour at Passy, Le Veillard, and so many others all guillotined or massacred in the name of principles he had so long approved and cherished. Franklin's last thoughts would then have been darkened by a funeral veil, and his serene soul, before the rebirth he hoped for, would have known in one day all bitterness.

Madame Geoffrin.

Madame Geoffrin.

AFTER all that I have said of the women of the eighteenth century, I should leave too great a gap if I did not speak of Mme. Geoffrin, one of the most celebrated, and whose influence was of the greatest. Mme. Geoffrin wrote nothing that has been published except four or five letters; a quantity of her sayings both apt and piquant have been quoted; but they would not suffice to keep her memory alive. That which characterises her particularly and causes her to be remembered by posterity, is her salon, the most complete, the best organised, and, if I may say so, the best governed salon of her day, the best established that there has been in France since the founding of salons; that is to say, since the hotel Rambouillet. The salon of Mme. Geoffrin was one of the institutions of the eighteenth century.

There are persons who doubtless imagine that it suffices to be rich, to have a good cook, a comfortable house in a good quarter, a great desire to see society and much affability in receiving it to make for themselves a salon. They succeed only in gathering a crowd pell-mell, in filling their salon, not in

creating it; and if they are very rich, very active,
much impelled by the sort of ambition that desires
to shine, and are at the same time well informed
as to the list of invitations to issue, and determined,
at any cost, to receive in their houses the kings or
queens of the season, they may obtain the glory
which a few Americans obtain every winter in Paris:
they can have brilliant *routs* to which people rush
and pass on, and forget the winter after. What
a distance between this process of invasion and the
art of real establishment! That art was never better
understood or practised than in the eighteenth century, in the bosom of that peaceful, regular society;
and no one carried it farther along, conceived it on a
grander scale, or applied it with greater perfection
and finish of detail than Mme. Geoffrin. A Roman
cardinal would not have put into it more diplomacy,
more subtle and gentle skill than she bestowed upon
it for thirty years. In studying it closely we are
more than ever convinced that there is always a
reason for a great social influence; and that under
these famous powers which are summed up for us in
a single name, there was much toil, much study and
much talent; in the present case of Mme. Geoffrin, we
must add, much good sense.

Mme. Geoffrin appears from the first as an old
woman; her youth disappears in a far distance that we
do not seek to penetrate. *Bourgeoise,* and very *bourgeoise* by birth, born in Paris in the last year of

MADAME GEOFFRIN
From a portrait by Hubert Robert

the seventeenth century, Marie-Thérèse Rodet was married, July 19, 1713, when fourteen years old, to Pierre-François Geoffrin, a substantial citizen, a lieutenant-colonel of the National Guard of those days, and one of the founders of the Manufactory of looking-glasses. A letter of Montesquieu, written in 1748, shows us Mme. Geoffrin at that date, assembling choice company at her house, and already the centre of a circle which for twenty-five years was to last and increase. Whence came this person so distinguished and so skilful, who, by her birth and position in the world, did not seem destined for the part she played? What was her early education? The Empress of Russia, Catherine II, having put this question to Mme. Geoffrin herself, received in reply a letter which ought to be added to all that Montaigne has said on education:

" I lost," she says, " my father and mother when in my cradle. I was brought up by an old grandmother who had much intelligence and a sound head. She had very little education; but her mind was so bright, so adroit, so active, that it never failed her; it took the place of knowledge. She talked so agreeably of things she knew nothing about, that no one wished her to know more; and when her ignorance became too visible, she got away from it by jests that disconcerted the pedants who had tried to humiliate her. She was so content with her lot that she considered knowledge a very useless thing for a woman. She used to say: ' I have done so well without it, that I have never felt the need of it. If my grand-daughter is stupid knowledge will make her self-conceited and intolerable; if she has intelligence and sensibility she will do as I have done: she will make up by cleverness and feeling for what she does not know; and when she comes to have more reason she will learn that for which she has the most aptitude, and learn it quickly.' So, in my childhood, she had me taught simply to read; but she made me read a great deal; she taught me to think and to reason; she taught me to know men, making me say what I thought, and telling me the judgment she formed upon them. She obliged me to give her an account of all my impulses and all my feelings; and these she corrected with such gentleness and grace that I never hid anything of what I thought and felt from her ; my interior was as visible to her as my exterior. My education was continual. . . ."

I said that Mme. Geoffrin was born in Paris: she never left it but once, in 1766, when sixty-seven years old, to make her famous journey to Warsaw. Moreover, she never quitted her own quarter; even when she drove into the country to visit a friend, she always came back at night and never slept away from home. She was of the opinion that "there is no better air than that of Paris"; and wherever she might have gone she would always have preferred her gutter of the rue Saint-Honoré, as Mme. de Staël preferred hers of the rue du Bac. Mme. Geoffrin adds one more name to the list of Parisian spirits who have been endowed in the highest degree with the social and affable virtues, and who are thus so easily civilisers.

Her husband seems to have counted for little in her life, except to provide her with the fortune which was the starting-point and the first instrumentality of the consideration she was fitted to acquire. M. Geoffrin is represented to us as old, and silently present at the dinners that were given in his house to men of Letters and of science. They tried, so the story goes, to make him read some book of history, or of travels;

but as he always took up the first volume without
perceiving that there were others, he contented himself by saying that "the work was interesting, but the
author repeated himself a little." It is told that reading
a volume of the Encyclopædia (or of Bayle), which
was printed in two volumes, he read across the page
from one column to the other, which caused him to
say that "while he thought the work very able, it
seemed to him a little abstruse." These, however, are
tales readily told of the effaced husband of a celebrated
wife. One day, a foreigner asked Mme. Geoffrin
what had become of the old gentleman who used always to be at her dinners and whom he no longer saw
there. Mme. Geoffrin replied: "That was my husband; he is dead."

Mme. Geoffrin had one daughter, who became the
Marquise de La Ferté-Imbault, an excellent woman, it
was said, but without the moderation, good sense,
and perfect decorum of her mother, who used to say:
"When I consider her I feel like a hen which has
hatched out a duckling."

Mme. Geoffrin, therefore, derived her training from
her grandmother, but she seems to me the only one
of her race. Her talent, like all true talent, was wholly
personal. Mme. Suard represents her as gently imposing respect "by her tall figure, her silvery hair
covered with a head-dress tied under the chin, her
dress, very noble and decent, and her air of good judgment mingled with kindness." Diderot, who had

just been playing a game of piquet with her at Grand-val, Baron d'Holbach's place, where she was dining (1760), wrote to a friend:

" Madame Geoffrin appeared very well. I have always observed the noble and simple taste with which that woman dresses : to-day, she wore a simple material, austere in colour, wide sleeves, linen of the finest and smoothest, and everywhere the utmost cleanliness."

She was then sixty - one years old. This old woman's attire, so exquisite in its modesty and simplicity, was peculiar to her, and recalls, in a way, the similar art of Mme. de Maintenon. But Mme. Geoffrin was not obliged to husband or repair the remains of a beauty that still shone by flashes in a half-light; she was frankly old at an early age, and she suppressed the autumn season. While most women are concerned to retreat in good order, prolonging their age of yesterday, she took the bull by the horns and installed herself, without haggling, in the age of the morrow. It was said of her that " all women dress as they did yesterday; no one but Mme. Geoffrin dresses for to-morrow."

Mme. Geoffrin is thought to have taken her lessons of the great world from Mme. de Tencin, and to have formed herself in that school. The assiduity of her visits being remarked, Mme. de Tencin is quoted as saying to a knot of her intimates: " Do you know what the Geoffrin comes here for ? She comes to see what she can collect out of my property." That " property " was worth some trouble, for it consisted of Fontenelle, Montesquieu, Mairan, and others of their kind.

Mme. de Tencin is much less remarkable as the author of romantic and sentimental tales (in which she may have been assisted by her nephews) than for her spirit of intrigue, her wily manœuvres, and for the boldness and range of her opinions. A woman of little worth, some of whose actions came near to being crimes, those who approached her were captivated by her gentle and almost kindly air. When her interests were not concerned, she could give safe and practical advice, by which others profited in their lives. She knew the end of the game in everything. More than one great statesman, even in our own day, would have been the better for keeping before his eyes this maxim, which she often repeated: "Men of intelligence make many mistakes in conduct because they never believe the world to be as stupid as it is." Nine of her letters that were published (all being addressed to the Duc de Richelieu during the campaign of 1743), show her to us in all the manœuvres of her ambition, working to seize power for herself and her brother the cardinal, during that brief moment when the king, emancipated at last by the death of Cardinal de Fleury, had not yet taken a formal mistress. Never has Louis XV been judged more profoundly, or with more clear-sighted and better-founded feelings of contempt than in those nine letters of Mme. de Tencin. As early as the year 1743, this intriguing woman has flashes of perception that pierce the horizon: "Unless God puts his hand in it visibly," she writes, "it is physically impossible that the State should not be overthrown." It was this able mistress whom Mme. Geoffrin consulted, and from whom she received good counsel, notably that of never refusing any connection, any offer of friendship; for if nine out of ten brought her nothing, the tenth might compensate for all; "and besides," said this woman of resource, "everything comes into use in a household when we ourselves know how to handle the tools."

Mme. Geoffrin did, in part, inherit the salon and methods of Mme. de Tencin; but in confining her ability to the sphere of private life she singularly extended it, and in a path that was wholly honourable. Mme. de Tencin moved heaven and earth to make her brother prime-minister: Mme. Geoffrin, putting politics aside, and never meddling in matters of religion, became herself, by her infinite art, by her spirit of consistency and propriety, a sort of skilful administrator or, as one might say, a great minister of society, one of those ministers who are all the more influential because they are less proclaimed and more permanent.

From the first, she conceived the idea of this machine called a salon to its full extent, and was able to organise it completely, with the gentlest and most imperceptible machinery, but skilful and kept in repair by continual watchfulness. She not only sought and welcomed men of Letters, properly so-called, but she was solicitous for artists, sculptors, and painters, seeking to bring them all into relations with one another and with people of the great world; in short she conceived the Encyclopædia of the century in action and in conversation around her. Every week she gave two dinners; one, on Monday, to artists: at that could be seen Van Loo, Vernet, Boucher, Latour, Naltier, Vien, Lagrenée, Soufftot, Lemoine, some amateurs of distinction and patrons of art, some literary men, like Marmontel, to sustain the conversation and make a bond between the rest. Wednesday was the dinner for the men of Letters; at which were present d'Alembert, Mairan, Marivaux, Marmontel, the Chevalier de Chastellux, Morellet, Saint-Lambert, Helvétius, Raynal, Thomas, Grimm, d'Holbach, and Burigny of the Academy of Inscriptions. One woman only was admitted besides the mistress of the house, and that was Mlle. de Lespinasse. Mme. Geoffrin had noticed that several women at a dinner distracted the guests, broke up and scattered conversation; and what she liked was unity—remaining herself its centre.

After dinner the house continued open for other guests, and the evening ended by a little supper, very simple but very choice, composed of five or six intimate friends, among them certain women, the flower of the great world. Not a foreigner of distinction lived in, or passed through Paris without aspiring to be received by Mme. Geoffrin. Princes came there as private individuals; ambassadors never stayed away when once they had a footing there. Europe was represented in the persons of Caraccioli, Creutz, Galiani, Gatti, Hume, and Gibbon.

We can now see that of all the salons of the eighteenth century that of Mme. Geoffrin was the most complete. It was more so than that of Mme. Du Deffand who, after the defection of d'Alembert and others consequent upon the departure of Mlle. de Lespinasse, had lost nearly all the men of Letters. The salon of Mlle. de Lespinasse, save for six or seven earnest friends, was made up of persons little bound together, taken here and there, but assorted by that brilliant woman with infinite art. The salon of Mme. Geoffrin represents, on the contrary, the great centre and gathering-place of the eighteenth century. In its decent conduct, its animated decorum, it makes a counterpoise to the little dinners and licentious suppers of Mlle. Quinault, Mlle. Guimard, and the financial magnates, the Pelletiers and the La Popelinières. Towards its close, Mme. Geoffrin's salon witnessed the rise, in emulation of and slightly in rivalry with it, of the salons of Baron d'Holbach and of Mme. Helvétius, which were composed partly of the cream of Mme. Geoffrin's guests, and partly of certain hotheads whom she had found too excitable to admit to her dinners. The century became, in the end, a little weary of being controlled by her and held in leading-strings; it wanted to speak out loud with joy at heart.

The spirit that Mme. Geoffrin brought into the ordering and management of the little empire she had so broadly conceived was a spirit of naturalness, or correctness, of delicacy, and of refinement, descending to the smallest details; an adroit, active, and gentle spirit. She had caused a plane to be passed over the carvings in her apartment; and it was the same in her moral existence: "Nothing in relief" seemed to be her motto: "My mind," she said, "is like my legs: I like to walk on level ground; and I do not want to climb a mountain for the pleasure of saying when I get there, 'I have climbed this mountain.'" She liked simplicity, and may, on occasion, have slightly affected it. Her activity was of a kind that is chiefly noticeable through good order; one of those discreet activities that act at all points silently and insensibly. Mistress of a household, she had an eye to everything; she presided; she sometimes scolded, but with a scolding that was hers alone; she desired that talk should be stopped in time; she policed her salon. With a single sentence, "That will do," she checked at the right moment conversations that were wandering towards hazardous topics, and heads that were getting heated; the latter feared her, and carried their outbreaks elsewhere.

She held it as a principle not to talk herself, except when necessary; and not to intervene unless at certain moments; and never for any length of time. It was then, however, that she gave wise maxims or told piquant tales and anecdotes on morals or actions, usually illustrated by some familiar image or expression. All this, however, was chiefly pleasing as it came from her lips; she knew this, and she used to say that she did not wish people "to preach her sermons, tell her tales, or touch her tongs."

Having posed so early as an old woman and as the "mamma" of the persons she received, she found a means of governing, a little trick or artifice, which became in the end a sort of mania. This was to scold; but to scold as a compliment. Not every one who wished could be scolded by her; it was the highest mark of her favour and guidance. He whom she liked the best was the most scolded. Horace Walpole, before he passed with colours flying into the camp of Mme. Du Deffand, wrote the following letter from Paris to his friend the poet Gray:

"(January 25, 1766) Mme. Geoffrin, of whom you must have heard a great deal, is a very extraordinary woman, with more common sense than I have almost ever met with. She has great quickness in reading characters at a glance, much penetration in going to the bottom of each one, and a pencil that never misses a likeness—which is seldom flattering. In spite of her birth and the absurd prejudices in France about nobility, she exacts for herself a great court and a well-maintained respect. She has succeeded in this by a thousand little artifices and many kind offices of friendship; also by a liberty and severity which seem to be almost her only object in drawing society round her; for she never ceases to scold those she has once cajoled. She has little taste and less knowledge, but she protects artists and authors, and she pays court to a small number of great people to gain influence that may be useful to her protégés. She got her training under the famous Mme. de Tencin, who taught her as a rule never to rebuff any one, for, said that clever matron, 'even if nine out of ten would not give themselves a farthing's worth of trouble for you, the tenth may become a useful friend.' She has neither adopted nor rejected that plan as a whole, but she has kept to the spirit of the maxim. In a word, she presents to us an epitome of empire which exists by means of rewards and penalties."

The office of majordomo of her salon was usually confided to Burigny, one of her oldest friends, and the most scolded of all. When there had been some in–fraction of the rules, some outbreak of imprudence in speech, she laid the blame on him for not keeping better order.

People laughed, and even joked with her about it, all the while submitting to a rule that was narrow and exacting, though tempered by much kindness and beneficence. This right of correcting she secured to herself by now and then placing in the pocket of a guest some good little pension—not forgetting the annual gift of the velvet breeches.

Fontenelle did not make Mme. Geoffrin the execu-trix of his will without reason. Mme. Geoffrin, pro-perly observed, seems to me to have been, by the nature of her mind, by the method of her proceedings, and by her class of influence, a female Fontenelle; a Fontenelle more active in beneficence (I shall return to that point later), but a true Fontenelle in caution, in her way of conceiving and regulating happiness, by a manner of speech, familiar at will, epigrammatic and ironical, but without bitterness. She is a Fontenelle who, for the very reason that she is a woman, has more **vivacity and more affectionate and kindly impulses.**

But, like him, she loved quietude and to walk on level ground. All that was ardent around her made her uneasy; she thought that reason itself was wrong when impassioned. She compared her mind, one day, to "a roll, which unfolds, unrolls by degrees." She was in no hurry to unroll it rapidly. "Perhaps at my death," she said, "the roll may not be wholly unrolled."

That wise slowness is a distinctive trait in her mind and of her influence. She feared too hasty emotions and changes that were too abrupt: "We must not," she said, "pull down the old house before we build the new one." She moderated the epoch, then beginning to be so ardent, as much as she could, and tried to discipline it. It was an offence to her if, at one of her dinners, things were said that might have sent the speakers to the Bastille. Marmontel perceived that he was lowered in her favour after his affair of *Bélisaire*. In short, she continued to represent the spirit, already philosophical but still moderate, of the first half of the eighteenth century so long as it did not cease to respect certain limits. I picture to my own mind this constant care and solicitude of Mme. Geoffrin, by an image: to the bust of Diderot by Falconet she added a wig (a marble wig, if you please).

Her beneficence was as great as it was ingenious; in her it was a true gift of nature: she had "the giving humour," she said. "Give and forgive" was her motto. Benefaction on her part was perpetual. She could not refrain from making presents to every one; to the poorest man of Letters as well as to the Empress of Germany; and she gave them with an art and a perfection of delicacy which would have made the refusal of them churlish. Her sensibility became perfected by the practice of kindness, and by an exquisite social tact. Her beneficence, like all her other qualities, had something singular and original about it that was hers alone. Many charming, unlooked-for instances of this, such as Sterne would have turned to profit, are told of her; I will relate but one:

It was remarked to her, one day, that everything in her house was perfect, except the cream, and that was not good. "How can I help it?" she said. "I cannot change my milkwoman." "What is there about your milkwoman that you cannot change her?" "Why, I gave her two cows." "A fine reason!" they cried all round her. The fact was, that one day when the milkwoman was weeping in distress at having lost her cow, Mme. Geoffrin had given her two; the extra one to console her for having wept; and from that day the giver felt that she could not change her milkwoman. This is rare, and it is delicate. Many persons would have been capable of giving a cow, or even two; but to keep an ungrateful or negligent milkwoman, in spite of her bad cream, is what few would have done. Mme. Geoffrin did it for her own sake; so as not to spoil the memory of her first kindly action. Just as she scolded, not to correct but for her own personal pleasure, so did she give, not to make worthy persons happy or grateful, but to content and please herself. Her benefactions were stamped by a certain roughness of humour; she held thanks in aversion: "Thanks," some one said, "caused her a kindly and almost real anger." About this she had a theory which she carried into paradox; she even went so far as to make a formal eulogy of ingratitude. What is very clear is that, even in giving, she chose to pay herself by her own hands, and enjoy *all alone* the satisfaction of obliging others.

Shall I say it? I think I find here, even in this excellent nature, that corner of selfishness and hardness so inherent in the eighteenth century. The pupil of Mme. de Tencin, the friend of Fontenelle, is visible even at the moment when she gives way to an inclination of her heart—she gives way to it, but without warmth, and still arranging all things. We know that Montesquieu also did a fine act of benevolence, after which he escaped abruptly and almost harshly from the thanks and tears of those he had obliged. Contempt for mankind is here shown even in benevolence. Is it taking the right moment to show contempt to choose that in which we uplift men, or touch their hearts, or make them better? In St. Paul's admirable chapter on Charity we find, among other characteristics of that divine virtue: "Charity seeketh not its own; . . . thinketh no evil." Here, on the contrary, this worldly and social benevolence sought its pleasure, its personal relish and satisfaction, mingling with them a little irony and malice.

I know all that can be said in favour of that respectable and charming virtue, even when it thinks of itself. Mme. Geoffrin, when questioned about it, had a thousand good answers, all as shrewd as herself: "Those," she said, "who seldom oblige, do not need working maxims; but those who oblige often ought to do so in the manner most agreeable to themselves, because we want to do conveniently what we wish to do every day." There is something of Franklin in that maxim; of Franklin correcting and rather blurring the too spiritual meaning of Charity as given by St. Paul. Let us respect, let us honour the natural and reasonable liberality of Mme. Geoffrin; but let us, at the same time, recognise that there is lacking in that kindness and that beneficence a certain celestial fire, just as there was lacking in the whole social spirit and art of the eighteenth century a bloom of imagination and poesy, a depth of celestial light. Never do we see above us the blue of the heavens and the radiance of the stars.

We have now obtained an idea of the form and quality of Mme. Geoffrin's mind. The dominant characteristics in her were justness, fitness, and good sense. Horace Walpole, whom I like to quote as a good judge above suspicion, saw much of Mme. Geoffrin before he belonged to Mme. Du Deffand; he enjoyed her extremely, and always spoke of her as having one of the best heads and best understandings he had ever met;

and also as the person who had the greatest knowledge
of the world.　Writing to Lady Hervey, after an attack
of the gout, he said:

" Paris, October 13, 1765.　Mme. Geoffrin came the other evening
and sat two hours by my bedside; I could have sworn it was my
Lady Hervey, so full of kindness was she.　And this together with so
much good sense, information, sound advice and timely.　She has,
especially, a way of reproving you that charms me.　I have never in
my life seen any one who detects so quickly the defects, vanities, and
false airs of others, or who exposes them with such clearness and con-
vinces you of them so easily.　I never before liked being reproved; but
now, you cannot imagine what a taste I have for it.　I have made her
my Confessor and Director both, and I begin to believe that I shall
be, in the end, a reasonable human being—which I never aimed at
being until now.　The next time I see her I mean to say: ' O! Common Sense, sit thou there; I have, until now, thought so and so; tell
me, is it, or is it not absurd ? '—As to all other kinds of sense and wisdom, I never liked them, and now I shall hate them for her sake.　If
it were worth her trouble to do so, I can assure you, Madam, she
might rule me like an infant."

At all times he speaks of her as Reason incarnate.
What he says shows us the species of charm, the singular, scolding charm that her common sense exercised
around her.　She liked to school her company, and
she usually made it like its lesson.　It is true that if
any one did not accept it, if he tried to get away from
her desire to advise and reprove him, she was not
pleased; and a dry little tone in her voice soon warned
him that she was piqued in her foible, in her claim
to be mentor and director.

A little note that she wrote to David Hume has
been lately printed as a specimen of her way of abus-

ing people when she was pleased with them; I suppress the faults of spelling—for Mme. Geoffrin could not spell, and made no secret of it:

"Nothing hinders you, my big rascal [*mon gros drôle*] from being a perfect dandy but playing stern virtue and not answering the love-letter I sent you by Gatti. In order to have all possible airs you seem to be giving yourself that of being modest. . . ."

Mme. de Tencin called the clever men of her society her "stupids" [*bêtes*]: Mme. Geoffrin continued to treat them as such, with a switch.

She judged her friends, her habitual guests, seriously and with accuracy. Certain scathing remarks that escaped her, not then in jest, have been preserved. It was she who said of the Abbé Trublet when some one spoke of him in her presence as a man of intellect: "He, a man of intellect! he is a fool rubbed with intellect." She said of the Duc de Nivernais: "He is a failure every way, soldier failure, ambassador failure, author failure." Ruthière read aloud in her salon his manuscript "Anecdotes on Russia"; she wanted him to throw it into the fire and offered to compensate him with a sum of money. Ruthière was indignant, and brought forward all the great sentiments of honour and disinterested love of truth: "How much more do you want?" was her only reply. We see that Mme. Geoffrin was gentle only when she pleased; and that her benignity of temper and beneficence covered some inward bitterness.

I have quoted Franklin in relation to her. She had maxims that seemed to come from the same good sense, calculating, ingenious, and wholly practical like his. She had engraved on her card-counters the words: "Economy is the source of independence and of liberty." And also the following: "Never let the grass grow on the path of friendship."

Her mind was one of those keen minds of which Pascal speaks; which are wont to judge at a glance, instantly, and which never return to what they have once been mistaken in. Such minds dread fatigue and *ennui,* and their sound, sometimes penetrating, judgment is not continuous. Mme. Geoffrin, gifted in the highest degree with that sort of mind, differed wholly in this respect from Mme. du Châtelet, for example, who liked to follow up and exhaust an argument. These delicate and quick minds are specially fitted for knowledge of the world and men; they like to let their eyes wander, rather than fix them on anything. Mme. Geoffrin needed, to save her from weariness, a great variety of persons and things. Too much intensity suffocated her; too great duration even of pleasure made it unbearable to her: " Of the most charming society she wanted only just so much as she could take at her own time and ease." A visit which threatened to be prolonged and to last for ever turned her pale as death. Once, when she saw the excellent Abbé de Saint-Pierre settle himself in her salon for a long winter's evening, she felt a momentary terror; then, inspired by the desperate situation, she drew the worthy man out so skilfully that she made him amusing. He was quite astonished himself, and when, at parting, she complimented him on his conversation he replied: "Madame, I am only an instrument on which you have played skilfully." Mme. Geoffrin was indeed a skilled virtuoso.

In all this, I have simply extracted from and summed up the Memoirs of the time. It is a greater pleasure than people suppose to read over again those authors of the eighteenth century who are called secondary, but who are simply excellent in their sensible prose. There is nothing more agreeable, delicate, and distinguished than the pages that Marmontel devotes in his Memoirs to Mme. Geoffrin, and the sketch of her society. Morellet himself, in speaking of her, is not only an excellent painter but an admirable annalist; the hand that writes is rather heavy, but the pen is clear and fine. None of them, down to Thomas, who was held to be too enthusiastic, fails to give very charming and very happy expression to their sentiments for Mme. Geoffrin. It is often said and repeated that Thomas was bombastic; but we ourselves, in our present style of writing, have become so turgid, so metaphorical, that Thomas, as I reread him, seems to me simple.

The great event of Mme. Geoffrin's life was the journey she made to Poland in 1766, to visit the king, Stanislas Poniatowski. She had known him when quite a young man, in Paris, and he, like many others, had received her assistance. He had hardly ascended the throne of Poland before he wrote to her: "Mamma, your son is king"; and he begged her earnestly to come and see him. She did not refuse, in spite of her advanced age. Passing through Vienna, she was the object of marked attentions from the sovereigns. It was thought that a small diplomatic mission was slipped into this journey. We have the letters of Mme. Geoffrin written from Warsaw; they are charming; they went the rounds of Paris, and it was not good form in those days to be ignorant of them. Voltaire chose that moment to write to her as to a power, begging her to interest the King of Poland in the Sirven family.

Mme. Geoffrin was so well balanced that this journey did not turn her head. Marmontel, in writing to her, had seemed to think that these attentions shown by monarchs to a private person must make a revolution in her ideas. Mme. Geoffrin recalls him to the true point of view:

"No, my neighbour" (neighbour, because Marmontel had an apartment in the same house) "no, not a word is true of all that; nothing at all of what you think will happen. Everything will remain just the same when I return, and you will find my heart such as you have ever known it, very sensitive to friendship."

Writing to d'Alembert, also from Warsaw, she says,

while congratulating herself (but without intoxication), on her lot:

"This journey ended, I feel I shall have seen enough
of men and of things to be convinced that they are
everywhere very much the same. I have my store-
house of reflections and comparisons well supplied
for the rest of my life. . . ."

And she adds a sentiment as touching as it is noble
about her royal pupil:

"It is a terrible position to be King of Poland. I
dare not tell him how unfortunate I think him; alas!
he feels it himself only too often. All that I have seen
since I quitted my *penates* makes me thank God that I
was born a Frenchwoman and a private individual."

On her return from Warsaw, where she had been
loaded with honours and attentions, she increased in
skilful modesty. We may believe that this modesty in
her was only a gentle manner, replete with good taste,
of bearing her self-gratification and her new fame.
But she excelled in such discreet and fitting conduct.
Like Mme. de Maintenon, she belonged to the race of
the self-glorifying modest people. When persons con-
gratulated and questioned her about this journey,
whether she answered them or did not answer, she put
no affectation into her words nor into her silence. Never
did any one know better than she—this Parisian *bourgeoise*—how to deal with great people, how to get out
of them all she wanted without either effacing herself
or presuming in any way, simply by keeping, with an

air of ease in all things and to all persons, within the limits of decorum.

Like all great persons she had the honour of being attacked. Palissot tried twice to arraign her on the stage as patroness of the Encyclopædists. But of all these attacks the one Mme. Geoffrin felt most keenly was the publication of the private letters of Montesquieu, which the Abbé de Guasco caused to be printed in 1767, for the purpose of being disagreeable to her. Some of Montesquieu's remarks against Mme. Geoffrin indicate pretty plainly what, indeed, we might otherwise divine, namely: that wherever there are men to be governed there is always something of intrigue and of manœuvring, even when women undertake it. Mme. Geoffrin had sufficient influence to stop the publication, and the passages relating to her were cancelled.

The last illness of Mme. Geoffrin brought about certain singular circumstances. While supporting the *Encyclopédie* with her gifts, she had always kept a corner in her mind for religion. La Harpe relates that she had at her beck and call a Capuchin confessor, a confessor with very wide sleeves for the convenience of her friends who might need them; for if she did not like to have her habitués get themselves put into the Bastille, still less did she like them to die without confession. As for her, while living with the philosophers, she always went to Mass, as if for assignation; and she had her seat in the church of the Capucines, as others had their *petite maison*. Age increased this serious or becoming inclination.

At the close of a Jubilee, which she observed with too much exertion in the summer of 1776, she was struck down by paralysis, and her daughter, profiting by her condition, shut the door to the philosophers, whose influence on her mother she dreaded. D'Alembert, Marmontel, Morellet, were harshly excluded. Imagine the clamour! Turgot wrote to Condorcet: "I pity that poor Mme. Geoffrin for undergoing such slavery, and for having her last moments poisoned by that villainous daughter." Mme. Geoffrin was no longer mistress of her actions; even after she came to herself, she felt that she had to choose between her daughter and her friends; the ties of blood carried the day: "My daughter," she said, smiling, "is like Godefroi de Bouillon; she wants to defend my tomb against the Infidels." She frequently sent to those Infidels her regards and her regrets; she also sent them gifts. Her mind grew feeble, but its character remained the same, and she roused up, now and then, to utter sayings that showed she was still herself. They were talking, one evening, round her bed of the means that Governments might employ to make their peoples happy; each person present suggested fine things: "Add," she said, "the care of *procuring pleasures for them;* a thing that is never enough thought of."

She died in the parish of Saint-Roch on the 6th

of October, 1777. The name of Mme. Geoffrin,
and her form of influence, recall to us, naturally, another interesting name, which it is now too late to
weigh with hers in this essay. The Mme. Geoffrin of
our time, Mme. Récamier, had, in excess of the other,
youth, beauty, poesy, the graces, a star on her brow,
and, let us add, a goodness, a kindness that was not
more skilful but more angelic. That which made
Mme. Geoffrin superior in her government of a *salon*
that was far otherwise extended and important, was a
firmer, and, in some sort more domestic judgment,
which made less efforts and advances, fewer sacrifices
to the tastes of others—in short, it was the unique
good sense of which Walpole has given us so clear an
idea, and a mind not only delicate and refined but just
and penetrating.

The Abbé Barthélemy.

The Abbé Barthélemy.

I SPEAK to-day of the author of *Le Voyage du Jeune Anacharsis,* the Abbé Barthélemy. That work, which made his reputation and which appeared in 1788, seems to have been laid aside for some time and judged with a severity that ought not to run into injustice. It had, when it appeared, brilliant success, which was concurrent with the first events of the Revolution, and lasted as long as our fathers lived. They were grateful to the Abbé Barthélemy for what he had taught them, in a few days' reading, of that Greek world and that ancient society then talked of constantly, but into which very few had actually penetrated. The Abbé Barthélemy was to them, in this respect, a teacher such as Rollin had formerly been, but one more fitted to the new era; a teacher, brilliant and agreeable, polished and fluent, enlightened, pleasing, and very animated; skilful in concealing the depth and accuracy of his knowledge beneath a grace that was almost worldly.

He himself, as a man, has a character distinct and modestly original in its delicate shading, among all the celebrated writers of the eighteenth century. He deserves to be known and studied in his private life.

Literary criticism, which is justly proud and happy to rise to the occasion when it meets a lofty subject, takes pleasure, nevertheless, from its own nature, in those medium subjects (not for that reason mediocre) which allow the social moral to penetrate them.

When old, having reached the end of an existence until then favoured and most equably gentle and peaceful, the Abbé Barthélemy suddenly found himself deprived by the Revolution of fortune, ease of life, and liberty; in those moments of deprivation and retirement, he formed the idea of writing his Memoirs; these remained unfinished, but so far as they go, they are the source from which we learn to know him best. His family lived at the South, in the pretty little town of Aubagne, between Marseilles and Toulon ; he himself was born at Cassis, during a visit his mother made there in January, 1716. He has given us a sunny idea of his childhood in the bosom of a united and tender family. He had a brother and two sisters; having lost his mother early, he found in his father an affection that was truly maternal. He studied at the College of the Oratorians at Marseilles; and if we had to select a pupil who expressed, in its best aspect, the form of education received at the Oratory, liberal, ornate, varied, sufficiently philosophical and morally decent, no better example could be chosen than Barthélemy. He had, even in college, brilliant successes, and showed tastes already academic; and he possessed, as it were from birth, a very marked literary senti-

J. J. BARTHELEMY.

JEAN JACQUES BARTHÉLEMY

After the bust by Houdon

ment. Apropos of one of the public exercises that took place in the great hall of the college, the audience being in part composed of the prettiest women of the town, he records that when he saw M. de la Visclède, secretary of the Marseilles Academy, enter, "I could see no one but him; my heart palpitated as I looked at him."

Such was Barthélemy at fifteen years of age; an equable soul, affectionate and refined; with a mind eager, inquisitive, quick; hungry for knowledge, putting nothing above the beautiful and noble studies that can be cultivated peacefully in the shade of Academies and Museums. We could almost think that something of the penetration and gentleness of the ancient Greeks, those first colonisers and civilisers of the Phocian country, had passed into him, and that he had tasted their honey too long ever to be weaned from it. "I destined myself," he says, "for the ecclesiastical profession"; for him the Church meant what it has been at so many epochs, a haven of peace and study, a shelter for the learned and innocent researches from which a scholarly and cultivated mind cannot bear to be distracted. The Bishop of Marseilles, who had been so admirable during the plague, the virtuous Belzunce, did not like the theological and semi-jansenist doctrines of the Oratorians; and it was through him that Barthélemy pursued his philosophical and theological studies with the Jesuits. But though he passed that way, he was never acclimated to it, and whenever he spoke of the Jesuits it was always with a slight touch of ridicule and aversion, naturally felt by the former pupil of the Oratorians and by the friend of the Duc de Choiseul.

The account that Barthélemy gives of the early years of his youth, passed in Provence at his various studies, learning Hebrew, Arabic, the history of medals, mathematics, and astronomy, is lively and piquant; he endeavoured to make it so by means of anecdotes well related. The study of mathematics and of astronomy in which he immersed himself for quite a long time, seemed to him afterwards one of the mistakes and dissipations of his youth. Without ambition, without strong passion, mingling liberal studies that were often intense, with the amusements of society, with readings among friends and little concerts, neglected and forgotten by his bishop, he lived at Aubagne in the bosom of his family, making, from time to time, little journeys to Marseilles or to Aix, which kept him in communication with the learned men of that region. But by this time, he was almost twenty-nine years of age; his brother's family was increasing, and the hour came when he was compelled to make a career for himself, and he started for Paris in June, 1744.

Among the letters of recommendation which he took with him was one to M. de Boze, one of the most influential of the Academicians, and the keeper of the Cabinet of Medals. The young abbé, invited to his dinners, given on Tuesdays and Wednesdays, became acquainted there with the learned men of the day, the men of Letters in the Academy of Inscriptions, and with several persons of the great world who piqued themselves on their erudition and knowledge of art; he felt at first in their presence something of the respect and emotion that he had felt fifteen years earlier on seeing M. de la Visclède.

"This profound respect for men of Letters," he says, "I felt to such an extent in my youth that I ever retained the names of those who sent enigmas to the *Mercure*. The result to me was quite an injury; I admired but I did not judge. For a very long time I never read a book without acknowledging inwardly that I was incapable of making as good a one. In my last years I have been bolder in regard to works relating to research and to antiquity ; I had then, by long labours, acquired rights to my own confidence."

Even supposing that the abbé, wishing to make his narrative lively, exaggerates a little his veneration and his trepidation, we at least see plainly the direction in which lay his vocation and the literary religion that was, as it were, infused into him. He grew bolder rapidly; he made himself known and liked by men who were more or less distinguished; and the more intelligence they had themselves the better he pleased them. Nature had done much for him; his manner of speaking was lively, easy, insinuating; intercourse with him was safe and charming. A contemporary, seeing him at the height of his fame, and having before his eyes the bust that Houdon made of him, describes him as follows:

" He had a very tall and well-proportioned figure. It seemed as if Nature wanted to match his form and his features to his morals and

his occupations.   His face had an antique character and his bust could
be rightly placed between those of Plato and Aristotle.   It is the work
of an able hand that knew how to put into his countenance that mixture of gentleness, simplicity, kindliness, and grandeur which render
visible, so to speak, the soul of this rare man."

Take out the word *grandeur,* and the names of Plato
and Aristotle, which are out of place, and it remains
true that the Abbé Barthélemy had a very fine head,
was a little too thin, but had all the external advantages
that attract and charm, with manners that made the
young scholar the most easy and natural of men of the
world: "The Abbé Barthélemy," wrote Gibbon, "is
very agreeable and has nothing of the antiquary about
him but his erudition"; and all those who knew him
said the same.

Before he became celebrated as a writer by his *Voyage du Jeune Anacharsis* (which he did not publish till
he was seventy-two years of age), Barthélemy was
long only an antiquary, and it was in that capacity
that he gained his first renown.   Arriving in Paris, and
welcomed, as I have said, by M. de Boze, who made
him his assistant in the Cabinet of Medals, and caused
him to become a member of the Academy of Inscriptions, he was forced to train himself, under a most
painstaking master, to extreme accuracy and to wearisome application.   But nothing ever discourages that
which comes in the line of a passion, and Barthélemy
had a true passion for medals, something of that sacred
fire which applies itself to many different objects, and

is well known to all those who have become possessed
by the taste for collections.

Having succeeded M. de Boze when the latter died,
he had no thought more dear than to enrich the King's
Cabinet, thus intrusted to him, with new and rare
treasures, and he was joyful when, in 1755, the Duc
de Choiseul (then Comte de Stainville), appointed
ambassador to Rome, offered to take him to Italy, lodge
him at the embassy in Rome, and to facilitate his
journey in every way. This was the beginning of a
lasting tie that became closer year by year, and was
broken only by death. The names of the Duc and
Duchesse de Choiseul and that of the Abbé Barthélemy
have become inseparable. There were grandeur and
magnificence in the benefactions of M. de Choiseul,
combined with a rare fund of delicacy; he won the
hearts of all those he obliged. The Abbé Barthélemy
had attraction, charm, constant amenity, a true and
attaching sensibility. " My fate " he said, " is to have
warm friends; it is a happiness of which I feel the full
extent."

The first impression that he received on arriving in
Rome and seeing the vast wealth of antiquities there
accumulated was amazement, and something like
discouragement:

" We can never hope," he cries, " to form such collections; we live
in a land of iron for antiquaries. It is in Italy that researches should
be made; never shall we conquer the Romans but in Rome. I blush
a hundred times a day at the infinitely petty things that are in our infinitely petty Cabinet of antiques; I blush that I showed it to strangers;

what must they have thought of the interest I took in those bronzes seven or eight inches high, in those two or three mutilated heads of which I wanted them to admire the grandeur and the rarity! Why did no one warn me?"

Yet he recovered, little by little, from this electrical shock; he found his bearings; he selected and discerned among the objects of his research: "In the beginning," he says, "I saw Rome through a petrified fog; to-day I see it through a cloud that lets some flashes of light through it." It was in devoting himself particularly to his principal object, medals, that he succeeded, little by little, in accumulating treasures. He delights in relating the stratagems, the diplomatic wiles, the manœuvres that he has to employ. More than one antiquary is pitiless, and will not part with his possessions. Barthélemy is then obliged to resort to the plots of Ulysses:

For example, there is in Verona an antiquary named Muselli, who has the medal of a certain almost unknown little king which Barthélemy covets for his Cabinet, and which the possessor will not give up. But this Muselli like most of the Italian *savants,* has a great desire to be connected in some way with the Academy of Inscriptions in Paris, and Barthélemy begs M. de Caylus to negotiate with the Academy in favour of the said Muselli so far as to make him their correspondent; arranging, however, that to him, Barthélemy, the letters are to be sent: "I shall then," he says, "go to Verona; if he gives me the medal, I will

give him hopes; if he refuses it, I will make him fear
my opposition to his desire; all this very politely. It
is a misfortune for me that he knows the value of his
treasure; you cannot snatch anything from Italians if
they once know the value of what they possess." All
this is said merrily, and in the tone of a man of the
world which never fails to accompany the learned man
in Barthélemy and gently to put aside the pedant.

At last, his harvest is garnered, his prize is won; he
feels that his journey has not been mere loss; that was
his fear at the beginning; a hundred times did he regret
having occasioned a useless expense: "That thought,"
he says artlessly, "poisoned moments which I might
have spent with more pleasure. But here I am now
more tranquil, thanks to a dozen or two of little bits
of bronze. It is certainly very senseless to have set
one's happiness on the increasing of a treasure in which
almost no one deigns to take an interest." It remains
evident, after reading his letters from Italy, that, in spite
of some success, he feels a little lost in that vast field;
his journey has humbled more than it has delighted him,
by revealing to his mind the full extent of much that he
must either ignore or touch superficially. He feels the
need of concentrating himself on his return; of shutting
himself up while vigour remains, and not coming out
of his retirement till he can bring with him some great
work.

During this journey in Italy, I fancy I see two instincts struggling together in the breast of the Abbé

Barthélemy: one is the pure instinct of the antiquary, of the lover of old fragments, the zealous collector of rare medals, which tells him to exhaust the material he finds there and remain; and the other is the instinct of the writer, the man of modern art and of style, who, at the sight of these scattered treasures, these monuments of a great past, these relics of a vast ruin superseded by a brilliant Renaissance, feels the necessity of gathering himself together, of returning to his industrious hive and there composing a work that shall be his, his only. It was, in fact, from this sojourn in Italy that we must date the idea of the *Jeune Anacharsis*.

Barthélemy first thought of making a Frenchman travel in Italy about the time of Leo X, and of painting, by this means, the rich and full Renaissance; but, on reflection, he decided that he was less qualified for that subject, which would draw him from his favourite domain and throw him into a world of art, of modern poesy and painting, into a whole order of subjects with which he was only moderately familiar. He therefore transported his idea to Greece, inventing the visit of a Scythian to that country in the days of Philip of Macedon. This was the germ of his work, which took him thirty years to prepare and then to write.

On his return from this journey to Italy his life settled down into a single course; he became inseparable from the Choiseuls and could no longer part his fortunes from theirs. In any picture made of the society and the salons of the eighteenth century he must be presented as the most accomplished type of the erudite, social abbé, having all the advantages that the position implies, and paying for them by his kind offices and accomplishments.

In every rich household in the eighteenth century there was always "the abbé," an accessory and yet indispensable personage, convenient for the master and mistress of the house, answering the questions of the children and their mothers, keeping an eye on the tutor, well-informed, active, domestic, assiduous, amusing, a necessary piece of furniture in the country. I do not know who it was that wagered he could go from door to door through the Faubourg Saint-Germain asking each porter: "Has the abbé come in?" "Will the abbé dine at home to-day?" and that to these questions the porter would answer as if he knew of course who was meant. The Abbé Barthélemy, by his own merit, and by the nature of the sentiments that bound him to the Choiseuls, was far above this class of abbé; or rather he personifies it to our eyes by a superior and almost ideal example.

On the return from Italy, M. de Choiseul put his young wife in charge of the abbé to accompany her and bring her to Paris. This young woman, of whom all descriptions agree, was, from her tenderest years, a dainty perfection of good sense, prudence, grace, and prettiness.

" Mme. de Stainville," the abbé says of her," though scarcely eighteen years of age, enjoyed the deep veneration that is usually accorded

only to a long exercise of the virtues: all in her inspired interest, her
age, her face, the delicacy of her health, the vivacity that animated her
words and actions, the desire to please which it was so easy for her to
satisfy (the success of which she carried to a husband the worthy
object of her tenderness and worship), the extreme sensibility that
made her happy or unhappy through the happiness or troubles of
others, and lastly, her purity of soul that never allowed her to suspect
evil. At the same time, persons were surprised to see so much en-
lightenment with such simplicity. She reflected at an age when
others scarcely begin to think."

The Abbé Barthélemy has on many occasions portrayed Mme. de Choiseul; he has put her with her
husband into his *Jeune Anacharsis* under the names
of Phédime and Arsame: "Phédime discerns at a
glance the different bearings of a subject; with a
single sentence she can express them. Sometimes
she seems to remember what she has never learned."

He was very sensitive to friendship, and very worthy
of it. He had many sweet and charming thoughts upon
it. In a little *Traité de Morale,* written for the use of
a nephew of M. de Malesherbes at the request of the
mother, he shows how amenity was the natural bent
of his character, and humanity the foundation of his
soul. He knows very well how to distinguish between
complaisance and friendship. Wishing to show that
among the different sorts of spirit that of display and
effusiveness is the most opposed to friendship, he says:
"Friendship would get on better with that refined and
delicate spirit which seems only to express itself to
give pleasure, and leaves more to be perceived than is
expressed. But observe that it pleases only in taking

the tone of true feeling, and it is necessary always to make plain that its seductive graces are not the fruit of worldly customs or of the hypocrisy of the heart." He desires friendship to be wholly sincere, wholly virtuous, and founded on the love of honour: "We need," he said, "in friendship, not a passing or imaginative fervour, but a steady and judicious warmth. When that warmth has had time to insinuate itself into hearts, when proofs have only rendered it more effectual, then the choice is made, then we begin to live in another *ourself.*" He speaks with feeling and with force. Friendship, and the continual solicitudes it brings with it, which embarrass some souls, are delightful to him. The details into which it must enter daily never weary him; far from causing him *ennui,* they seem to him a source of pleasure:

"Let us consecrate to friendship," he says, "all the moments of which other duties allow us to dispose ; delicious moments that come so slowly, and go so fast; in which all that is said is sincere, all that is promised is durable; moments when hearts, unconstrained and bared, know how to give importance to the smallest things, and confide to one another without reluctance secrets that draw their ties the closer; moments, in short, when silence itself proves that souls can be happy in the silent presence of each other; for this silence brings neither distaste nor *ennui* We say nothing, but—we are together."

He was one of those moderate and sensible souls who, amid slow and patient study and a pronounced taste for social enjoyments and familiar pleasantry, have within them a vein of tenderness, and who, in their hours of revery, feed themselves on passages from Euripides, Racine, or Saint-Augustine.

And why should he not have given himself wholly
to the Choiseuls, who forestalled his slightest desires
with so much grace and beneficence? During his last
days in Rome he saw and desired to possess a dozen
little figurines in terra-cotta, which had recently been
discovered in a marble tomb; but the price demanded
was excessive. He related this by chance to a friend
in Mme. de Choiseul's presence; and the next day he
found the twelve little figurines on his table with no
intimation whence they came. Such deeds on the
part of a gracious fairy were perpetual. On his return
to Paris, he fitted up for himself a lodging and a study.
Mme. de Choiseul, aided this time by Mme. de Grammont as her accomplice, obtained the key during his
absence, and the philosophical study, decorated, by
the touch of a wand, with all sorts of pretty furniture
and even bits of embroidery by their own hands, was
metamorphosed, in an hour, into a charming bower.
This graceful deed was for the moment the talk of all
Paris (November, 1762).

In these years Barthélemy justified the attentions he
received by the manner in which he treated certain
points of erudition before the public at the solemn sessions of his Academy. In April, 1763, at the public
session after Easter, he read a dissertation on the Coptic
language:

" We knew what it was to be beforehand," says Gibbon, " and
every one blamed the choice of such a knotty subject, which seemed
only suitable for private meetings. But we saw with pleasure mingled

with surprise how interesting our abbé made it to the women and persons of society who heard it, by the graces of his style, the acuteness
of his criticism, and his correct and luminous principles."

" The women themselves," we find it stated in the
Memoirs of Bachaumont, " were delighted with that
lecture." Here we come upon the class of talent, and
also upon what was to prove the general defect of the
Abbé Barthélemy in his *Anacharsis,* namely, rather
too much condiment in his erudition, and an elegant
weakening of antiquity with worldly graces.

He was too highly favoured in these years not to
rouse envy. During the ministry of the Duc de Choiseul, pensions, benefices, sinecures were poured upon
him continually, to the point of giving him an annual
revenue of nearly 40,000 *livres.* When he was named
secretary-general of the Swiss Guard, a place which
alone brought him 20,000 *livres,* those present at a Car-
nival ball a few days later beheld a tall, thin, ungainly
man, representing a caricature of him masked, and
wearing a costume partly of the Swiss Guard, but with
breeches and a black cloak. A scene was acted between the mask and a stranger : " Who are you, noble
mask ? " asked the latter; " what profession do you
belong to, abbé or guardsman ? " " To one or the
other, whichever you please," replied the mask, " provided it gives me 30,000 *livres* per year." The Duc de
Choiseul was very angry and wanted to discover the
actor. The abbé recovered the good opinion of the
public by his moderation, and by resigning a small

pension which he received from the *Mercure*. This slight sacrifice, made at the right moment and without effort, pacified the Encyclopædists, with whom Barthélemy was not always on good terms because he did not belong to them.

After the fall of the Duc de Choiseul, when the office of colonel-general of the Swiss Guard was taken from him, Barthélemy sent in his resignation as secretary-general; and he persisted in it in spite of the efforts made to get him to withdraw it. They finally gave him, without his requesting it, a pension of 10,000 *livres* on the office he resigned. He was thus enabled to live with the noble exiles at Chanteloup, be faithful, as he should be, to friendship, and yet have a handsome revenue, which he disposed of generously and without ostentation.

If the letters, or rather the gazettes, which the Abbé Barthélemy wrote to Mme. Du Deffand from Chanteloup had been preserved, letters which gave an account of their doings from day to day, we should have true memoirs of the private life of the great world in the eighteenth century. We can get some idea of the correspondence from a little mock-heroic poem by Barthélemy, entitled *La Chanteloupée,* which is otherwise very frivolous. We find in the Correspondence of Horace Walpole a remark about the Abbé Barthélemy and a word of praise that needs some explanation. One of Walpole's friends, General Conway, being in France and, in spite of his expressed

desire, not succeeding in making the acquaintance of
the Duc and Duchesse de Choiseul who were little inclined to it, Walpole writes to him:

"Though the Choiseuls hold themselves aloof from
you, I hope that their Abbé Barthélemy is not subjected
to the same quarantine. Besides great knowledge he
has infinite wit and *polissonnerie,* and he is one of the
best sort of men that there is in the world."

The word *polissonnerie* is written in French and
underlined. Walpole evidently did not fully understand what the word signifies; it is probable that he
meant to speak of the gay and lively playfulness that
the abbé showed in a drawing-room. At supper with
Mme. Du Deffand, or in writing to her of the doings
at Chanteloup, this abbé of good society had a slight
touch of Gresset about him.

The actual facts of the Abbé Barthélemy's merits as
an antiquary, and before the publication of his *Anacharsis,* escape my search; what can be said in general
is, that he rendered true service to the knowledge of
medals [and the coins of antiquity]; that he contributed
to raise them from the condition of mere curiosities,
and to make them one of the regular and consecutive
supports of history. In sixty years of practice, more
than four hundred thousand medals passed through
his hands. Bringing to this study, as to all those he
undertook, a philosophical mind, he nevertheless preserved himself from what was called the philosophy of
the century; and, as much, perhaps, from a sense of

propriety as from reflection, he at all times considered the attacks on religion, in which the brilliant men and the principal writers around him indulged, as fatal and ruinous.

After the death of the Duc de Choiseul in 1785, he lived in Paris,' dividing his time between his Cabinet of Medals, his Academy and a few salons, that of Mme. de Choiseul being his centre. He carefully avoided all quarrels and disturbances; we find him advising Walpole, in a certain case, to give no pretext for war to Voltaire. He, himself, has the honour, I believe, of not being once mentioned in the Works of that monarch and literary despot of the eighteenth century. When, at the age of seventy, his friends advised him no longer to put off the publication of his *Jeune Anacharsis,* the work of his whole life, he hesitated long; and when he finally decided to let it appear, in 1788, that is to say on the eve of the States-General, his hope was that the attention of the public, being occupied elsewhere, would turn slowly and only little by little to the book, and therefore that it would have neither a success nor a failure: "I wished," he says, "that it might slide silently into the world."

In what I have thus far said, I have sought to present the Abbé Barthélemy in his surroundings and general mode of life; and to show the mild and tempered distinction of his nature; by so doing it becomes easier to speak of his work.

He wanted for his *Jeune Anacharsis,* as I have said,

a gentle, almost silent success, something like the manner in which it had been composed; and it obtained, from the very day it was published, a dazzling success. Yet, the States-General were just convoked and the year 1789 was opening in the midst of boundless expectation. Sièyes had published his pamphlet, "What is the Tiers-État?" Political discussion was becoming inflamed on all sides; but, amid the soughing of that impetuous, rising wind which was not yet a hurricane, the French Academy was receiving the Chevalier de Boufflers; the Abbé Delille recited in public sessions with applause, portions of a poem on Imagination, and the young Anacharsis entered the port of Athens with all sail set. It was the last great literary success of the eighteenth century, at the moment when the whole of French society was issuing from its happy lake, its peaceful Mediterranean, through unknown straits, whence the Genius of the new Era was to launch it with a powerful hand upon the ocean.

With his elegant and polished young Greek, who to-day seems to us so cold, the Abbé Barthélemy obtained a success like that of Bernardin de Saint-Pierre. Men of the world, the *élite,* and also the people of Letters, and women, were all seized, in an instant, with enthusiasm. Mme. de Krüdner, who at that date was still only an ambassadress and a pretty woman, copied and learned by heart long passages of *Anacharsis;* Mme. de Staël, who had just written her *Lettres sur Jean-Jacques Rousseau* and who was dawning into celebrity, addressed to the abbé at a supper couplets that sounded the names of Sappho and Homer. I find a quantity of verses addressed by amateurs to the learned abbé, among them some to the air of *Prends, ma Phillis.* In short, the success, save for a few isolated protestations, was sudden and universal. Frenchmen were grateful to an author who had continually thought of them while painting Athenians, and they applauded enthusiastically the gratifying resemblance.

The defects and the good qualities of the book are fully explained by the manner in which it was composed, and by the style of mind of the writer. At the time when he conceived the idea of his work Barthélemy had just read the ancient authors; he then re-read them, pen in hand, "noting down on cards all the points that threw light on the nature of the governments, the habits and morals, and laws of the people, the opinions of philosophers." It was these precise and careful notes that he set himself to rearrange and unite by an ingenious plot and a pleasing narrative. "Antiquity," he thought, "is only a study of various accounts. The more we see of monuments, the more texts we have at hand, the better we are able to explain them one by the other." Here we see his method, which was that of collection and mosaic.

Having chosen his young Scythian traveller, to make him talk and judge of Greece in the days of Epaminondas and Philip of Macedon, he takes much trouble to introduce questions that the sight of Greece, at that

time, would not have roused; but he does it to elude
and adroitly set aside certain other questions, and to
produce a sort of rigid appearance of truth, for which,
to-day, we do not thank him. Nevertheless, those who
in their youth took pleasure (and I am one of them) in
reading *Anacharsis*, have, from duty and gratitude,
certain favourable reasons to present.

In Barthélemy's work there is a quality which we
value too little in our day—namely, composition, connection, unity. The rather lively and elegant Introduction which epitomises the history of the earlier ages of
Greece, makes the frontal of the abbé's monument.
The *Voyage*—the Journey, properly so-called—begins
joyfully and with emotion, by a visit to Epaminondas,
the most perfect of ancient heroes; it ends, in the last
chapter, with a portrait of the young Alexander: the
whole narrative is enclosed between that first visit in
Thebes, where the subject of Greece appears in all its
glory, and the battle of Cheronæa, at which perished
the liberties of Greece. Within these confines we
have many instructive digressions, returns into ancient
history; conversations in libraries; erudite but not per-
plexing dissertations; meetings with celebrated men,
who are painted with a good deal of truth and character; chapters that are quite charming in their tempered style, such as the visit made to Xenophon at
Scillus. In a word, though the current in *Anacharsis*
is never rapid, it suffices to carry along a reader who
is not too impatient, and who will pardon a lack of

vigour and originality for the sake of elegance and sweetness combined with accuracy.

Barthélemy has nothing of Montesquieu in his view of Greece. "Every author must follow his own plan," he said; "it did not enter into mine to send a traveller into Greece to take them my thoughts, but to bring back theirs to me as much as possible." It is a question, however, whether the thoughts of the Greeks, expressed by them and translated to us without previous explanation, are sufficiently suited to our use. We could wish that instead of minutely describing the Constitutions and the government of Athens, Barthélemy had made us feel more vividly the marked differences between them and modern society— slavery, on which they were founded, oppression of conquered races, civic rights reserved exclusively to a small number of the inhabitants, in the very place where, as we are told, the multitude ruled.

Barthélemy, by introducing a personage of the past, and making him constantly speak, cut himself off from the resource of modern and really statesmanlike considerations; but, had he spoken in his own name, he would also have ignored them; they did not enter into the nature of his mind. He kept to mundane and superficial analogies, and, if I may say so, to the Parisian resemblances which the names of Aspasia or Alcibiades suggested; he never cut to the depths in his comparisons. We find in Grimm's *Correspondance* a few pages written after reading *Anacharsis,* which

treat of the government of Athens; that short chapter,
on the eve of the French Revolution, says more about
that government than all the notes so minutely dove-
tailed together by Barthélemy. After stating the
principal features of the government of Athens and
the spirit of the Athenian people, after pointing out
the influence, often sovereign, of their greatest men,
Themistocles, Pericles, etc., Grimm (or the writer
of the chapter, whoever he was) boldly drew this
conclusion:

"It is therefore permissible to say that the most
democratic democracy that ever has been, perhaps, in
the world, had no more certain means of sustaining
itself than to cease at times to be so; and that each
time it was least democratic in fact it enjoyed a more
brilliant fortune and one more truly to be envied."

Barthélemy has none of the comprehensive views of
a statesman and a philosopher; nor has he those of a
painter. His style, as I have said, has gentleness, and
in places emotion and sensibility. I could quote
many passages carefully worked up and graceful in
effect; such, for instance, as the famous description of
the spring-time at Delos: "In the happy climate
where I dwell, spring is like the dawn of a beautiful
day." But even there, we feel it is a theme, treated
and caressed deliberately by a skilful, polished pen,
rather than a picture grasped by the imagination or
vividly seized from nature. It is the work of a descriptive Isocrates, and nothing more.

Chateaubriand, in his first, confused work, his *Essai sur les Révolutions,* started, in a way, from the *Voyage du Jeune Anacharsis* to make continual comparisons of antiquity with the modern world; but, after the first steps in the tracks of his predecessor, how he makes us feel that he penetrates far beyond him! His brilliant and energetic talent begins at once, and at all hazards, to give sword-thrusts through his subject, and from that sword the lightnings dart. It would seem that all new talent, new genius, must enter thus into subjects sword in hand, like Renaud into the enchanted forest; and that it needs to strike boldly until it has broken the charm: the conquest of the true and of the beautiful is at this cost.

After Chateaubriand had visited Greece she had a painter among us. I do not say that he painted simply, or in the manner that she herself, in her best days, would have preferred; I say only that with the means and system of colour which were his, he imparts to us vividly the *sensation* of Greece. He arrives in Athens; he mounts at once to the Acropolis; like a conqueror he chooses his camp; he establishes his sovereign point of view. Re-read that page of his *Itinéraire.* Thence he describes the hills, the monuments about him; he evokes, he re-creates in idea the ancient city, the theatre resounding with applause, the fleets issuing from the Piræus, the days of Salamis or of Delos. There is nothing more glorious under the sun nor more luminous than that picture. With

Barthélemy, with his young Anacharsis, who is supposed to arrive for the first time in Athens, we have nothing of the kind; we follow him through the streets, one by one, but without a *coup d'œil*. We feel that our guide is troubled, he finds his way with effort; at last we reach the steps that lead to the Acropolis; slowly we mount, and wearily. The general *coup d'œil* comes too late, and is feeble. All this tells us that Barthélemy has read, but not seen.

I do not wish, however, to lay too much stress on his defects; we feel them too much in our day; but in his day he had grace and a relative usefulness. The idea that men have formed of Greece, of that celebrated literature and country, has not always been the same in France; it has passed in the course of three centuries through many variations and vicissitudes. If, formerly, we made ourselves too effeminate and smiling an image of ancient Greece, are we not making too hard and savage a one to-day? In the sixteenth century, on the morrow of the Renaissance and in the intoxication that followed it, our French poets imitated the Greeks without sobriety, and without taste; they missed the grandeur through their very excess of imitation; they succeeded in rendering adequately only the lesser authors, the graceful odes, the Anacreonics, a few idylls fallen from the treasury of the "Anthology." Amyot by devoting himself to Longinus and Plutarch, propagated the literature of Greece far better by making its prose more liked.

In the seventeenth century Greece was not as well comprehended, nor as faithfully pictured as we imagine; Boileau, who did, strictly speaking, understand Longinus and Homer, was, nevertheless, far more Latin than he was Greek. Racine, imitating with genius and drawing his inspiration from his own heart, reproduced from the old tragic masterpieces nothing, if I may say so, but their pathetic and sentimental beauties, which he sought to assimilate with French elegances. Fénelon alone, without thinking of copying or of inventing, and solely from a natural simplicity of taste, found Greece beneath his pen and easily reproduced it.

In the eighteenth century Bernardin de Saint-Pierre, without ever having studied the Greek language, is the one who, on certain of his pages, has divined and best revealed the Greek genius. André Chénier attained to a perception of Greece, by race, by study, and by talent, and he takes us there, even into many a by-way. But before he was known, before his Elegies, confided to love or to friendship, could be repeated, after his death, by the lips of admirers, a growing taste, more or less intelligent, for the antique had sprung up at the close of the eighteenth century; and it was that taste, I might almost say that fashion, which *Le Voyage du Jeune Anacharsis* fostered and quickened. There was a moment when Greece, through the Abbé Barthélemy, was the rage in all Parisian salons and boudoirs. We find in the Memoirs of Mme. Vigée-Lebrun (the graceful painter) the story of a supper improvised after a reading of *Anacharsis;* all the guests were draped in Greek costumes: even the cooking had a savour of antiquity. A cake was served made with the honey and raisins of Corinth; they drank the wine of Cyprus; they even tried, I think, a Lacedemonian broth. Le Brun-Pindare recited imitations of Anacreon.

Those imitations of Le Brun are more Greek than Barthélemy permitted himself to be. When he had a passage from Sappho or Sophocles to translate into verse for his *Voyage,* he had recourse to the muse of the Abbé Delille. The Greece of the Abbé Barthélemy corresponds well, in fact, with what appears to be the Roman country in the *Georgiques* of the other accomplished abbé. The literary usefulness of the two was of the same order and the same kind.

Chateaubriand, Paul-Louis Courier, and Fauriel have, since then, sufficiently corrected us of those ideas of Greece, redolent of the vicinity of Chanteloup, Ermenonville, and Moulin-Joli. For some time past another Greece has become the fashion, a Greece more complete, they assure us, more real, better based upon the original; often, however, too wanting in elegance. I applaud with all my heart such importations when they are faithful and conscientious; telling myself, at the same time, that they seem to proclaim, by this looking backward, a certain famine in the present, and that they must not be prolonged. The conclusions that I draw from this long series of attempts, which have, each in turn, gone to extremes, seldom reaching the exact

point, are that we cannot transplant one literature into
another, nor the genius of one race and language into
the genius of a different people; that to know Greece
and the Greeks well, we should read them much and
say but little—unless with those who read them also;
and that to draw something from them into the current usage of our day, the surest way is to have talent
and imagination in French.

If the Abbé Barthélemy had had more of that natural
originality, of that living inspiration, we could pardon
him certain infidelities in execution. In spite of all
his care, in spite of his determination not to take one
step without his erudite notes, his book must be considered, at least in certain parts, a modern and personal production. It was thus that, towards the end,
during the sojourn at Delos, he could not refrain from
giving himself free rein: the man is revealed; he puts
into the mouth of Philocles his own ideas on happiness, on society, on friendship; he inserts, by extracts,
his former little treatise on Morals that he wrote, many
years earlier, for the nephew of M. de Malesherbes.
We all know that he sang the praises of M. and Mme.
de Choiseul in his work, under the names of Arsame
and Phédime; and it is noticeable that he praises them
at three different periods: in the first chapter, in the
last chapter but one, and in the middle and very heart
of his work; thus distributing, intentionally, these dear
parts of his soul into the principal sections of his life-
long work. When Barthélemy published the book,

M. de Choiseul was dead; Mme. de Choiseul still lived and was destined to survive the friend who lauded her so delicately.

The *Voyage du Jeune Anacharsis* had been published some months and its success had mounted to the clouds; a place became vacant in the French Academy by the death of the grammarian Beauzée, and Barthélemy, chosen unanimously to succeed him, was received at the public session on Saint Louis's day, August, 1789. The Chevalier de Boufflers replied to him, and took the honours of the session by a brilliant analysis of the *Jeune Anacharsis,* whose author he compared to Orpheus. In Barthélemy's speech certain neologisms attracted notice. He said, in speaking of the States-General, and the hopes, already clouded, to which they had given birth : " France . . . sees her representatives ranged around the throne, whence are descending words of consolation *that have never before fallen from such a height.''* The singularity of that sentence, according to Grimm, was much applauded. Barthélemy inaugurated the parliamentary style. In another place he said, lauding the invention of printing, and sacrificing slightly to the enthusiastic ideas of the moment: " Eternal day has dawned, and its effulgence, becoming ever brighter, will penetrate successively all climes."

Barthélemy must have had, at the bottom of his heart, less ease and confidence in auguring good for the future. It was he who said, in a letter of Calli-

medon to Anacharsis, speaking of popular prejudices
and superstitions: "My dear Anacharsis, when we
say that an age is enlightened, that means that more
ideas are found in certain towns than in others; and
that in those the principal class of citizens is better
educated than it once was." As for the multitude,
"not excepting," he said, "that of Athens," he believed it almost incorrigible and little perfectible,
adding with discouragement: "Never doubt it: men
have two favourite passions that philosophy cannot
destroy—that of error, and that of slavery." While
thinking thus he was not misanthropic; nor was he
inclined to blacken human nature. "In general," he
said, "men have less wickedness than weakness and
inconstancy."

The events of the Revolution came, blow after blow,
to sadden his heart, and destroy the structure, hitherto
so secure, of his fortune. Until then he had led the
most well-arranged and comfortable of existences; he
now saw it daily fall to pieces, bit by bit, and escape
him. He had the right spirit to stifle his own complaints, reflecting on the oppression of all and the
common calamity:

"I speak to you only of literature," he writes to M. de Choiseul-
Gouffier in March, 1792, "because all other subjects are grievous and
torturing. I turn my mind from them as much as possible. We are
at a point where we cannot think of the past nor of the future, and
scarcely of the present. I go to the Academies, and to very few
houses, sometimes to solitary promenades; and when night comes I
say to myself: ' There is another day gone by.' "

Soon the Academies, his true homes, failed him; they were abolished. Nothing remained to him, except his Cabinet of Medals. But such sanctuaries, in revolutionary days, are not inviolable or sacred. In all public establishments where a certain number oi men are employed, there is always one, usually of inferior rank, who has piled up, during years of silence, heaps of gall and envy, and when the day of revolution comes, that man will rise against the others, who may not even have known him until then, and become their enemy and denouncer. This is what happened at the Bibliothèque du Roi. An employé, named Tobiezen-Dubi, denounced all his superiors, and his information was accepted. Barthèlemy was taken, September 2, 1793, to the prison of the Madelonnettes.

Mme. de Choiseul, as soon as she received the news, bestirred herself and took steps to influence the representative Courtois, who went to the Committee of Public Safety. There he pleaded earnestly for the inoffensive old man, whose literary success, applauded by all, was still so recent. He found an echo to his words on all sides, with one solitary opposing voice; that of an author, formerly much protected at Court, Laignelot, who had written the tragedy of *Agis* some years before the publication and success of *Anacharsis,* and who had since then nurtured a professional jealousy of it. Barthélemy left the prison after a confinement of only sixteen hours.

The Minister of the Interior, Paré, in an honourable

letter (written in the style of *Anacharsis*), hastened to inform the old man, that in order to atone for that momentary severity, he was appointed director-general of the Bibliothèque. Barthélemy was touched, but he declined the office; he was satisfied to remain among his medals: he even returned, at this close of his life, to his favourite study with that renewal of love for it which many an old man feels for the first occupations of his youth. But the springs of life were worn out in him. It was noticed that the desire to please, "which was perhaps his dominant passion," abandoned him gradually; an habitual gloom enveloped his soul; the Revolution seemed to him, and he so called it, a "revelation," which disconcerted all the moderately indulgent ideas he had hitherto formed of human nature. Friendship alone and the thought of Mme. de Choiseul still brightened him, and his last care, in his last days, was for her, desiring to spare her the emotion that the news of his condition would cause her.

Mme. de Choiseul, after the death of her husband in 1785, retired to a convent in the rue du Bac; chiefly to economise in order to pay his debts and thus protect his memory. After the suppression of the convents, and under the Directory, she lived in an entresol of the Périgord mansion in the rue de Lille, where she died in November, 1801, under the Consulate, surviving her friend six years.

The Abbé Barthélemy died in April, 1795, in his eightieth year. At one of the sessions of the Con-

vention that followed his death, Dusault, the former
friend of Jean-Jacques and the translator of Juvenal,
mounted the tribune and pronounced a Eulogy upon
him, in which he recommended the nephews of the
deceased to the care of the nation. "Barthélemy," he
said, in the sentimental language of the day, through
which a sincere affection made itself felt,

"Barthélemy was an excellent man in all respects. Those who knew
him knew not which to admire most, his immortal *Anacharsis,* or
the whole tenor of his life. A single remark of his discloses the sweetness of his philanthropic soul: 'Why is it not given to a mortal,' he
exclaimed, 'to be able to bequeath happiness?'"

To the shocking maxim of loving our friends as
though we might some day hate them, Barthélemy
liked to substitute another, more human, more con-
soling, from one of his ancient authors: "Hate your
enemies as though you were some day to love them."

Louis XV.

Louis XV.

L OUIS XV, though endowed with a noble presence, and many apparent graces, showed himself, from his earliest years, the weakest and most timid of beings. It has often been said—but never often enough, that his was the most vacant, the most contemptible, the most cowardly, of the hearts of kings. Nothing is better fitted to make known his moral nature than certain letters written by Mme. de Tencin to the Duc de Richelieu during the year 1743.

Informed by her brother, the cardinal, of all that went on at the King's Council, this clever and intriguing woman reports it to the Duc de Richelieu, then with the army in Holland. Only her own sentences, given verbatim, can fully expose the opinion she entertained of the king.

"Versailles, June 22, 1743—You ought, I think, to write to Mme. de Châteauroux, and tell her to try to drag the king out of the torpor he is in about public affairs. What my brother has been able to say to him on that subject is useless: it is, as he sent you word, like talking to a rock. I cannot conceive how a man can wish to be *nil* when he could be something. No one but you could conceive the point to which things have now come What passes in his kingdom seems not to concern him; nothing affects him; in the Council he is absolutely indifferent; he assents to whatever is laid before him. Verily, it is enough to drive any one to desperation to have to do with such a man. Whatever the case may be, his apathetic nature leads him to the side on which there is least trouble, though it may be the worst side. . . . The news from Bavaria is bad. . . . They say the king avoids being told what takes place, and says it is better to know nothing than to hear disagreeable things. Fine *sang-froid* truly! "

Would the king go, or would he not go to the army ? A whole system of machinery had to be prepared and set in motion to effect it:

" My brother," writes Mme. de Tencin, " is inclined to think it would be useful to put him at the head of his troops. Not, between ourselves, that he is fit to command a company of grenadiers; but his presence would do much; the people love their king from habit; they will be enchanted to see him take this step—to which he will have been incited. His troops will do their duty better; and the generals will not dare openly to neglect theirs any longer."

I might multiply these crushing quotations : "Nothing in this world resembles the king," she writes, summing him up in one sentence. Such was Louis XV, in his full force and virility, on the eve of what the people were about to call his heroism.

The young king, who was sickly for a long time in childhood, and whose life seemed to hang by a thread, was brought up with excessive precautions; all effort was spared him, more, even, than is usually spared a prince. Cardinal de Fleury directed his education wholly in the line of indolence and effeminacy. That old man of over eighty, partly from habit, partly from wiliness, kept his royal pupil perpetually in leading-strings; turning him aside from all that re-

sembled an idea or an enterprise, watchful to uproot
in him the least volition or desire; thus he had
accustomed him to nothing but the easiest things.
Nature, moreover, had done nothing to help the
young king to surmount this senile and effeminate
education. There was no spark in him except that
which early declared itself for things of sense. The
young courtiers, the ambitious men who surrounded
him, saw with vexation this tutelage of the cardinal,
this insipid childhood, this schoolboy rôle prolong itself in a king who was over thirty years of age ; they
saw that there was only one means of emancipat-
ing him, and that was to give him a mistress. He
had had them for years, but always as a lad and
under the good pleasure of the cardinal ; he needed
one, they thought, who would be really mistress, and
would make him his own master.

To this end they managed matters, and it may be
said that Louis XV in this novel hunt had no more to
do than the sluggard kings in the other kind of hunts,
who shot the game when it was brought before them.
They aided him, for his start in this direction, to
choose successively three sisters, daughters of Mme.
de Nesle, so much did habit and a species of routine
rule him even in his inconstancy.

Cardinal de Fleury being dead, intrigues were carried on with renewed ardour; the question was, inasmuch as the king had no will of his own, to know
what hand would seize the tiller. It was then that

Mme. de Tencin, anxious to advance her brother, the cardinal, to the head of the ministry, wrote to the Duc de Richelieu to urge Mme. de Châteauroux (the third of the Nesle sisters) to " drag the King from his torpor." The idea prevailed, and Mme. de Châteauroux did, for one moment, make Louis XV a phantom hero and the idol of the people. She had heart; she felt a generous inspiration and she imparted it. She tormented this king, who seemed to regret he was a king, by talking to him of State affairs, of his interests, of his fame. "You kill me," he kept saying. "So much the better, sire," she answered. "A king must be resuscitated." She did resuscitate him; for a short time she succeeded in making Louis XV conscious of honour and scarcely recognisable.

We are now not so far from Mme. de Pompadour as we seem. This was the king whom she watched (while still Mme. d'Étioles) when hunting in the forest of Sénart, and set herself to love. She dreamed of Henri IV and Gabrielle. Mme. de Châteauroux dying suddenly [poisoned, rumour said, by those who wished to keep her from the king], she told herself that it was she who should take her place. A plot was at once laid by her friends. The details are lacking, but what is certain is that, with that total want of initiative that characterised Louis XV, it was necessary to do for her what had been done for Mme. de Châteauroux and her sisters, namely, *arrange* the affair for him. In such cases, especially with princes, offi-

cious go-betweens are never lacking. Mme. de Tencin,
after seeing her first instrument, Mme. de Châteauroux,
broken, concurred in replacing her by Mme. d'Étioles.
The Duc de Richelieu, on the contrary, was opposed
to the latter, having another candidate in view, a great
lady; for it seems that to be mistress of the king the
great requisite then was that she should be a lady of
quality; and the accession of Mme. de Pompadour, *née*
Poisson, was a total revolution in the manners and
morals of the Court. In this sense, especially, there
was scandal, and the great shade of Louis XIV was
invoked. M. de Maurepas, with the Richelieus and
their class, revolted at the idea of a *bourgeoise,* a *grisette,* as they called her, usurping the power hitherto
reserved for wantons of noble blood. Maurepas,
satirical first and last, remained in opposition, and
consoled himself by writing verses for twenty-five
years. Richelieu, ever, a courtier, made his peace,
and was reconciled.

The year 1745, that of Fontenoy, was for Mme.
d'Étioles one of triumph and also one of great metamorphoses. Her liaison with the king was "arranged"; she awaited only the moment of its public
announcement. The king was with the army, writing her letters upon letters. Voltaire, who was stay-
ing with her at Étioles, lent himself to the pretty play
of Henry IV and Gabrielle and rhymed madrigals
upon madrigals. Bernis, faithful to the taste of the
day, addressed her as "that virtuous beauty"; with

which title the young Pompadour made her entrance into Versailles as one " whose heart was taken captive by a faithful hero."

All this seems strange and almost ridiculous now; but if we study Mme. de Pompadour attentively we shall see that there is truth in this way of looking at the matter, and that it is representative of the real taste of the eighteenth century. Mme. de Pompadour was not precisely a *grisette,* as her enemies affected to say, and as Voltaire repeated on one of his malicious days: she was a *bourgeoise,* the flower of finance, witty, elegant, graced with many gifts and many talents, but with a manner of feeling that lacked the grandeur and coldness of aristocratic ambition. She loved the king for himself; as the handsomest man of his kingdom, as the one who seemed to her most lovable; she loved him sincerely, sentimentally, if not with deep passion. Her ideal, on arriving at Court, was to charm him, amuse him, by a thousand diversions derived from the arts or from the intellect; to make him happy and keep him constant by a varied round of enchantments and pleasures. A landscape by Watteau, games, comedies, pastorals in shady nooks, a continual embarkation for Cythera, such was her coveted framework. But once transplanted to the slippery ground of a Court, she could realise that ideal only very imperfectly. She, who was naturally obliging and kind, was forced to arm herself against enmities and treacheries, and to take the offensive to save herself from

being overthrown; and later, she was forced by necessity into politics and into making herself a minister of
State.

She loved the arts and the things of the intellect as
no mistress of a king had ever done before. Arriving
at that position, eminent but little honourable (much
less honourable than she thought it), she at first considered herself as destined to aid, summon around her,
and encourage, suffering merit and men of talent of
all kinds. Her sole glory lies there, her best title
and her excuse. She did everything to bring forward
Voltaire, and to make him agreeable to Louis XV,
whom the petulant poet disgusted by the very vehemence and familiarity of his laudations. She thought
she had found a genius in Crébillon and honoured him.
She favoured Gresset, she protected Marmontel, she
welcomed Duclos, she admired Montesquieu and
showed her admiration openly. When the King of
Prussia gave ostentatiously a very modest pension to
d'Alembert, she advised Louis XV, when he sneered
at the amount of the pension (1200 *livres*) compared
with the "sublime genius" it professed to reward, to
forbid the philosopher to accept it and to grant him an
annuity that was double that sum. This Louis XV
dared not do, for pious reasons, because of the "Encyclopædia." It was not her fault that no one can
speak of the "age of Louis XV" as they do of that of
Louis XIV. She would fain have made this king, so
little affable, so little *giving*, a friend of the Arts, of

Letters, and liberal as a Valois. "What was François I like?" she asked the Comte de Saint-Germain, who claimed to have lived through several centuries; "there is a king I should have loved." But Louis XV could not bring himself to the idea of regarding men of Letters and intellect as of any importance, or of admitting them on any footing at all in his Court:

"It is not the fashion in France," said this monarch of routine, one day when they cited to him the example of Frederick the Great; "besides, as there are so many more *beaux-esprits* and great seigneurs here than in Prussia I should be forced to have a very large dinner-table to assemble them all." Then he counted on his fingers: "Maupertuis, Fontenelle, La Motte, Voltaire, Fréron, Piron, Destouches, Montesquieu, Cardinal de Polignac" — "Your Majesty forgets," some one said, "d'Alembert and Clairaut," — "And Crébillon," he added, "and La Chaussée" — "And Crébillon *fils*," said another, "he is more amiable than his father; besides, there is the Abbé Prévost, and the Abbé d'Olivet." "Well!" said the king, "for twenty-five years *all that* might have been dining or supping with me!"

Ah! *all that* would indeed have been mightily out of place at Versailles; but Mme. de Pompadour would have liked none the less to see them there, and to have brought about some bond of opinion between the monarch and the men who were the honour of his reign.

In the *entresol* of her apartment at Versailles, lived
Dr. Quesnay, her physician, the patron and founder
of the sect of the Economists. He was a very original
man; brusque, honest, sincere in the midst of a Court;
grave, with "an air of mimicry," and ever finding ingenuous parables through which to speak the truth.
While the king was above with Mme. Pompadour,
Bernis, Choiseul, and the ministers and courtiers who
governed with her, the Encyclopædists and the Economists, were below, with Quesnay, talking freely of all
things, and settling the future. It would seem as if
Mme. de Pompadour herself had a consciousness of
the gathering storms above her head when she exclaimed in the famous words: *Après moi le Déluge !*
It was that *entresol,* full of ideas and doctrines, which
held the cataracts that, sooner or later, were to burst
upon them from the skies. On certain days round
Quesnay's dinner-table could be seen sitting together
Diderot, d'Alembert, Duclos, Helvétius, Turgot, Buffon, *all that,* as Louis XV said: "and Mme. de Pompadour," Marmontel relates, "not being able to invite
that group of philosophers to her salon, would come
down herself to see them at table, and talk with
them."

One day, when M. de Marigny, Mme. de Pompadour's brother, was in Quesnay's apartment, the talk
fell on the Duc de Choiseul:

"'He is nothing but a coxcomb,' said the doctor, 'if he were a little
better-looking he would be just made for a favourite of Henri III. The

Marquis de Mirabeau [father of the great Mirabeau] and M. de La Rivière were present. 'This country,' said Mirabeau, 'is in a bad way;
there are no energetic sentiments, and no money to supply their place.'
'It cannot be regenerated,' said La Rivière, 'unless by a conquest like
that of China, or by some great internal overthrow; but woe to those
who live here then! the French populace strikes hard.' 'Those
words,'says the good Mme. Hausset, Mme. de Pompadour's waiting-
woman, who relates the scene in her Memoirs, 'made me tremble
and I hastened to leave the room; so did M. de Marigny, without
showing that he was affected by what was said.' "

Join these prophetic words to those which escaped
Louis XV himself when talking of the opposition of the
Parliament: "Things as they are will last my time."
That was the end of the world to him.

Did Mme. de Pompadour contribute as much as it has
been said she did to the ruin of the monarchy ? She
certainly did not hinder it. Yet the character of Louis
XV being what it was, it may have been the best thing
that could happen to such a king to fall into the hands
of a woman "born sincere, who loved him for himself,
who was just of mind, and upright in heart—qualities
that are not to be met with every day." Such, at least,
is Voltaire's opinion, judging Mme. de Pompadour after her death. In spite of everything, she was certainly the mistress who suited the reign; the only one
that could have lessened the crying disparity between
the least literary of kings and the most literary of
epochs. As mistress and friend of the king, as pro-
tectress of the arts, her mind was wholly on the level
of her rôle and her position; as a politician she failed,
she did harm; but not more harm, perhaps, than any

other favourite might have done at that epoch when France was without a single real statesman.

Looking carefully at the condition of the country at the close of the ministry of Cardinal de Fleury, it is difficult to avoid believing that if the Duc de Choiseul and Mme. de Pompadour had not come to an understanding and given some consistency and some sequence to the policy of France, the Revolution, or rather the social dissolution, would have taken place thirty years earlier than it did, so nerveless were all the powers of the State. And at that time, the nation, the men of ' 89, who were being trained, by the sight of all this baseness, to a love of the public good, would not have been ready to gather up the fragments of the old inheritance while giving the signal for the new era.

Louis XV, contemptible as he was in character, was not without intelligence or good sense. Many clever sayings of his are quoted; piquant and sometimes shrewd repartees, such as the princes of the house of Bourbon are noted for. He seems to have had good judgment, if that term is not too exalted to signify the sort of immobility and sloth in which he liked to keep his mind; but what he wanted, above all, was to be governed. He was a Louis XIII transplanted into the eighteenth century with all the vices of his time; as feeble, as cowardly, and much less chaste than his ancestor; and who never found his Richelieu. He could not have found him except in a handsome woman; and such combinations—that of the genius of a Richelieu in the body of a Pompadour are not, perhaps, in the order of things possible. Yet, at a certain moment, Mme. de Pompadour knew that her rôle as mistress was ended; she felt there was but one sure means of maintaining her influence,— that of being the necessary friend and minister, the one who could relieve the king of the trouble of willing in the affairs of State. She then became such or as nearly such as the circumstances required of her; she forced her nature, which was far more fitted for the government of little coteries and minor pleasures.

Here mythology ceases and history begins, an ignoble history! After she had made the king dismiss MM. d'Argenson and de Machault, she governed conjointly with M. de Bernis and M. de Choiseul. Then it was that the world saw the political system of Europe overturned, the ancient alliances of France set aside, and a whole series of great events lying at the mercy of the inclinations, the antipathies, the frail and egotistical good sense of a charming woman.

Then was seen a most singular spectacle: that of an heroic and cynical King of Prussia in a struggle with three women, three *sovereigns* rabid for his ruin, whom he characterised, all three of them, energetically—the Empress Elizabeth of Russia, the Empress Maria Theresa, and Mme. de Pompadour, dealing with them as a man who is accustomed neither to love the sex nor fear it. Louis XV said naïvely of that king, whose ally he had not known how to be, and of whom he was so often the humiliated and defeated enemy: "He is a crazy man who will risk his all on the cast of a die, and who may win the game, though he is without religion, morals, or principles." It is amusing to see that Louis XV thought he himself had more morals and principles than Frederick; and he did have, in fact, rather more, inasmuch as he believed he had.

The state of public opinion in France at the beginning of this Seven Years' War, so lightly undertaken, was not what it became a year later. The new alliance with Austria, conceived in defiance of the old historical maxims, filled all minds and flattered all hopes. The Empress Maria Theresa, in her passionate and courageous struggle against the aggrandisement of Prussia, employed special coquetry in her endeavour to win France, not disdaining to make herself the "friend" of Mme de Pompadour; and the decision was formed at Versailles to "be for Austria" precisely as we declare for friends against all opponents in some society or coterie quarrel. Bernis, Mme. de Pompadour's right hand, was recalled from Venice and ordered to draw up and negotiate the treaty of alliance. In spite of his first objections as a man of sense, he did not long resist the general movement that carried away the whole community; he was dazzled himself, and finally believed that he was furthering the greatest political transaction since the days of Richelieu.

The history of the change that one year brought about in the minds of every one, more particularly in his own, can best be understood from the letters of Bernis, then minister of Foreign Affairs, to the Comte de Stainville (afterwards Duc de Choiseul), ambassador to Rome. The war began by successes: the taking of Port-Mahon, the victory of Hastenbach, the early advantages of the Duc de Richelieu, seemed to promise an easy victory to the new diplomatic combination. Bernis kept all such hopes until the moment when the Duc de Richelieu concluded with the Duke of Cumberland the hasty convention of Kloster-Zeven, September 8, 1757. From that moment the chances of war turned and became unfavourable. Three months later, (December 13th) Bernis writes to Choiseul:

" One does not die of grief, inasmuch as I am not dead since September 8. The blunders committed since that date have been heaped up in such a way that one can hardly explain them except by supposing evil intentions. I have talked with the greatest force to *God and his Saints* (Louis XV). I produce a slight rising of the pulse, and then the lethargy returns; great sad eyes are turned upon me, and all is said."

He sees that there is neither king, nor generals, nor ministers, and the charge seems to him so just that he consents to be included in the category of those who do not exist:

" I seem to myself to be the minister of the Foreign Affairs of Limbo. Try and see, my dear count, whether you can do better than I in kindling the spark of life, which is being extinguished here. As for me, I have dealt all my great blows; henceforth I shall take the course of becoming paralysed like the rest in regard to feeling, without ceasing to do my duty as a good citizen and an honest man."

In France, at this date, there was no direction, no management, no control, either in the armies or in the Cabinet. Insubordination and want of discipline were everywhere; no one was either feared or obeyed. The rivalry and disunion of the Duc de Richelieu and the Prince de Soubise led to the disasters at the end of the campaign. In the midst of these reverses, which affected so deeply the military honour of France and the future of the monarchy, Louis XV remained totally apathetic:

" There is no other such instance of playing a vast game with as much indifference as he would show to a game of cards. . . . Sensitive, and, if I may dare to say it, sensible as I am, I am dying on the rack, and my martyrdom is useless to the State. . . . May it please God to send us a *will* of some kind, or some one who will have it for us! I would be his valet, with all my heart. . . ."

It is not possible, even after the lapse of a century, to read a certain letter from Bernis to Choiseul (March 31, 1758,) without blushing. Never was the decadence of the monarchy of Louis XV so bare to sight; we feel, from the very character of the evil, that the dissolution of everything was near at hand: "We must change our moral habits," he cries, "and that work which demands centuries in other lands could be done in a year in this land, if there were doers to do it." That remark is profoundly true, applying, I do not say to morals, but to the sentiments and to the spirit of our nation, which we have seen, more than once, completely reversed, in a moment of time, under the impulsion of a powerful mind. In Paris, the exasperation of the public mind had reached a climax in that summer of 1758:

"I am threatened, in anonymous letters," writes Bernis, "to be torn in pieces by the populace, and though I do not fear such threats, it is certain that coming evils, which all can foresee, may easily realise them. *Our friend* [Mme. de Pompadour] "runs quite as much risk as any of us."

There were two distinct epochs in Mme. de Pompadour's career and influence: the first, the most brilliant and the most favoured, was on the morrow of the Peace of Aix-la-Chapelle, (1748): then she was completely in her rôle as a young, adored woman; happy in the peace, in the arts, in the pleasures of the mind, protecting and counselling all fortunate things. Then came the second epoch, very confused, but chiefly fatal and disastrous; this was the whole period of the Seven Years' War; the period of Damiens' attempt on the king's life, the defeat at Rosbach, and the victorious insults of Frederick the Great. These were hard years, that aged before she was old this frail and gracious woman, dragged into a struggle that was too strong for her. Yet my own impression, resulting to-day from a simple glance at this distance, is that things might have gone even worse, and that Mme. de Pompadour aided by M. de Choiseul, did, by means of the "Family Compact," redeem some of her own faults, and the humiliation of France and its monarchy.

It would seem that the nation itself felt this; and felt it, above all, after the brilliant favourite had fallen very low; for when she died at Versailles, April 15, 1764, the regret of the people of Paris, who would have stoned her a few years earlier, was universal. One of those who seems to have regretted her least was Louis XV; it is related of him that as he watched from a window the removal of the coffin from the Château of Versailles to Paris, he remarked (it being a stormy day): "The marquise will have bad weather for her journey." His ancestor, Louis XIII, said at the hour of the execution of his favourite, Cinq Mars: "Dear friend must be making a horrible grimace just now." Compared with such a speech, that of Louis XV seems quite touching in its feeling.

The death of Mme. de Pompadour was a severe loss to the arts, and they have consecrated her memory. If Voltaire, as a man of letters, could say of her to his friends, "She was one of us," artists had still stronger reason to say it. Mme. de Pompadour was herself a distinguished artist. Directly, and through her brother, M. de Marigny, whom she caused to be appointed Superintendent of Buildings, she exercised a most active and happy influence. At no epoch was art more living, more related to social life, which expressed itself in it, and modelled itself by it. Diderot, giving an account of the Salon of 1765, and speaking of an allegorical picture by Carl Van Loo,

which represented the Arts in despair supplicating
Destiny for the recovery of the marquise, says:

"She protected them indeed; she loved Carl Van
Loo, she was the benefactress of Cochin; the engraver
Gai had his tools at her house. Too happy would
the nation have been had she confined herself to
amusing the sovereign with such relaxations, and in
ordering from artists their pictures and statues."
Then, after describing the painting, he concludes,
rather harshly, it seems to me:

"Van Loo's Suppliants obtained nothing from Destiny, which
proved more favourable to France than to the Arts. Mme. de Pompadour died at the moment when they thought her out of danger.
Well! what remains of that woman who exhausted us in men and
money, left us without honour or energy, and who overturned the
whole political system of Europe? The Treaty of Versailles, which
will last as long as it may; Bouchardon's *Amour,* that will be forever
admired; a few of Gai's engravings, which will astonish antiquaries in
years to come; a good little picture by Van Loo, which people will
look at occasionally, and a handful of ashes!"

Some other things remained, and posterity, or at
any rate the amateurs who to-day represent it, seem to
ascribe to Mme. de Pompadour's influence, and to
range under her name many more objects worthy of
attention than Diderot enumerates. I shall rapidly
indicate a few of them.

Mme. de Pompadour had a fine library, especially
rich in dramatic works; a library chiefly composed of
French books, that is, of books she read, most of
them bound with her arms (three towers), on the

cover; some with broad lace-work ornamenting the flat surfaces [*avec de larges dentelles qui ornent les plats*]. These volumes are still sought for, and bibliophiles give her a choice place in their golden book, beside the most illustrious collectors whose names have come down to us. She carried her love of this art so far as to print with her own hands, at Versailles, a tragedy by Corneille, *Rodogune* (1760): of which only twenty copies were printed. These were mere caprices, some may say; but they prove the taste and the passion for letters in this woman who "would have loved François I."

In the Cabinet des Estampes is a collection entitled *Œuvre de Mme. de Pompadour;* which contains more than sixty of her engravings and etchings. They are for the most part allegorical designs, intended to celebrate some of the memorable events of the day; but there are others that come more within the idea we have of the charming artist: "Love cultivating a myrtle," "Love cultivating laurels." The Loves appear under many aspects; Military Genius itself is represented as Love meditating among flags and cannon. Not content with reproducing on copper with acids the engravings of Gai on stone, Mme. de Pompadour seems to have done some engraving herself on delicate stones—agate and cornelian. Her etchings, at any rate, were retouched with the graving-tool. Here, as in printing, she put her pretty hand to the actual work; she is of the trade; and just as the bibliophiles inscribe her on their list, and the typographers on theirs, the engravers have a right to class in their ranks, with the title of co-worker, "Mme. de Pompadour, etcher."

The Manufactory of Sèvres owes much to her; she looked after it actively; she often took the king there; and he, for once, felt the importance of an art to which he owed magnificent dinner-services worthy to be offered as gifts to sovereigns, Under the fostering influence of Versailles, Sèvres soon had original marvels fit to compete with old Dresden and Japan. Nowhere does the style called "Pompadour" shine with more fancy and delicacy, or more in its true place, than in the porcelain of that date. This glory of hers, due to a fragile art, is more durable than many others.

While her brother, M. de Marigny, summoned Soufflot from Lyons to entrust him with the erection of Sainte-Geneviève (the Pantheon), she herself was deeply interested in the establishment of the École Militaire, to which she contributed her own money. Among the very few authentic letters that we have of hers is the following, addressed to a friend, the Comtesse de Lutzelbourg, January 3, 1751:

"I think you must be very pleased with the edict just issued by the king to ennoble the military. You will be still more so with one that is soon to appear for the establishment of five hundred gentlemen, whom the king is to have trained in the military art. This royal school will be built quite close to the Invalides. This establishment will be all the finer because His Majesty has been working over it for a year, and the ministers have had no part in it, and, indeed, knew nothing of it until he had arranged it to his fancy. . ."

If the king ever thought of it alone and without the suggestions of his ministers, there can be no doubt that to Mme. de Pompadour he owed the inspiration, for he was not a man to originate such ideas himself. That this was the fact appears in another, and later, letter from Mme. de Pompadour to Paris-Duverney, who was the one who first suggested the idea to her.

" No, indeed, my dear simpleton, I shall not allow to perish in port an establishment which ought to immortalise the king, render happy the nobles, and make known to posterity my attachment to the State and to the person of His Majesty. I have told Gabriel to-day to arrange for the necessary workmen to finish the work. My revenue for this year has not yet come in; but I shall employ it all in paying the journeymen every fortnight. I do not know whether I shall find any security for repayment, but I know very well that I shall risk one hundred thousand *livres* for the welfare of those poor lads."

Such in her prosperous days was this enchanting, ambitious, frail woman, who was also sincere, who remained kind in her prosperity, faithful (I like to think so) in her sin, serviceable where she could be, yet vindictive when driven to it; a woman who was truly of her sex after all; of whose private life her waiting-woman has left us an account that is neither overwrought nor crushing.

That book of Mme. du Hausset leaves a singular impression; it is written with a degree of *naïveté* and ingenuousness which preserves a sort of virtue in the close vicinity of vice:

"'That is what the Court is, corrupt from the greatest to the smallest,' I said one day to Madame, who spoke to me of certain facts within my knowledge. 'I could tell you many more,' she said, 'but in that little chamber where you often sit you must overhear plenty.'"

Mme. de Pompadour, after the first dazzling moments of her fairyland were over, judged her situation for what it was; and though she continued to love the king, she retained no illusion as to his character, nor as to the sort of affection of which she was the object. She felt that she was to him a habit, and nothing else. "It is your staircase that the king loves," the little Maréchale de Mirepoix said to her: "he is so in the habit of going up and down it. But if he found another woman to whom he could talk of his hunting and his affairs as he does to you, it would be all the same to him at the end of three days." Mme. de Pompadour repeated those words to herself as being the exact and melancholy truth. She had everything to fear at every minute, for, with such a man, *everything was possible*. A smile from him, a more or less gracious look proved nothing:

"You do not know him, my dear," she said one day to Mme. du Hausset, with whom she had been talking of some rival with whom her enemies were trying to supplant her: "if he meant to put her to-night into my apartment, he would treat her coldly before the world, and treat me with the greatest affection." He acquired that dissembling habit from his early education under Cardinal de Fleury. "Ah!" she exclaimed one day with a secret sense of her misery, "Ah! my life is like that of the Christian, a perpetual struggle. It was not so with the women who obtained the good graces of Louis XIV."

Mme. de Pompadour may be considered as the last in date of kings' mistresses, correctly so-called. After her it is impossible to descend and enter decently into the history of the Du Barry. The kings and emperors who have succeeded one another in France until our day have been either too virtuous, too despotic, too gouty, too repentant, or too good fathers of families to permit themselves such inutilities; at the most, one perceives a few vestiges. The race of kings' mistresses may therefore be said to be, if not extinct, at least greatly interrupted, and Mme. de Pompadour remains to our eyes the last in sight in our history, and the most brilliant.

All this while, there was,—let us remember it in order not to be unjust in our severity,—there was in the bosom of that very Versailles, and of that corrupt Court, a little reserved corner, a sort of asylum of all the virtues and domestic pieties, in the person and in the family of the Dauphin, father of Louis XVI. This estimable prince, and all who surrounded him, his mother, his wife, his royal sisters, all his household, made the most absolute and the most silent contrast to the scandals and the intrigues of the rest of the Court. It is a striking contrast to compare his premature end and his death, so courageously Christian, with the miserable death-scene of the king, his father. We are told that during his last autumn on earth (1765), he wished to see again the little grove at Versailles which bore his name and where he had played in childhood; on seeing the trees half-stripped, he said, with a sort of presentiment: "Already the fall of the leaf!" Then he added, instantly: "But we can see the skies better."

The Dauphin, son of Louis XV, whatever homage we may render to his virtues, was not of those of whom we can say otherwise than by a poetic fiction: *Tu Marcellus eris.* All in him reveals a saint, but it was a king that the monarchy and France required. Louis XVI, heir to his father's virtues, did not know how to be a king; and nothing justifies us in supposing that the father, had he lived, was of the stuff to make one. It is clear to all, that, with the death of Louis XV, the monarchy was condemned already, and the race cut off. Let us see now how Louis XV died.

We cannot say: "Thus die voluptuaries," for the voluptuous often end with firmness and courage. Louis XV did not die like Sardanapalus; he died as Mme. Du Barry died later, flinging herself with clasped hands at the feet of the executioner and crying out: "One instant more!" Louis XV said something of the same kind to the Faculty assembled around him.

The man who watched, and wrote down upon the spot, the pusillanimities of the king during his last illness was M. de Liancourt, Grand-Master of the Wardrobe; the same whom every one has since known and venerated under the name of the Duc de La Rochefoucauld-Liancourt, who did not die till 1827.[1] This was the witness; one of the most virtuous of citizens; a man of '89, the kind of man that was, at that epoch, being developed in all ranks, but particularly among the enlightened and generous young nobles. A spectacle

[1] This paper, the manuscript of which is preserved in the Bibliothèque de l'Arsenal, is very long, and gives a detailed account of the base intrigues that went on around the deathbed of Louis XV. It breaks off abruptly before the death took place. Only a few brief extracts, relating to Louis XV himself, can be given here.—Tr.

" Wednesday, April 27, 1774, the king being at Trianon, felt un-well, with pains in his head, chills, and lumbago. The fear he always had of being ill, or the hope of feeling better by exercise, induced him to make no change in the orders given the night before. He started for the hunt in a carriage, but feeling worse, stayed in the coach and did not mount his horse. He complained of illness, and returned about half past 5 o'clock to Trianon, and shut himself up with Mme. Du Barry. . . . In the night he felt worse and sent to wake up Lemonnier [his physician] and Mme. Du Barry. Anxiety and fear laid hold of him, but Lemonnier, who knew his propensity to be frightened by nothing at all, considered his anxiety as no more than the effect of his natural disposition. So with regard to the pains of which the king complained, he reduced them in his own mind by three-fourths. This is what always happens to effeminate persons; they are like liars, who by dint of having abused the credulity of others lose the right to be believed when they really ought to be. Mme. Du Barry, who knew the king as well as Lemonnier, thought as he did about the pains of which the king complained, but she regarded as an advantage to her

like that of the deathbed of Louis XV was well fitted
to stir noble hearts and turn them sick at the sight
of such base intrigues. If we wish to know the

all the care she could give him, and the solicitude she could show for
him. . . .

" It got to be three o'clock, and no one had been admitted to the
king's room. It was only imperfectly known that he was not well,
but by the little news that transpired people judged it was merely a
slight indisposition. Mme. Du Barry had informed M. d'Aiguillon
(prime minister, whose tool she was), who was at Versailles, and by
his advice she formed the project of keeping the king at Trianon as
long as his indisposition lasted. By this means she would be enabled
to spend more time alone with him, and, more than that, to gratify her
aversion to M. le Dauphin, Mme. la Dauphine, and Mesdames [the
king's daughters], by keeping the king away from them, and rendering their conduct toward him embarrassing to them. The uncertainty felt by Lemonnier as to the result of this indisposition, the
inconvenience of the service in so small a room, the scandal and in-
decency to which this prolonged stay would give rise—nothing of all
this could turn Mme. Du Barry from this unreasonable and indecent
project, formed especially to defy the royal family. . . .

" When I say that Mme. Du Barry willed, I mean that M. d'Aiguillon
willed, for this woman, like three-quarters of the women of her kind,
had no will. All her wills were fancies, and all those fancies were
diamonds, ribbons, money. The homage of all France would have
been quite indifferent to her. She was wearied by the business her
odious favourite (Aiguillon) wished her to attend to, and had no
pleasure except in squandering on gowns and jewels the millions which
the business of the controller-general supplied to her in profusion.
Whether from fear, liking, or weakness, she was given over to the
despotic will of M. d'Aiguillon, who employed her to assist him in
wreaking vengeance on his enemies, and otherwise using for his own
ends all the influence she possessed over the apathetic weakness of the
king. . . .

" However, the fever continued during the night with some force; it
even increased; the pains in the head grew worse, and it was announced
that at eight o'clock in the morning the king would be bled. . . .

" It was now midday; the doctors who had been summoned began to

Duc de La Rochefoucauld-Liancourt, the results of his life can be seen everywhere, his memory lives again in numerous institutions of benevolence. It was he

appear. We of the wardrobe were also called in. I found the king surrounded by a crowd of physicians and surgeons, all of whom he was questioning with indescribable anxiety and lack of courage about his state, about the progress of his illness, about the remedies they would give him in such or such a case. The doctors reassured him, and diagnosed his illness as catarrhal fever. But they showed much more uneasiness in the way they treated him than in what they said; They had already announced that they should make the second bleeding at half past three o'clock; and perhaps a third at midnight, or early next morning, if the second did not relieve the pains in the head. The king, whose repeated questions had driven the doctors to make him this answer, showed much displeasure: 'A third bleeding!' he said; 'why that means an illness! A third bleeding will bring me very low; I will not have a third bleeding. Why this third bleeding? . . .

"The cowardice of the doctors which made them give up the third bleeding if the second did not produce great relief, did not prevent them from thinking it would probably be necessary; and to satisfy both their promise and their conscience, they decided to make the second bleeding so abundant that it would take the place of a third. Consequently, they drew from the king the amount of four large *palettes* full. Kings must be accustomed to see their fame and their health the plaything of the intrigues and self-interest of all who surround them. The king again showed himself for just what he was during and before this bleeding; his fear, his pusillanimity were inconceivable; he had vinegar brought to hold under his nose, and said, when he saw the surgeon approach, that he should faint; he made four men hold him, and gave his pulse to all the Faculty to feel, asking the same questions of the doctors at every instant: about his illness, about the remedies, about his state: 'You tell me I am not so ill, and that I shall get well soon,' he said to them, 'but you do not believe a word of it ; you ought to tell me.' They protested that they were telling him the truth; but for all that the king did not whine, nor complain, nor cry out the less. His fears and his terror were not those of a touching anxiety, but those of a cowardly and revolting weakness. . . .

"The quantity of doctors who surrounded him had made me pity him

who, thanks to his office as Grand-Master of the Wardrobe, entered the bedroom of Louis XVI in the middle
of the night, and woke him to tell him of the taking

earlier in the day. Fourteen persons, each of whom had the right to
approach and examine the patient, seemed to me a positive torture.
But the king did not think so; anxiety and fear made the importunity
precious to him. The Faculty was composed of six physicians, five
surgeons, and three apothecaries; he would have liked to see the number increased. He made all fourteen of them feel his pulse six times an
hour; and if the whole of the numerous Faculty were not in the room
he sent for those who were absent, that he might be constantly surrounded by all of them; as if he hoped that with such satellites disease
would not dare to approach his Majesty. I shall never forget that when
Lemonnier told him it was necessary to show his tongue, he stuck it
out at its full length, putting his hands before his eyes because the light
hurt them, and he kept it out more than six minutes, only drawing it
in to say (after Lemonnier's examination): 'Your turn, Lassonne':
'Yours, Borden': Yours, Lorry': 'Yours, and yours,'—until he had
called up, one by one, all the doctors, who each testified in his own
manner the satisfaction he felt at seeing the beauty and colour of that
precious and royal morsel. It was the same a moment later, with his
stomach, which it was necessary to feel; he made each physician, each
surgeon, each apothecary defile before it, submitting eagerly to the examination, and calling them up, one after the other, in order. . . .
"It was now ten o'clock at night. The king had been changed from
his large bed to a small one, for the convenience of taking care of him.
His debility, his pains, his sluggishness were increasing; and, in spite of
the opinion held by all of his fears and his timidity, it seemed very evident that he was at the beginning of some great illness. All Versailles
was convinced of this, except those who chose not to be. The doctors
were equally convinced, and their silence showed it. They spoke only
to each other, and they put off pronouncing an opinion on the nature
of the illness till the morrow.
"The royal family, very uneasy, came back after their supper to see the
king, and were preparing to remain very late in a side chamber to see
how the night would turn, when, all of a sudden, the light brought
close to the king's face without the usual precaution, revealed red
blotches on his forehead and cheeks. The doctors who surrounded

of the Bastille: "Why, it is a revolt!" cried the king: "No, sire," he answered, "it is a revolution." Such was the man who, young and condemned by the

the bed, when they saw those blotches, some of which had risen above the skin in pustules, looked at one another with one accord, and their astonishment was a confession of their ignorance. Lemonnier had seen the king for four days with pains in his loins, with faintness and nausea, and the other four had seen those symptoms increasing since midday, yet none of them, in spite of the feeling of the pulse, had suspected that the disease could be smallpox. Every one in the room saw it at that moment, and it was needless to be a doctor to be convinced of it.

"The doctors left the room immediately, and announced to the royal family the nature of the illness, saying that it was well understood, that the king was well prepared for it, and that all would go right. The first care of every one was to induce M. le Dauphin, who had never had the smallpox, to leave the apartment. Mme. la Dauphine took him away. M. le Comte de Provence, M. le Comte d'Artois and their wives went away also. Mesdames alone remained. They had never had the smallpox either, and they were afraid of it; but they would not yield to the representations we made to them; they showed themselves immovable in the purpose they had formed of not abandoning their father. It is difficult to believe that this act of filial piety excited very little public interest. Those who spoke of it contented themselves by saying it was very right; but three-quarters of the people never spoke or thought of it at all. This indifference, this coldness to an action that was truly fine and touching, and one they would have highly praised in private persons, was produced by the dull, meagre lives of Mesdames, who were known to be without desires for good, without soul, without character, without sincerity, without love for their father. People were convinced that it was either to make themselves talked of, or else mechanically that they subjected themselves to so evident a danger. Their customary idleness made some persons think they did it for an occupation; others believed that Mme. de Narbonne and Mme. de Durfort, two well-known intriguers, had urged Madame Adélaïde and Madame Victoire to this conduct, hoping to gain in the end some good from it themselves; as for Madame Sophie, who was a species of automaton, as lacking in mind as she was in character, she followed, with her usual apathy, the will and projects of her sisters.

"But the best reason of all for the little impression made upon the

duties of his office to witness the last moments of
Louis XV, was seized with the idea of writing down
what he witnessed that posterity might profit by it.

Court and upon Paris by the really estimable conduct of Mesdames was
the man himself, who was the object of their self-devotion.   The
king was so degraded, despicable, so thoroughly despised, that nothing
done for him had the right or power to interest the public.   What a
lesson for kings! They need to learn that while we are obliged, in
spite of ourselves, to pay them outward marks of respect and submission, we judge their actions sternly, and we avenge ourselves for their
authority over us by the most profound contempt when their conduct
has no aim for the public good, and is not worthy of our admiration.
But as for this king, no stern effort was needed to judge of him as he
was judged by his whole kingdom."

PORTRAITS OF THE
EIGHTEENTH CENTURY

Collation of Texts

For the benefit of those readers who may want to compare these translations to the original, the following table indicates the sources and dates of each essay. A detailed collation has not been included in the collection as being specialized in interest and too cumbersome to tabulate. It has, however, seemed vital to an understanding of Sainte-Beuve's original articles to give the date and reference to the ones which appear here. The references are to the standard current editions of his works.

C.L.   *Causeries du Lundi* (1870 edition) 15 vols.
P.L.   *Portraits littéraires* (1862 edition) 3 vols.

Volume I

1. DUCHESSE DU MAINE
   Dec. 23, 1850   C.L. III, 208-228
2. MADAME DE STAAL-DELAUNAY
   Oct. 21, 1846   P.L. III, 439-454
3. LE SAGE
   p. 77-90   Aug. 5, 1850   C.L. II, 353-364
      90-96   C.L. Index vol.
      96-105   Aug. 5, 1850   C.L. II, 365-374
4. MONTESQUIEU
   p. 109-134   Oct. 18, 1852   C.L. VII, 41-62
      134-156   Oct. 25, 1852   C.L. VII, 63-84
5. ADRIENNE LE COUVREUR
   Dec. 24, 1849   C.L. I, 199-220
6. VOLTAIRE
   p. 187-199   Oct. 20, 1856   C.L. XIII, 1-16
      199-212   July 8, 1850   C.L. II, 267-285
      212-214   Dec. 16, 1850   C.L. III, 187-190
                                   (Article: Frederick the Great)
      214-215   Mar. 14, 1853   C.L. VII, 479
                                   (One paragraph re-worked)

6. VOLTAIRE (continued)

215-216	Dec. 16, 1850	C.L. III, 194-196
216-218	Sept. 1, 1856	C.L. XII, 407-409
		(Article: Margrave de Bareith)
218-219	Sept. 8, 1856	C.L. XII, 419-423
		(Article II: Margrave de Bareith)
219-221	Dec. 16, 1850	C.L. III, 196-198
221-222	Oct. 27, 1856	C.L. XIII, 21
222-226	Nov. 8, 1852	C.L. VII, 106-109
226-236	Oct. 27, 1856	C.L. XIII, 23-25

p. 228   One paragraph is in none of these texts.

7. MARQUISE DU DEFFAND

p. 239-250	Mar. 11, 1850	C.L. I, 412-421
250-269	May 9, 1859	C.L. XIV, 219-237
269-281	Mar. 11, 1850	C.L. I, 421-431

8. EARL OF CHESTERFIELD

	June 24, 1850	C.L. II, 226-246

9. BENJAMIN FRANKLIN

p. 311-335	Nov. 15, 1852	C.L. VII, 127-148
335-355	Nov. 22, 1852	C.L. VII, 128-166
355-375	Nov. 29, 1852	C.L. VII, 167-185

10. MADAME GEOFFRIN

	July 22, 1850	C.L. II, 309-329

11. THE ABBÉ BARTHÉLEMY

p. 407-424	Dec. 6, 1852	C.L. VII, 188-205
424-439	Dec. 13, 1852	C.L. VII, 206-223

12. LOUIS XV

	Sept. 16, 1850	C.L. II, 488-511
		(Article: Madame de Pompadour)
	Feb. 15, 1846	P.L. III, 512-539

The article is badly out of order with the second woven into the first and also giving p. 465-472.